AF167587

# Lecture Notes of the Institute for Computer Sciences, Social Informatics and Telecommunications Engineering    618

The LNICST series publishes ICST's conferences, symposia and workshops.
LNICST reports state-of-the-art results in areas related to the scope of the Institute.
The type of material published includes

- Proceedings (published in time for the respective event)
- Other edited monographs (such as project reports or invited volumes)

LNICST topics span the following areas:

- General Computer Science
- E-Economy
- E-Medicine
- Knowledge Management
- Multimedia
- Operations, Management and Policy
- Social Informatics
- Systems

Joseph Bamidele Awotunde ·
Agbotiname Lucky Imoize · Cheng-Chi Lee
Editors

# Emerging Technologies for Developing Countries

7th International Conference, AFRICATEK 2024
Ilorin, Nigeria, August 6–8, 2024
Proceedings

Springer

*Editors*
Joseph Bamidele Awotunde 🆔
University of Ilorin
Ilorin, Nigeria

Agbotiname Lucky Imoize 🆔
University of Lagos
Lagos, Nigeria

Cheng-Chi Lee 🆔
Fu Jen Catholic University
New Taipei City, Taiwan

ISSN 1867-8211 ISSN 1867-822X (electronic)
Lecture Notes of the Institute for Computer Sciences, Social Informatics
and Telecommunications Engineering
ISBN 978-3-031-93556-5 ISBN 978-3-031-93557-2 (eBook)
https://doi.org/10.1007/978-3-031-93557-2

This Springer imprint is published by the registered company Springer Nature Switzerland AG
The registered company address is: Gewerbestrasse 11, 6330 Cham, Switzerland

If disposing of this product, please recycle the paper.

# Preface

We are pleased to introduce the proceedings of the seventh edition of the European Alliance for Innovation (EAI) International Conference on Emerging Technologies for Developing Countries (AfricaTek 2024) co-organized with the University of Ilorin, Nigeria. The theme for this year's edition was Artificial Intelligence and Innovative Technologies for Sustainable Development. This year's theme brought together researchers, policymakers, and industry leaders involved in AI Applications for Sustainable Development, Innovation in Healthcare, Environmental Monitoring and Conservation, Collaborative Approaches for Global Impact, Emerging Technologies for Sustainability, Smart, Sustainable Cities, and Climate Change Management. Coupled with innovations in renewable energy, smart infrastructure, and digital communication, these technologies are poised to accelerate progress towards achieving the United Nations Sustainable Development Goals (SDGs).

After a rigorous review process, AfricaTek 2024 consisted of 15 full papers out of 42 submitted papers. There were 3 guest speakers for oral presentation, and the conference tracks were: Track 1 - Emerging Technologies and Sustainability Aspects; Track 2 - Ethical Considerations in AI for Sustainable Development; and Track 3 - Smart, Sustainable Cities and Climate Change Management. AfricaTek 2024 featured one keynote speech with two technical workshops. Syed Abdul Rehman Khan delivered the keynote speech from Tsinghua University, China. The two workshops organized were Grantsmanship: how to write an Acceptable Grant, and Effect of the Mentor-Mentee Programme on Ph.D. Student's Success delivered by Christiana O. Abikoye, and R. G. Jimoh, respectively. The Grantsmanship workshop aimed to equip participants with essential skills in crafting competitive grant proposals. It focused on understanding funder expectations, structuring proposals effectively, developing strong narratives, and aligning project goals with funding priorities, increasing the chances of securing funding successfully. The Mentor-Mentee workshop aimed to explore how mentoring enhances Ph.D. students' academic growth, research skills, and overall success through guidance, support, and collaboration.

The unwavering support of our amiable Vice Chancellor Wahab Olasupo Egbewole, SAN, and the entire management was essential for the success of the AfricaTek 2024 conference. We sincerely appreciate their constant support, provision, and guidance. Working with such an outstanding organizing committee for their hard work in planning and supporting the conference was a great pleasure. Most especially, we thank the LOC Chair, R. G. Jimoh, Local Co-Chair Christiana O. Abikoye, and Imoize A. L. for their support and guidance all the time. We thank the Dean of the Faculty of Information and Communication Science Azeez A. L., and other faculty staff. Our special thanks go to the Conference Manager, Katarína Antalová, and the Venue Manager Stella Dao for their help, support, and kindness. Finally, we thank our dynamic authors, who submitted their papers to AfricaTek 2024 and allowed us to review and present them at the conference.

The outcome and insightful presentation of AfricaTek 2024 provided a good platform for presenters, researchers, developers, and policymakers to discuss Artificial Intelligence and Innovative Technologies for Sustainable Development in African nations. It is believed that the upcoming AfricaTek conference will be equally successful and stimulating, as suggested by the contributions presented in this volume.

July 2025

Joseph Bamidele Awotunde
Agbotiname Lucky Imoize
Cheng-Chi Lee

# Organization

## Steering Committee

Imrich Chlamtac      University of Trento, Italy

## Organizing Committee

### General Chair

Mohammad S. Obaidat      University of Jordan, Jordan

### General Co-chair

Awotunde Joseph Bamidele      University of Ilorin, Nigeria

### TPC Chair

Akash Kumar Bhoi      Sikkim Manipal University, India

### Sponsorship and Exhibit Chair

Francisca Oladipo      Thomas Adewumi University, Nigeria

### Local Chair

Gbenga R. Jimoh      University of Ilorin, Nigeria

### Workshops Chair

Mohammad Hammoudeh      King Fahd University of Petroleum and Minerals, Saudi Arabia

### Publicity and Social Media Chair

Idowu D. Oladipo      University of Ilorin, Nigeria

**Publications Chairs**

Awotunde Joseph Bamidele          University of Ilorin, Nigeria
Imoize Agbotiname Lucky           University of Lagos, Nigeria
Lee Cheng-Chi                     Fu Jen Catholic University, Taiwan

**Web Chair**

AbdulRaheem Muyidden              University of Ilorin, Nigeria

**Posters and PhD Track Chair**

Maria José Sousa                  Instituto Universitário de Lisboa, Portugal

**Panels Chair and Local Co-chair**

Christiana O. Abikoye             University of Ilorin, Nigeria

**Demos Chair**

Roseline O. Ogundokun             Kaunas University of Technology, Lithuania

**Tutorials Chair**

Abdullateef .O. Balogun           Universiti Teknologi PETRONAS, Malaysia

# Technical Program Committee

Abidemi Emmanuel Adeniyi          Bowen University, Nigeria
Gbemisola Janet Awotunde          Landmark University, Nigeria
Sunday Adeola Ajagbe              University of Zululand, South Africa
Samarendra Nath Sur               Sikkim Manipal Institute of Technology, India
Adewale Lukman                    University of North Dakota, USA
Peace Falola                      University of Ibadan, Nigeria
Roseline Oluwaseun Ogundokun      Landmark University, Nigeria
Hammed Adeleye Mojeed             Gdańsk University of Technology, Poland
Akshat Agrawal                    Amity University, Gurugram, India
Moses Abiodun Kazemm              Landmark University, Nigeria
Matthew Adigun                    University of Zululand, South Africa
Samuel Ajibade                    Istanbul Ticaret University, Turkey

| | |
|---|---|
| Olukayode Oki | Walter Sisulu University, South Africa |
| Latifat Odeniyi | Koladaisi University, Nigeria |
| Skhumbuzo Zwane | University of Zululand, South Africa |
| Blessing Olorunfemi | Redeemer's University, Nigeria |
| Adeyemo Adetoye | Bowen University, Nigeria |
| Manjushree Nayak | NIST University, India |
| Adedoyin Oyebade | Bowen University, Nigeria |
| Odunayo Falana | Bowen University, Nigeria |
| Gbeminiyi Falowo | Redeemer's University, Nigeria |
| Saumya Das | Sikkim Manipal Institute of Technology, India |
| Emmanuel A. Balogun | Ajayi Crowther University, Nigeria |
| Alaa Khadidos | King Abdulaziz University, Saudi Arabia |
| Micheal Olaolu Arowolo | University of Missouri, USA |
| Segun Jegede | Kent State University, USA |
| Olanrewaju Rasaki | Mohammed VI Polytechnic University, Morocco |
| Grace Ajiboye | Precious Cornerstone University, Nigeria |
| Adekunle Ejidokun | Kampala International University, Uganda |
| Meenu Vijarania | KR Mangalam University, India |
| Samson Akinpelu | University of Kwazulu-Natal, South Africa |
| Shakirat Aderonke Salihu | University of Ilorin, Nigeria |
| Fatima Enehezei Usman-Hamza | University of Ilorin, Nigeria |
| Halleluyah Aworinde | Bowen University, Nigeria |
| Sachi Nandan Mohanty | VIT-AP University, India |
| Abayomi Agbeyangi | Walter Sisulu University, South Africa |
| Ikeola Olatinwo | University of Ilorin, Nigeria |
| Abdullateef O. Balogun | Universiti Teknologi PETRONAS, Malaysia |
| Victor Alexander Okhuese | Dublin City University, Ireland |
| Oludare Adebisi | Abiola Ajimobi Technical University, Nigeria |
| Adebayo Paul Olujide | University of Ilorin, Nigeria |

# Contents

**Environmental Monitoring, Smart Agriculture and Smart Education**

# Smart, Sustainable Cities and Climate Change Management

# Perceptions of South African Residents on Alternative Energy Sources in Mitigating Load Shedding

Omowunmi Mary Longe[1]([⊠]) [iD] and Abieyuwa Ohonba[2] [iD]

[1] Department of Electrical and Electronic Engineering Science, University of Johannesburg, Johannesburg 2006, South Africa
omowunmil@uj.ac.za
[2] School of Economics, University of Johannesburg, Johannesburg 2006, South Africa

**Abstract.** There have been growing concerns in South Africa over the consistency of frequent electricity power interruptions commonly known as load shedding. This has resulted in significant and unprecedented negative impacts on the lives and livelihoods of its residents. This paper, therefore, examines the effects of load shedding on South African residents and their opinions on using alternative energy sources, such as solar home systems, as an instrument for mitigation. Employing qualitative methodology, this study leverages the strengths inherent to provide a comprehensive analysis. The findings reveal that all respondents have experienced load shedding and 90% indicated to have been negatively affected by it, which mirrors the experiences of the broader South African population. While there is a marked interest, about 75% among respondents in adopting alternative energy solutions to mitigate the impact of load shedding, financial constraints and the high costs associated with these technologies pose significant barriers to widespread adoption. The study concludes that effective mitigation of load shedding and its detrimental effects on the South African populace requires concerted efforts from power utility providers, retailers, and manufacturers of alternative energy technologies, as well as coordinated actions by the government and both the public and private sectors.

**Keywords:** Alternative Energy Sources · Load Shedding · Lives and Livelihoods · Qualitative Methodology · Renewable Energy

## 1 Introduction

South Africa faces significant challenges with its energy supply, including regular disruptions of electricity supply, generally known as load shedding. Load shedding can be described as the controlled and temporary interruption of electric power supply by the grid operators/utility operators, undertaken to balance the demand and supply of electricity and prevent system overloads or failures, thereby ensuring the overall stability and functionality of the electrical grid [1]. Every stage of load shedding implies

© ICST Institute for Computer Sciences, Social Informatics and Telecommunications Engineering 2026
Published by Springer Nature Switzerland AG 2026. All Rights Reserved
J. B. Awotunde et al. (Eds.): AFRICATEK 2024, LNICST 618, pp. 3–16, 2026.
https://doi.org/10.1007/978-3-031-93557-2_1

a corresponding shedding of its equivalent power in thousands of megawatts. Stage 1 load shedding implies that the national power utility provider, Eskom, sheds 1000 MW of load power from the grid, and Stage 8 load shedding implies that the power utility provider sheds 8000 MW of load power from the grid. This has often resulted in several negative consequences, like reduced productivity and loss of income and revenue to individuals, households, and businesses [2–4]. To mitigate these issues and ensure a more reliable energy supply, the country can turn to alternative energy sources. Since the first occurrence of load shedding and rolling blackouts in South Africa in 2008 [5, 6], its residents have been suffering from increasing stages of load shedding from stage one to stage eight [7], which has greatly affected the lives and livelihoods of South Africans [3–5]. The power utility draws a schedule by which consumers are cut from the national grid's power supply, as depicted on Eskom's mobile application for load shedding called EskomSePush [8]. Therefore, the load shedding schedule is often communicated on the EskomSePush application ahead of its implementation to the customers, except for a few cases where certain sudden breakdown or recovery of power plants causes sudden adjustments to the schedule and make the utility provider incapacitated to follow the initial schedule reflected on the app. However, customers, in most cases, welcome sudden recoveries that may eliminate their load shedding schedule than sudden breakdowns.

The challenges of load shedding have made residential, commercial, and industrial consumers of electricity in the country seek alternatives to meeting their electricity demands through battery backups and inverter systems, solar systems and farms, and wind power plants/farms, among the common options. Some consumers use the energy alternatives during load shedding while some go off-the-grid because their type of businesses would be greatly negatively impacted by an off-and-on power supply [9].

The National Energy Regulator of South Africa (NERSA) has defined the new stages of load shedding in South Africa and increased it to stage 16 should the need arise, as shown in Fig. 1 with data obtained from [10]. All the stages are scheduled; that is, customers are notified by the System Operator before their occurrence. Load curtailment for stages 1 to 3 must be within the period and for the duration notified and instructed, while for stages 4 to 10, it must be according to the agreed notification period or reduced to essential loads, and for stages 11 to 16, will mean reduction to essential loads or at the instruction of the System Operator [10].

Figure 1 shows that the deteriorating state of the national load shedding increases as the stage increases. The implication of this is that consumers' denial of access to electricity consumption grows as the national load shedding increases over time. This denial of the electricity supply is not without its consequences for consumers and the electricity-generating industry. Also, the curtailing effects of load shedding, which initially increased very slowly against the consumers' satisfaction but later increased significantly, may leave consumers seeking alternative sources of energy to meet their energy needs.

Therefore, this paper studies the impact of load shedding on consumers and the use of alternative energy sources to mitigate its effects on the lives and livelihoods of energy consumers in South Africa. Some residents in rural areas suffer from poor quality (low voltage/current) power supply even when there is a supply of electricity from the grid. Also, the study showed that though some people may want to use clean alternative energy

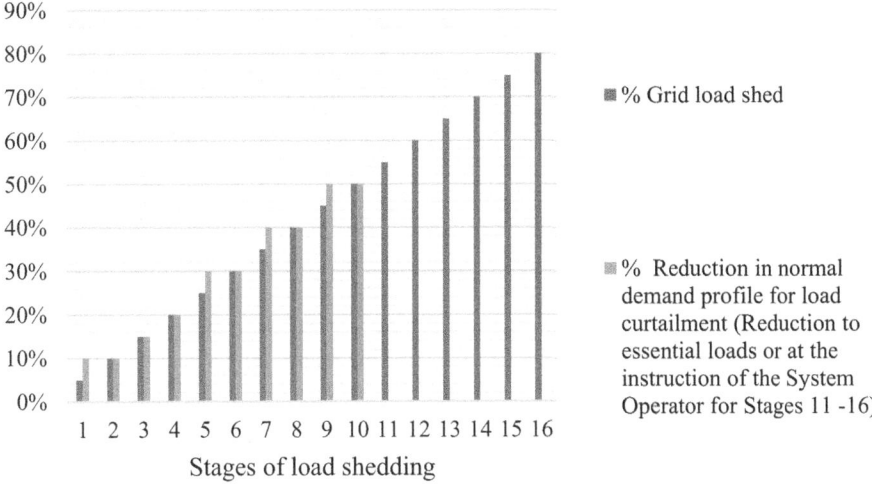

**Fig. 1.** New national load shedding stages as defined by NERSA (data obtained from [10].

sources to mitigate the effects of load shedding on their lives and livelihoods, they do not have the financial capabilities to do so. Therefore, this paper investigates the impact of load shedding on consumer satisfaction in South Africa, and the effect of alternative energy sources on their livelihoods. The findings of this study also show that everyone in South Africa, irrespective of where they live, is experiencing load shedding.

The rest of this paper is structured as follows: the literature review in Sect. 2 and the methodology, results, analysis, and discussion, and the conclusion in Sects. 3, 4, and 5, respectively.

## 2 Literature Review

Energy is a key factor that has a profound impact on the growth and development of households and, ultimately, the economy. Accordingly, understanding the determinants of household energy choices is crucial for developing effective strategies to address energy challenges and promote sustainable development.

Theoretically, from an energy economics perspective, the economic theory of household behaviour provides the framework for this study. The basic premise of this theory is that household decisions on production and consumption are based on the utility or satisfaction that is derived from the goods or services [11]. These choices are dependent on several factors, including income, price, and substitutes, among others. Importantly, the type of good or service is a key factor in household decisions and choices [12]. Consequently, energy can be classified as an 'essential good' (compared to a luxury good). Therefore, consumers will seek substitutes to meet their essential energy needs if they are unsatisfied with their current service. Stemming from the theory of household behaviour, the energy ladder hypothesis has been used to explain the use of changes in energy sources from one level to another [13]. This implies that individuals or households move from lower energy sources like coal to higher energy sources like electricity as their income increases. However, we argue that the energy ladder hypothesis may more likely occur in rural and low-income households and may not necessarily eluci-date the energy choices in South Africa because of the necessity of electricity for most of their daily activities. Accordingly, the energy stacking model that posits the use of multiple energy sources could be more plausible [14]. However, both models can be seen as complementary rather than substitutes. In the context of this study, the unstable supply of electricity in the country could influence households' choice of alternative sources, whether through the energy ladder or energy stacking channels.

In the empirical literature, a large and growing body of literature has explored the adoption of alternative energy sources due to various factors like economic and envi-ronmental concerns. In developed countries, there has been an increase in the use of renewable energies like wind, solar energy, and bioenergy. However, households are still mainly dependent on grid electricity. For example, in Germany, there has been an increase in energy autonomy in some municipalities but not in households, where the electricity is relatively stable [15]. Similarly, a study in Spain found that while there have been transitions from coal to more sustainable renewable energies like wind and nuclear power, households are still largely dependent on the government's grid for electricity [16].

In developing countries, some studies have shown that there has been increased inter-est in alternative energy uses. In Nigeria, Rwanda, Kenya, and Ethiopia, there is evidence of an increase in the dependence on off-grid electricity consumption, especially solar systems and petrol/diesel generators, though the latter is not environmentally friendly [17, 18].

In South Africa, some studies have focused on off-grid electricity in rural areas due to the lower rate of electrification in rural areas than in urban areas [18–20]. Other studies have provided evidence of increasing indications of substitution to solar panel systems, especially for middle and high-income households [19–22].

The main contribution of this paper, therefore, is to provide more recent perceptions on the substitutes for household off-grid energy in a period of increasing load-shedding in South Africa.

## 3  Research Design and Methodology

The research design employed in this study is a qualitative research methodology as it would offer more detailed information about the opinions of people on the topic of study by harnessing the gains thereof. In [23], a qualitative methodology was defined as a research methodology that can help researchers generate hypotheses and enhance further investigation and understanding of quantitative data since it gathers participants' experiences, perceptions, and behaviour. Also, it is considered a tool to gain insights into the constructions of human realities [24] since every human has a right to their opinion on any matter. Hence, the convergence or divergence of these opinions can give us more clarity on the issue. Qualitative analysis, as a stand-alone method and in combination with a quantitative method, has been used to successfully conduct research in different disciplines [25–27]. The research question that guides this study is to find out if load shedding can be enough motivation for South African residents to adopt alternative energy sources for their energy needs.

### 3.1 Data Collection, Sampling, and Ethics

The research instrument used for this study comprises structured questions that were typed and shared with the participants. Their responses were recorded in print so that they could be analysed effectively later. The data collected from this study are stored without the personal details of any of the participants in the University of Johannesburg's repository.

The sampling method adopted for this research is convenience sampling, also called availability sampling, as it allows the researcher to choose the participants from a sample of people who can easily be accessed by the researchers [28, 29]. This sampling method can be used for qualitative, quantitative, and mixed methods of research.

The four principles of ethics, namely beneficence, non-maleficence, autonomy, and justice, were taken into consideration in this research. Participation in the study was voluntary, and participants were free to opt-out at any time when completing the questionnaire. The survey was conducted without any risk to the participants and the researchers. While the participants may not have any direct benefit from participating in the research, they can benefit from government policies that may arise from the implementation of the findings of this research.

Qualitative researchers have argued that data saturation, that is, the point at which new data no longer provide additional insights or themes can be achieved with a relatively small sample size [30, 31]. It is clear, however, that the reported experiences and insights are specific to these participants. Therefore, the sample size of participants was considered satisfactory to allow for knowing the rich textured understanding of the phenomena being investigated, and yet small enough to give room for a deep case-oriented analysis [31]. As it turned out in this study, a data saturation point was reached with 40 participants, as it became clear that no new meta-themes were emerging.

This study was conducted by engaging 40 participants within South Africa, with 80%, 17.5%, and 2.5% of them living in urban, rural, and semi-urban areas of the nation, respectively, with their employment type, at the time of completing the questionnaire, presented in Fig. 2. The unemployed respondents constitute 71% in the rural area and 19% in the urban area. This is similar to the general statistics of South Africa having a higher unemployment population in rural areas than in urban areas [32].

The majority, that is, 53% of South Africans earn their income from salaries [33]. Hence, salaries are a good tool for determining the affordability of alternative energy sources by the respondents. Other sources of income in South Africa in order of decreasing contribution to total household income are grants, businesses and others, remittances, and pensions [34]. The net monthly income of the respondents is presented in Fig. 3.

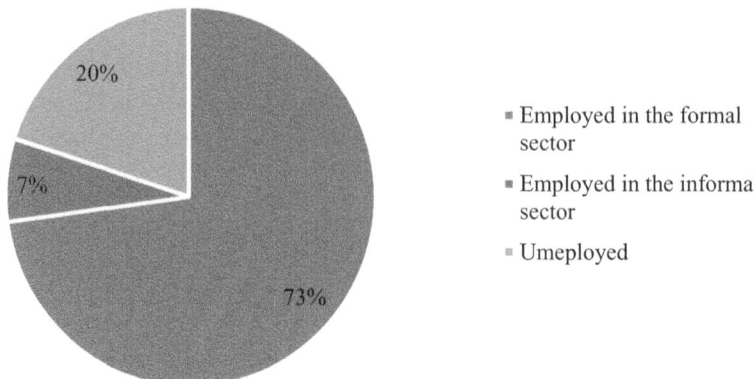

**Fig. 2.**  Employment statistics of the respondents.

Their levels of highest qualification obtained, and ages are presented together in Table 1. This is to show that the respondents are mature and have some level of education to be able to rightly articulate the questions and answer correctly seeing that the least education obtained by the respondents is a secondary school certificate.

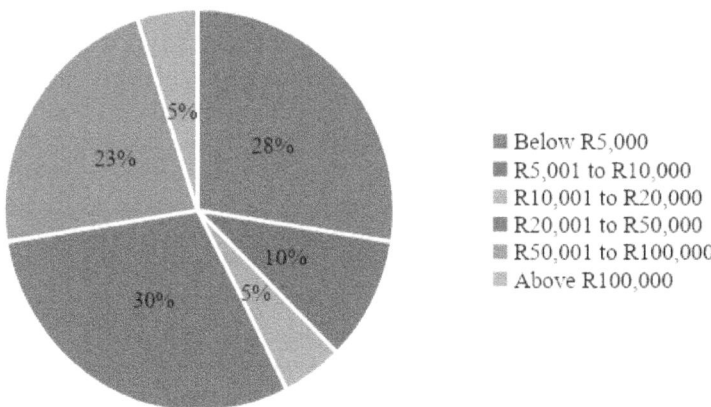

**Fig. 3.**  Net monthly income of respondents.

Our basic model for this study on consumer livelihoods depends on the effect of load shedding households, the impact of Eskom's coal generation on the environment, the cost of electricity bill, solar power generation and feed-in to the grid, carbon footprint, and support the Just Energy Transition agenda.

**Table 1.** Highest qualification obtained and ages of respondents.

| Highest Qualification Obtained by Respondents | | Age Groups of Respondents | |
|---|---|---|---|
| PhD | 15% | 21–30 years old | 35% |
| Masters | 20% | 31–40 years old | 20% |
| Bachelors | 47.5% | 41–50 years old | 20% |
| Advanced Diploma | 2.5% | 51–60 years old | 20% |
| Diploma | 5% | 61–70 years old | 5% |
| Secondary School | 10% | Older than 70 years old | - |
| Primary School | - | | |
| No Formal Education | - | | |

## 4    Results and Discussion

There have been issues with unsatisfactory energy availability factors from the power utility provider in the country, leading to rolling blackouts and load shedding affecting every class of consumers. This necessitated the President of the country to create a portfolio called Minister of Electricity in the Presidency and appoint an engineer to head the ministry [30]. It has, however, contributed to some positive changes in the sector, though not satisfactory as load shedding hasn't been fully mitigated as it often gets worse during the winter months.

For ease of understanding, the responses have been evaluated, analysed, and aggregated/grouped to enable some quantitative presentation of results where possible while limiting the researchers' bias in the study. The structured interview questions comprised open-ended and closed-ended questions, and all the participants were asked the same question to enable ease of analysis. Qualitative answers by the respondents are italicised in this paper to differentiate between the authors' texts and participants' texts, except in the cases of mathematical parameters and equations.

The type of sources of energy that the respondents are using to meet their energy needs is presented in Table 2. This shows that South African residents are gradually exploring alternative energy sources due to the inconveniences caused by load shedding in their lives and livelihoods. In addition, this study makes use of descriptive analysis to investigate the effect of alternative energy sources on the energy consumers' livelihood in South Africa. Table 2 provides a descriptive analysis of our study. Table 2 revealed that tapping from the national grid is the most preferred source of energy. However, the emerging options, as indicated from the responses, proved that customer dissatisfaction with load shedding is on the increase even though it is marginal.

**Table 2.** Choices of electricity supply as sampled in the study.

| Sources of electrical power | Consumer demands | Preference ranking | Weighted average |
|---|---|---|---|
| National Grid | 90% | 1 | 0.77 |
| Inverter with battery | 12.5% | 2 | 0.11 |
| Inverter with generators | 10% | 3 | 0.09 |
| Batteries | 2.5% | 4 | 0.02 |
| Solar panels | 2.5% | 4 | 0.02 |

Source: Authors' Computation, 2024.

The reasons consumers seek alternative sources of energy are highlighted in Table 3, whereby each respondent can have more than one reason, and it shows that the effects of load shedding on their households is the highest factor since it disrupts daily household activities such as cooking, studying, virtual workers, entertainment, heating, ventilation, and air-conditioning devices, etc.

These responses offer explanations to achieve consumer livelihood and show that most people would seek an alternative energy source for personal benefits, such as reducing the effects of load shedding on their households and their monthly electricity bills. Hence, any solution from the government, public, and private sectors to mitigate load shedding should consider consumer preferences if it will be widely adopted. The low response on climate-related reasons shows that most of the respondents, though they all have one form of education or the other, are not motivated by sustainability and environmental friendliness as they are about their comfort.

**Table 3.** Reasons respondents are considering alternative energy sources.

| Reasons for considering alternative energy sources | % of Responses | Preference Ranking |
|---|---|---|
| To reduce the effect of load shedding on my household | 75% | 1 |
| To reduce the impact of Eskom's coal generation on the environment | 20% | 4 |
| To reduce the cost of my electricity bill | 57.5% | 2 |
| To sell my excess solar power generation to the grid | 15% | 6 |
| To reduce carbon footprint | 22.5% | 3 |
| To support the Just Energy Transition agenda | 17.5% | 5 |
| To earn carbon credits and other incentives from Eskom | 10% | 7 |
| To imitate others | 2.5% | 8 |

Source: Authors' Computation, 2024.

Due to the increase in the installation of solar home systems (SHS) in South Africa and the forecast by the International Energy Agency that most of the increase in electrification in Sub-Saharan Africa would come from off-grid energy solutions [33], the participants were asked about the size of the solar home system (SHS) they would like to install for their buildings. Although only one respondent was not interested in the SHS solution, the rest of the respondents have these common answers:

- *SHS to provide lighting in the house*
- *SHS to provide lighting and entertainment (e.g., TV and DSTV decoder)*
- *SHS to power bulbs, computer systems, and Wi-Fi router*
- *SHS to power the entire house during load shedding*
- *SHS to move completely off-the-grid*
- *SHS to power in-house and security lights*
- *SHS to power the lounge*
- *SHS to power the living room and kitchen*

When asked what would encourage them to procure an alternative energy system, their responses include the following:

- *Lower prices*
- *Affordable prices*
- *Government subsidy*
- *Bank financing or loan*
- *Provision of instalment payments by the manufacturers, wholesalers, or retailers*
- *Possibilities for tax rebates on SHS installation*
- *Free installation of SHS by the manufacturers*
- *Very low price such that I can fully acquire it without a loan or instalment payment*

These responses show that most people would need financial support or incentive for them to own an SHS in South Africa.

They were further asked about the type of policies they opined would enhance their adoption of alternative energy use, and their responses include the following:

- *The presence of government tax incentives for local manufacturers and importers of SHS components.*
- *Establishing renewable energy standards in the country.*
- *Establishment of consumer-friendly Feed-in tariffs for building-to-grid and vehicle-to-grid integrations.*
- *Increased education and awareness about alternative energy sources on television, radio, and social media platforms by governments and non-governmental organisations.*
- *Increased funding for research and development on renewable energy sources in the country.*
- *Skills transfer from the developed countries for local production of equipment for installing SHS in South Africa.*
- *Reduced or no tax policy by the government on renewable energy companies and households using renewable energy to power their houses.*
- *Review of curriculum to teach renewable energy technologies in secondary schools to develop local skills for the SHS industry.*

These opinions show that the government of South Africa still has a lot to do in developing and implementing policies that will encourage the populace to use more renewable energy sources to meet their energy needs. For instance, the feed-in policy adopted by the government of the Western Cape [34] needs to become a national policy whereby the national government of South Africa develops policies, standards, processes, and incentives to promote grid-tied distributed renewable energy generation as shown in [35] which can also help to mitigate load shedding. Given that the probability $P$ of an occurrence is generally given as:

$$Probability = \frac{Number\ of\ occurrence\ of\ the\ event}{Total\ number\ of\ possible\ occurrence\ of\ the\ event} \tag{1}$$

Therefore, the probability that a respondent in this study would like to purchase an alternative energy source is $39/40 = 97.5\%$. However, the probability that they will be able to afford an alternative energy source for their households is $23/40 = 57.5\%$. Therefore, most of them are likely to require some sort of financial support for them to have alternative energy sources on their premises.

When inquired about what technical energy solution they would recommend to the government to mitigate load shedding, the following responses were received:

- *Additional coal power plants*
- *Integration of big renewable energy plants to the grid*
- *Reviving failing coal power plants*
- *Try all possible energy technologies that can end load shedding in the country*
- *Nuclear power plants*
- *Integrations of electric vehicles to the grid*
- *Explore possibilities of hydropower plants where possible*
- *Inclusion of biomass generation plants*

These responses show that some respondents are more concerned about ending load shedding than clean energy generation since they want additional/reactivating coal power plants to be connected to the grid to power the country.

From the survey conducted, the highest stage of load shedding that the respondents have experienced is presented in Fig. 4. The newly approved sixteen stages of load shedding by NESRA [10] may bring unprecedented hardship to grid customers, except there is an intervention. This may result in more customers procuring alternative energy sources for themselves.

These results show that stage 5 load shedding is the least load shedding experienced by the respondents, while stage 6 load shedding is the most common highest stage of load shedding experienced by the respondents. There are more occurrences of even-numbered load shedding stages than odd-numbered load shedding stages in the country.

Furthermore, 77% of the participants responded in the affirmative to the question of whether load shedding has affected their livelihoods negatively, as shown in Fig. 5.

However, when asked if load shedding has affected their levels of productivity in any of their endeavours, 90% responded in the affirmative, while 7.5% said that they weren't sure, and just 2.5% said 'No.' Some of the areas in which load shedding affected their productivity include the following:

- *Inability to attend all online classes*
- *Inability to complete some assignments*

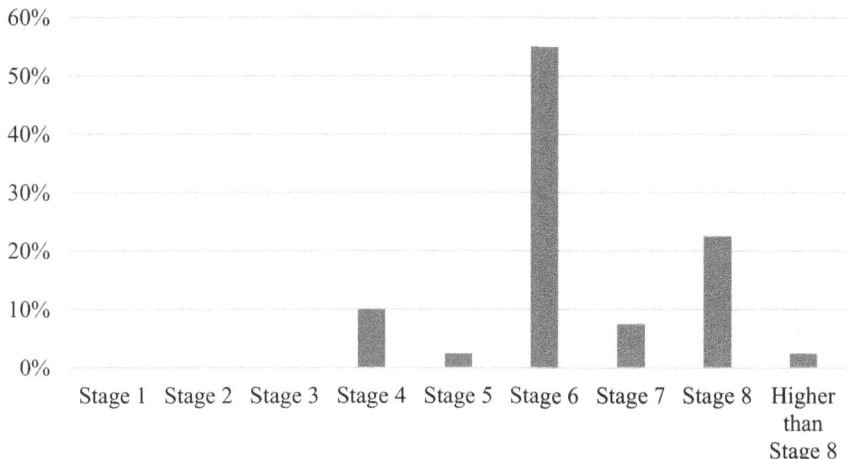

**Fig. 4.** Highest stage of load shedding experienced by the respondents.

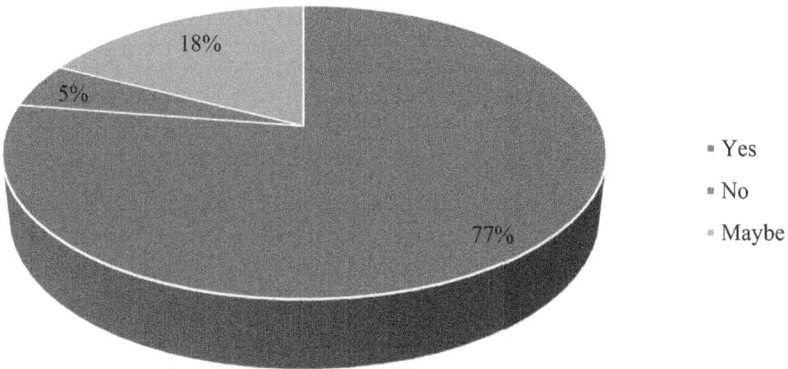

**Fig. 5.** Response to the negative effects of load shedding participants' livelihoods.

- *Inability to meet some work targets*
- *Altered some family social gatherings*
- *Inability to eat what you wanted during load shedding*
- *Poor network connectivity during load shedding*
- *Inability to submit some assignments in due time*
- *Security issues when load shedding happens in the night and on a night shift or returning late from work*

The effects of load shedding on some South African residents and their choice of alternative energy sources have been reported in this section to convey the objectivity of the research findings. The menace of load shedding needs to be addressed as a matter of urgency in South Africa to limit its consequences on the lives and livelihoods of residents as also shown in other works of literature [2–4].

# 5  Conclusion

This paper has explored the perceptions of some residents of South Africa on the effects of load shedding and their plans to mitigate it by acquiring alternative energy sources. The study showed that although all the respondents have experienced load shedding at one time or another, their willingness to mitigate it with solar home systems has been impeded by the challenge of affording SHS for their premises. Hence, financial and policy interventions from government, public, and private stakeholders are required to enhance access to universal electricity in the country and mitigate and/or end load shedding in the country.

Future work would include a wider sample space and population for a quantitative study. Also, the direction and extent of the impact of load shedding on livelihoods cannot be verified because an in-depth econometric analysis is required to achieve this. This will be investigated in our subsequent work.

# References

1. Eskom: What is load shedding? https://loadshedding.eskom.co.za/LoadShedding/Description. Accessed 18-06-2024
2. Erero, J.C.: Impact of loadshedding in South Africa: a CGE analysis. J. Econ. Polit. Econ. **10**(2), 78–94 (2023)
3. Masinga, F., Madzivhandila, T.: Loadshedding impact on food spoilage: an analysis of household experiences in South Africa. Afr. J. Govern. Dev. Sabinet Afr. J. **12**(2), 182–197 (2023)
4. Goldberg, A.: The economic impact of load shedding: the case of South African retailers. Mini-Dissertation, University of Pretoria (2015)
5. Altman, M.: The impact of electricity price increases and rationing on the South African economy. Department for International Development (DFID) Initiative, United Kingdom (2008)
6. Eskom: Our Recent Past - Shift performance and grow sustainably (2024). https://www.eskom.co.za/heritage/history-in-decades/eskom-2003-2012/. Accessed 29-03-2024
7. Eskom: Finding and Interpreting Schedules (2018). https://loadshedding.eskom.co.za/LoadShedding/ScheduleInterpretation. Accessed 29-03-2024
8. ESP: EskomSePush (ESP) (2024). https://esp.info/. Accessed 29-03-2024
9. Businesstech: More big companies are moving away from Eskom's grid (2022). https://businesstech.co.za/news/energy/589934/more-big-companies-are-moving-away-from-eskoms-grid/#:~:text=All%20of%20SAB's%20Breweries%20in,operation%20entirely%20off%20the%20grid. Accessed 29-03-2024
10. National Energy Regulator of South Africa (NERSA): Part 9: Code of Practice – Load Reduction Practices, System Restoration Practices and Critical Load and Essential Load Requirements Under Power System Emergencies (2024). https://www.nersa.org.za/wp-content/uploads/bsk-pdf-manager/2024/04/NERSA-Approved-Version-of-NRS-048-9-2023-Edition-3.pdf. Accessed 18-04-2024
11. Vermeulen, F.: Collective household models: principles and main results. J. Econ. Surv. **16**(4), 533–564 (2002)
12. Frederiks, E.R., Stenner, K., Hobman, E.V.: Household energy use: applying behavioural economics to understand consumer decision-making and behaviour. Renew. Sustain. Energy Rev. **41**, 1385–1394 (2015)

13. Masera, O.R., Saatkamp, B.D., Kammen, D.M.: From linear fuel switching to multiple cooking strategies: a critique and alternative to the energy ladder model. World Dev. **28**(12), 2083–2103 (2000)
14. Waleed, K., Mirza, F.M.: Examining fuel choice patterns through household energy transition index: an alternative to traditional energy ladder and stacking models. Environ. Dev. Sustain. **25**(7), 6449–6501 (2023)
15. Weinand, J.M., Ried, S., Kleinebrahm, M., McKenna, R., Fichtner, W.: Identification of potential off-grid municipalities with 100% renewable energy supply for future design of power grids. IEEE Trans. Power Syst. **37**(4), 3321–3330 (2020)
16. García-Gusano, D., Iribarren, D.: Prospective energy security scenarios in Spain: the future role of renewable power generation technologies and climate change implications. Renew. Energy **126**, 202–209 (2018)
17. Mugisha, J., Ratemo, M.A., Keza, B.C.B., Kahveci, H.: Assessing the opportunities and challenges facing the development of off-grid solar systems in Eastern Africa: the cases of Kenya, Ethiopia, and Rwanda. Energy Policy **150**, 112131 (2021)
18. Monyei, C.G., Adewumi, A.O., Jenkins, K.E.H.: Energy (in) justice in off-grid rural electrification policy: South Africa in focus. Energy Res. Soc. Sci. **44**, 152–171 (2018)
19. Longe, O.M., Rao, N., Omowole, F., Oluwalami, A.S., Oni, O.T.: A case study on off-grid microgrid for universal electricity access in the Eastern Cape of South Africa. Int. J. Energy Eng. **7**(2), 55–63 (2017)
20. Masuku, B.: Rethinking South Africa's household energy poverty through the lens of off-grid energy transition. Development Southern Africa, pp. 1–24 (2024)
21. Cheruiyot, K., Lengaram, E., Siteleki, M.: South Africa's energy landscape amidst the crisis: unpacking energy sources and drivers with 2022 South African census data. Sustainability **16**(2), 682 (2024)
22. Mulaudzi, S.K., Bull, S., Makhado, R.A.: Potential of households' solar PV consumption in South Africa. Afr. J. Sci. Technol. Innov. Dev. **14**(3), 730–739 (2022)
23. Tenny, S., Brannan, J.M., Brannan, G.D.: Qualitative Study. [Updated 2022 Sep 18]. In: StatPearls [Internet]. Treasure Island (FL): StatPearls Publishing (2024)
24. Cropley, A.: Introduction to Qualitative Research Methods: A Practice-Oriented Approach. University of Hamburg, Editura Intaglio Publishing House (2022)
25. Longe, O.M.: An assessment of energy poverty and gender nexus towards clean energy adoption in rural South Africa. Energies **14**(12), 3708 (2021)
26. Golzar, J., Noor, S., Tajik, O.: Convenience sampling. Int. J. Educ. Lang. Stud. **1**(2), 72–77 (2022)
27. Scholtz, S.E.: Sacrifice is a step beyond convenience: a review of convenience sampling in psychological research in Africa. South African J. Indust. Psychol. 1–12 (2021)
28. Statistics South Africa: Statistical Release - General Household Survey 2022. https://www.statssa.gov.za/publications/P0318/P03182022.pdf. Accessed 17-04-2024
29. South African Government News Agency: Dr Kgosientsho Ramokgopa appointed Minister of Electricity in the Presidency, 6 March 2023. https://www.sanews.gov.za/south-africa/dr-kgosientsho-ramokgopa-appointed-minister-electricity-presidency#:~:text=President%20Cyril%20Ramaphosa%20has%20announced,in%20the%20Presidency%20for%20Electricity. Accessed 17-04-2024
30. Creswell, J.W.: Research Design: Qualitative, Quantitative, and Mixed Methods Approaches, 4th edn. SAGE Publications Inc, London (2013)
31. Vasileiou, K., Barnett, J., Thorpe, S., Young, T.: Characterising and justifying sample size sufficiency in interview-based studies: systematic analysis of qualitative health research over a 15-year period. BMC Med. Res. Methodol. **18**(148), 1–18 (2018)
32. Statistics South Africa: Quarterly Labour Force Survey: Quarter 1 2024. https://www.statssa.gov.za/publications/P0211/P02111stQuarter2024.pdf. Accessed 18-06-2024

33. International Energy Agency: World Energy Outlook 2023. https://iea.blob.core.windows.net/assets/86ede39e-4436-42d7-ba2a-edf61467e070/WorldEnergyOutlook2023.pdf. Accessed 18-04-2024

34. Western Cape Government: Solar PV for Home and Business (2023). https://www.westerncape.gov.za/110green/energy/solar-pv-home-and-business. Accessed 18-04-2024

35. Longe, O.M., Ouahada, K., Rimer, S., Ferreira, H.C., Vinck, H.: Distributed optimisation algorithm for demand side management in a grid-connected smart microgrid. Sustainability **9**(1088), 1–16 (2017)

# Development of Microservice Application
# for Environment Monitoring

J. Zaafira[1], T. Ananth Kumar[1] ⓘ, Sunday Adeola Ajagbe[2,3,4(✉)] ⓘ,
Adedayo Amos Olayiwola[4] ⓘ, Ijeoma Noella Ezeji[2] ⓘ, and Matthew O. Adigun[2] ⓘ

[1] Department of Computer Science and Engineering, IFET College of Engineering, Villupuram,
India
[2] Department of Computer Science, University of Zululand, Kwadlangezwa 3886, South Africa
saajagbe@pgschool.lautech.edu.ng
[3] Department of Computer Engineering, First Technical University, Ibadan 200255, Nigeria
[4] Computer Engineering Department, LAUTECH, Ladoke Akintola University of Technology,
Ogbomoso, Nigeria

**Abstract.** Utilizing microservices, the Internet of Things (IoT), and advanced machine learning algorithms, this study addresses the escalating global demand for sustainable and effective environmental monitoring systems. The focus is on augmenting data gathering, processing, and visualization, with the study delving into the development and deployment of a microservice-based application dedicated to environmental monitoring. Initial data analysis is conducted using simpler models like Logistic Regression. Advanced predictive models, such as XGBoost and AdaBoost, are developed and applied to forecast environmental parameters. Comparative analysis using Random Forest ensures the robustness and accuracy of the chosen models. These models collectively enhance the environmental monitoring system's capability to provide real-time insights and support decision-making processes. The paper showcases the efficacy of machine learning techniques such as Random Forest, Logistic Regression, AdaBoost, and XGBoost in anticipating and evaluating environmental data. Drawing on a dataset sourced from IoT sensors, the research demonstrates the potential for precise and real-time environmental monitoring. The methodology section provides a comprehensive outline of the project strategy and scientific techniques, accompanied by a thorough review of relevant literature to identify potentials and gaps in the field. The proposed microservice architecture is not only robust and scalable but also adaptable to diverse applications, contributing significantly to the discourse on environmental monitoring. The study's results suggest promising avenues for further research in this emerging area and lay a solid foundation for enhancing data-driven decision-making in environmental management.

**Keywords:** Microservices · Environment Monitoring · IoT · Machine Learning · Microservice Architecture · Sustainability · Data Analysis

J. B. Awotunde et al. (Eds.): AFRICATEK 2024, LNICST 618, pp. 17–34, 2026.
https://doi.org/10.1007/978-3-031-93557-2_2

# 1 Introduction

There is an urgent demand for creative solutions in the sector of environment monitoring due to the quick advancement of technology and the growing worries about environmental issues [1]. This paper provides a novel way to develop a robust and flexible microservice application for environment monitoring by utilizing microservices, Internet of Things (IoT), and machine learning [2]. It provides the issue statement, the context and motivation for research, and the research objectives that guide work in this introduction [3]. Understanding and maintaining the ecological health of planet depend heavily on environmental monitoring [4]. The scalability, adaptability to changing environmental circum- stances, and real-time data collecting of traditional monitoring methods—many of which depend on manually operated systems—are all limited. The emergence of IoT technology presents a singular chance to transform environmental monitoring through the amalgamation of sensor data, cloud computing, and data analytics into a unified and adaptable system [5]. The pressing need to solve global environmental issues like air quality, ecosystem health, and climate change is what drives [6]. For the purpose of formulating policies and making educated decisions, timely and accurate data collection and analysis are essential [7]. Goal is to improve the capabilities of environmental monitoring by creating a microservice-based system that facilitates effective data collecting, processing, and display.

Numerous issues impede the efficacy of the current environmental monitoring methods. Data silos, restricted scalability, and inadequate flexibility to various environmental conditions and data sources are some of these difficulties [8]. Furthermore, there is still work to be done on the smooth integration of machine learning algorithms for analytical and predictive activities [9]. In order to overcome these obstacles, research aims to develop a microservice-based system that offers a stable and adaptable framework for real-time environment monitoring in addition to overcoming the current constraints [10].

This study sets forth the following objectives:

(1) Develop a Microservice Architecture: Designing and implementing a microservice architecture specifically for environmental monitoring is the main goal of project [12, 13]. With the help of microservices for data processing, storing, displaying, and gathering, this architecture will be modular, scalable, and easily integrated with IoT sensors.

(2) Leverage Machine Learning Techniques: In order to forecast and evaluate environmental data, want to use cutting-edge machine learning algorithms including Random Forest, Logistic Regression, AdaBoost, and XGBoost [14].

   i. Random Forest

   For both classification and regression tasks. Can be used to predict environmental conditions like air quality index, temperature trends, etc., by learning from historical data. Handles large datasets and can capture complex interactions between variables. It is robust to overfitting due to its ensemble nature.

   ii. Logistic Regression

   Primarily for binary classification tasks. Useful for predicting the likelihood of certain events, such as whether a particular pollutant level exceeds a safe threshold.

Simple and interpretable model, efficient for binary outcomes, and can be used as a baseline model.

iii. AdaBoost

Used for boosting weak classifiers in classification tasks. Enhances the performance of simple models to improve the accuracy of predictions related to environmental parameters. Combines multiple weak learners to form a strong classifier, thus improving prediction performance.

iv. XGBoost

Both for classification and regression tasks, known for its high performance and speed. Can be used for various predictions in environmental monitoring, such as forecasting pollution levels, predicting weather patterns, etc. Efficient, scalable, handles missing values well, and provides high predictive accuracy due to its gradient boosting framework.

These algorithms will reveal patterns, irregularities, and possible hazards in the environment.

(3) Evaluate Performance: The assessment of the microservice-based system's and machine learning models' effectiveness in actual environmental monitoring situations is a crucial component of research. The system and models' scalability, accuracy, and efficiency in real-world applications will all be evaluated.

By fulfilling these goals, research hopes to offer a comprehensive and innovative response to the problems that conventional environmental monitoring systems present [15]. The main goal is to support data-driven, more sustainable approaches to environmental management, which will help to maintain and safeguard the ecological health of world [16].

The remaining part of this paper was organized as follows: Sect. 2 serves as the starting point for field inquiry and enabled better understanding of the existing literature in microservice application environment in which research is situated. Section 3 detailed the tools and methodologies employed to achieve research objectives. Among the pivotal algorithms, the Random Forest Algorithm and Logistic Regression Algorithm offered robust methods for data analysis and prediction for Handling Diverse Data Types, Robust to Overfitting, Feature Importance, Resilience to Outliers, Handling Missing Data, Ensemble Learning for Stability, Predictive Accuracy, Parallelization. Further- more, exploration of AdaBoost and XGBoost algorithms exemplified commitment to providing a comprehensive overview of Machine learning techniques are utilized in various aspects of environmental monitoring to analyze data, make predictions, and improve decision-making processes here are some applications and areas where machine learning is commonly employed in environmental monitoring are air quality monitoring, remote sensing, climate change monitoring etc. In this paper, laid out the specifics of microservices architecture can enhance scalability, flexibility, and maintainability in modular design, Monitoring and logging. With clarity, articulated the intricacies of System Architecture, Data Processing, Model Training and Testing, Performance Evaluation, and Measurement Setup. Each element was finely tuned to ensure the scalability, resilience, modularity, and flexibility of the system – key factors in enabling efficient and effective environmental monitoring.

## 2  Literature Review

This section acts as the foundation of this research paper, providing readers with a thorough grasp of the corpus of knowledge already available in the topic. Here, to explore the key elements of environment monitoring and microservices, talking about the ideas, tools, and techniques that have influenced the field and pointing out the gaps that indicate areas that still require investigation.

**A. Overview of Environment Monitoring and Microservices**
Concerns about climate change and environmental sustainability have led to a growing interest in the diverse topic of environment monitoring. In this regard, microservices have become a potent technological tool for developing and putting into operation effective environmental monitoring systems. Microservices have been applied to environment monitoring in a number of studies, with their scalability, modularity, and adaptability being highlighted. The creation of microservice architectures specifically suited for environment monitoring is a major field of study. These designs usually consist of a network of interconnected microservices that handle different functions, such as gathering, storing, processing, and displaying data. Empirical studies have demonstrated that these architectures provide a dispersed and adaptable approach, hence augmenting the capacity of monitoring systems to conform to diverse environmental circumstances and requirements.

**B. Key Concepts, Technologies, and Algorithms in the Field**
The collection, processing, and analysis of environmental data using cutting-edge technology and algorithms is a crucial component of environment monitoring. The environmental monitoring industry has seen a significant transformation in recent years, largely due to the Internet of Things (IoT). To obtain real-time data on variables like temperature, humidity, and air quality, IoT devices and sensors can be spread over large geographic areas. The requisite infrastructure for data processing and analysis is provided by microservices in the cloud, where the data is transferred. The interpretation of complicated environmental data has benefited greatly from the application of machine learning techniques, notably neural networks. Long-Short-Term Memory (LSTM) networks and Recurrent Neural Networks (RNNs) have shown to be excellent tools for environmental monitoring applications due to their ability to recognize anomalies and forecast time series. These algorithms enable prompt interventions and decision-making by recognizing trends, spotting abnormalities, and accurately predicting changes in the environment.

Data Curation Process for LSTM and RNN.

- Data Collection:

  Data was collected from IoT sensors deployed in various locations to monitor environmental parameters such as temperature, humidity, air quality, and noise levels. The sensors captured data at regular intervals, creating a time-series dataset. The data included multiple features relevant to environmental conditions.

- Data Preprocessing:

Cleaning: The raw data was cleaned to remove any noise or outliers. Missing values were handled using techniques such as interpolation or imputation.

Normalization: To ensure that the data fed into the LSTM and RNN models was on a similar scale, normalization (e.g., min-max scaling) was applied.

Feature Selection: Relevant features were selected based on their importance to the prediction task. This included both primary environmental parameters and derived features.

Sequence Creation: The time-series data was split into sequences of fixed length. Each sequence served as an input to the model, with the corresponding output being the parameter to be predicted at the next time step.

- Data Splitting:

Training and Testing Sets: The dataset was divided into training and testing sets to evaluate the performance of the models. A common split is 80% for training and 20% for testing.

Validation Set: A portion of the training set was further split into a validation set to tune the model hyperparameters and avoid overfitting.

### C. Internet of Things (IoT)

The method which data is gathered and sent in the context of environment monitoring has been completely transformed by the IoT, or IoT for short [11]. IoT is the network of interconnected devices, sensors, and systems that provide real-time data collection and analysis. IoT devices are strategically placed to collect data from a variety of sources, such as weather stations, soil moisture sensors, and air quality sensors, in environmental monitoring. After that, this data is sent to cloud-based platforms or central servers so that it may be processed and examined. IoT's capacity to deliver high-resolution, real-time data is advantageous for environmental monitoring. This helps scholars and decision-makers to make well-informed decisions about resource allocation, disaster management, and environmental policies. Furthermore, the ability to remotely monitor and operate the sensor network eliminates the need for labor-intensive and costly manual data collecting [11].

### D. Machine Learning Models for Microservice Environment

The software used to implement machine learning algorithms determines how effective the algorithms are. A number of software libraries and frameworks have become well-known in the field of machine learning for environment monitoring. Two stand out among them: TensorFlow and Keras. Google created TensorFlow, an open-source machine learning framework that is now widely used in both industry and academics. It is a great option for creating machine learning models, especially those for environmental monitoring, because of its scalability and adaptability. On top of TensorFlow, however, is an open-source neural network library called Keras. A high- level API is offered for creating and refining deep learning models. Because Keras makes building sophisticated neural networks easier, it's a top option for researchers and developers in the field. The choice of Machine Learning algorithms such as Random Forest, Logistic Regression, AdaBoost, and XGBoost was likely informed by their effectiveness in anticipating and evaluating environmental data. These algorithms are commonly used in various predictive modeling tasks due to their ability to handle complex datasets and provide accurate predictions.

i. Random Forest Algorithm

The Random Forest algorithm is an effective method for group learning. It functions by building numerous decision trees and integrating the results. Random Forest is used in environmental monitoring to provide forecasts by combining data from many sources. Provided a comparative benchmark for evaluating the performance of different models, helping to identify the most accurate and reliable predictive model. There are four main parts in the algorithm's operation: first, it takes random samples from the dataset, builds a decision tree for each sample, gets a prediction from each decision tree, and then chooses the forecast that receives the most votes as the eventual prediction. This ensemble approach is a useful tool in environmental data analysis since it improves forecast accuracy.

ii. Logistic Regression Algorithm

One popular classification approach that works well for binary classification issues is logistic regression shown in Fig. 1. It can be used to divide data into discrete groups when it comes to environmental monitoring. Based on certain input features, it can be used, for instance, to assess the safety or contamination of water quality. Because of its ease of use and interpretability, logistic regression is a vital tool for environmental researchers.

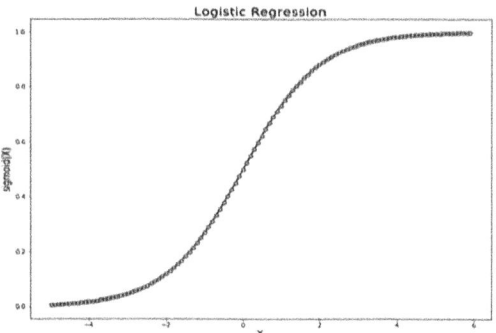

**Fig. 1.** Logistic Regression.

iii. AdaBoost Algorithm

AdaBoost is an ensemble learning technique that builds a more robust and accurate model by aggregating the predictions of several base classifiers. AdaBoost was used to enhance prediction accuracy by combining weak classifiers into a strong ensemble model. In order to give the difficult samples more weight, repeatedly modifies the weights of examples.

that were mistakenly classified. AdaBoost can be used in environmental monitoring to improve forecast accuracy, especially when handling imbalanced datasets or challenging classification issues.

iv. XGBoost Algorithm

   The sophisticated gradient boosting algorithm XGBoost is renowned for its effectiveness and forecasting ability. It is frequently utilized in practical applications and machine learning contests. XGBoost can be used for environmental/monitoring tasks such as anomaly detection, feature selection, and time series prediction. XGBoost, a powerful gradient boosting algorithm, was used for both classification and regression tasks. It was particularly effective in predicting air quality levels and other environmental parameters by learning from historical data.

   Application Point: After initial feature selection, XGBoost was applied to create robust predictive models. Its ability to handle large datasets and capture intricate patterns made it suitable for forecasting trends and identifying periods of high pollution or adverse environmental conditions.

   It is a useful tool in data analysis because of its capacity to manage missing values and carry out efficient tree pruning. Algorithms and technology are essential to contemporary environmental monitoring. These tools facilitate precise data gathering, analysis, and prediction other machine learning algorithms and ensemble techniques such as Random Forest, Logistic Regression, AdaBoost, and XGBoost, as well as the smooth integration of IoT devices.

The workflow integrating these algorithms can be described as:

1. Feature Selection and Initial Analysis:

   Logistic Regression- helped select the most relevant features from the dataset.

2. Predictive Modeling

   XGBoost- was deployed to create accurate predictive models for environmental parameters.
   AdaBoost- was used to refine these models by improving their predictive performance.

3. Model Evaluation:

   Random Forest- was used to compare the effectiveness of XGBoost and AdaBoost, ensuring the most accurate and reliable model was selected for the environmental monitoring system.

   Using technology and algorithms to their advantage, academics and decision-makers may make wise decisions to protect.

**E. Identification of Gaps in the Current Literature**
Although the integration of environment monitoring with microservices has advanced significantly in previous research, there are still a number of unanswered questions that need to be answered. The need for better data security and privacy in the context of microservices for environment monitoring is one obvious requirement. In order to protect data integrity and privacy, research in this field should concentrate on strong

encryption and access control measures because environmental data frequently carries significant significance and sensitivity. Moreover, there is still unrealized potential in integrating microservices into current environmental monitoring infrastructures. The benefits of microservices could be extended to many legacy monitoring systems; however, the process of conversion and integration has some problems that need to be carefully considered. To sum up, this literature analysis has given a thorough overview of the combination of microservices and environment monitoring. The review has identified gaps in present research, opening the door for more investigation into the field, and emphasized the importance of microservice architectures in achieving scalability and flexibility. It has also highlighted the role of IoT and machine learning in data gathering and analysis. These realizations set the stage for the rest of this work, where describe microservice application for environment monitoring and its implementation.

## 3  Methodology

### A. Dataset Processing in a Typical Microservice Application for Environment Monitoring

Data from different field-deployed sensors is collected, stored, processed, and visualized in an environment monitoring microservice application. Temperature, humidity, air quality, and other environmental factors are just a few of the many parameters that these sensors can record. With the help of the microservices design, the application is divided into smaller, scalable, independently deployable parts, each handling a single job. In this system, data collection, data storage, data processing, and data visualization are the four main microservices that are essential.

   i. Data Collection Microservice: The application's entry point, the Data Collection microservice, collects data from a network of sensors distributed over various geographic regions. The crucial connection between the digital world and the physical sensors is established by this microservice. It is in charge of sensor connectivity, data collecting, and preliminary quality assessment of the incoming data streams. Reliable environmental monitoring is based on accurate, timely, and secure data collection, which is ensured by a well-implemented Data Collection microservice. The collection of data from the many sensors and sources installed in the monitoring environment is the responsibility of this microservice. It guarantees that information is gathered instantly and sent safely to the central system.

  ii. Data Storage Microservice: The responsibility for storing the gathered data falls to the Data Storage microservice. It saves the information in a database so that it may be retrieved and analyzed later. The efficient handling of massive data volumes by this microservice guarantees the availability of historical records for long-term trend analysis and decision- making. Ensuring the integrity of environmental data and generating significant insights over an extended period of time require strong data storage. After being gathered, data is safely kept in a specific microservice for data storage. This part offers effective data retrieval for analysis while guaranteeing data integrity.

iii. Data Processing Microservice: The Data Processing microservice takes over to convert and analyze the data after it has been safely saved. This microservice uses machine learning methods and algorithms to sift through the raw data and find patterns and important information. It is in charge of feature extraction, data normalization, and cleaning—all essential processes for precise environmental monitoring. During this stage, anomaly detection, predictive modeling, and intricate computations may be used to find patterns and possible environmental problems. An essential part of system is data processing. This microservice prepares the dataset for model training and testing, processes the raw data, and extracts features. It uses preprocessing, cleaning, and transformation methods to make sure the data is ready for machine learning.

iv. Visualization Microservice: The Visualization microservice serves as an intermediary between decision-makers or end users and the processed data. It provides the analyzed data in an easy-to-use and visually appealing format. Users can learn more about trends and environmental conditions by interacting with interactive charts, dashboards, and maps. Making data-driven decisions requires visualization because it makes it possible for people to successfully comprehend and analyze the data. Visualization is crucial for monitoring and decision-making. This microservice offers real-time visualization tools, enabling users to interpret and analyze the data through intuitive graphs, charts, and dashboards.

## B. Key Features

In addition to the core microservices, a well-designed microservice application for environment monitoring boasts several key features that enhance its functionality and effectiveness.

i. Scalability: Systems for monitoring the environment frequently have to adjust to shifting workloads and growing sensor networks. A key component that enables microservices to manage growing workloads and data volumes without sacrificing performance is scalability. Microservice instances can be added or removed as needed, allowing the system to develop and remain effective all at once.

ii. Resilience: The mission-critical application of environmental monitoring places the highest priority on data integrity and system availability. Resilience should be considered when designing the microservices that the system can function even in the event of errors or disruptions. The fundamental elements of a resilient microservice architecture include redundancy, failover methods, and disaster recovery strategies.

iii. Modularity: Modularity allows for the independent development, deployment, and scaling of microservices. Each microservice operates as a standalone unit, making it easier to maintain and update the system. This flexibility enables rapid development and adaptation to changing environmental conditions or evolving sensor technologies.

iv. Flexibility: Environmental monitoring requirements can change over time, prompting alterations in the microservice application. Microservices can be added or removed with ease because to a flexible architecture, which enables the system to adapt to changing requirements and technological advancements. It also encourages compatibility with other systems and data sources, which raises the monitoring application's overall efficacy. To sum up, an environment monitoring program built on a microservices architecture makes use of modularity, scalability, robustness, and flexibility to deliver precise, timely, and useful environmental condition information. This method, which is centered on data collection, storage, processing, and visualization, provides a solid answer to the intricate problems associated with environmental monitoring in a constantly changing global context. These microservice apps will be essential to efforts as technology develops to monitor and protect environment.

### C. Implementation
This project's implementation phase is essential to putting the theories and techniques covered in the earlier sections into practice. The details of system architecture, data processing methods, model testing and training approaches, performance evaluation metrics, and measurement setup are covered in detail in this section. All of these elements work together to make microservice-based environment monitoring program run smoothly.

i. System Architecture

This system architecture is the cornerstone around which the whole application is constructed. It is intended to make it easier for several microservices, each in charge of handling different tasks in the environment monitoring procedure, to operate together seamlessly are depicted in Fig. 2. Because of the scalability built into system architecture, expanding or adding new microservices to meet the needs of expanding data sources and processing demands is possible. Moreover, it demonstrates resilience, guaranteeing that the system continues to function despite malfunctions or network problems. Another fundamental tenet of architecture is flexibility and modularity, which make it simple to replace or integrate new technologies.

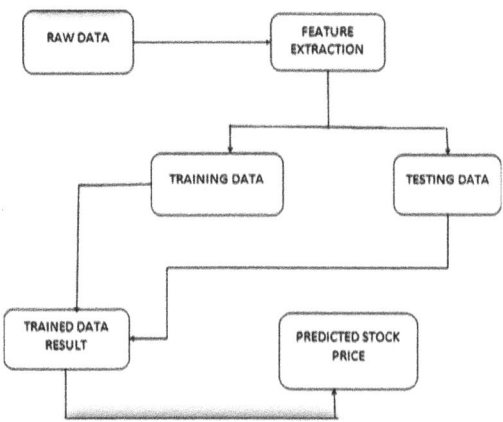

**Fig. 2.** Architecture for proposed system.

ii. Data Processing

The core of system is data processing, which transforms and gets ready for machine learning on raw data gathered from several sensors. The following are the duties performed by the data processing microservice: Feature Extraction: The data processing microservice uses a variety of methods, such as statistical analysis and domain-specific feature engineering, to extract relevant characteristics from the raw data. When creating precise prediction models, these characteristics are essential Training and Testing data: Training and testing datasets are created from the processed data. The testing dataset is put aside for model evaluation, whereas the training dataset is utilized to train machine learning models. The choice of suitable data split ratios is carefully thought out.

Predicted CO2 Emissions: Predicting CO2 emissions is one of system's primary goals. In order to ensure that the dataset has all the information needed for model training, the data processing microservice prepares it for this particular prediction task. By integrating well-known data processing tools and libraries, the data processing microservice enables effective, automated data transformation while preserving data integrity.

iii. Model Training and Testing

The fundamental component of predictive analysis is machine learning models. In order to forecast CO2 emissions and other environmental characteristics, Implement and train models in this phase. The following are the essential elements of model testing and training:

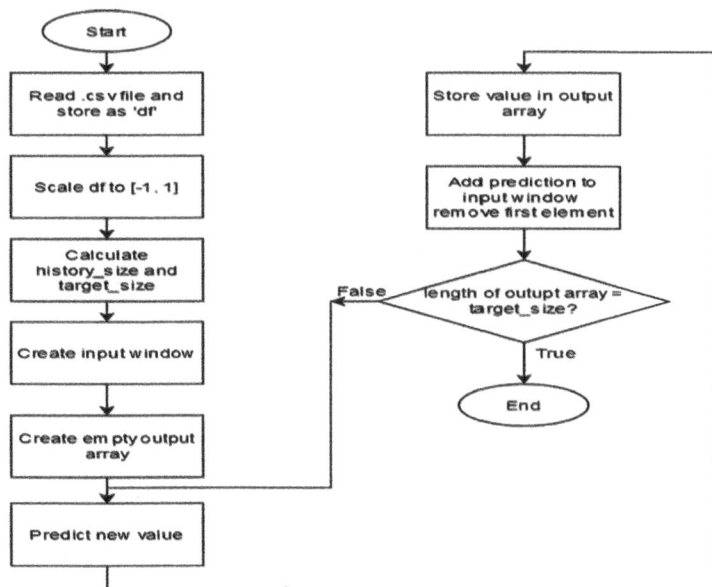

**Fig. 3.** Flowchart describing the prediction script of the multi-step regressive model

**Single-Step Prediction:** Develop models for single- step prediction, providing immediate estimates of CO2 emissions based on real-time sensor data.

**Multi-step, Single Shot Prediction:** In some scenarios, it is essential to predict multiple steps into the future with a single model. Implement such models to provide multi-step predictions in one go.

**Multi-step, Regressive Prediction:** For more complex analysis, build regressive models that predict multiple steps sequentially, offering a comprehensive understanding of environmental trends.

To guarantee the correctness and generalizability of the models, great care is taken in the selection of machine learning methods, hyperparameter tweaking, and model evaluation and the Fig. 3 explains the Flowchart describing the prediction script of the multi-step regressive model to improve the Performance. The model's performance is validated using cross- validation techniques on a variety of datasets.

iv. *Performance Evaluation*

It uses a strong performance evaluation system to guarantee the accuracy and dependability of predictive models. Important components in evaluating performance comprise.

**Regularization:** To prevent overfitting, incorporate regularization techniques in models.

**Parallel Processing:** leverage parallel processing capabilities to enhance model training speed, making it more efficient.

**Handling Missing Values:** Robust strategies are implemented to handle missing data, ensuring minimal data loss.

**Cross-Validation:** Models are evaluated through k-fold cross-validation to assess their generalization capabilities.

**Effective Tree Pruning:** In the case of tree-based algorithms such as Random Forest, effective pruning is applied to optimize model complexity.

Performance measures like R-squared, Root Mean Square Error (RMSE), and Mean Absolute Error (MAE) are used to evaluate the accuracy and predictive power of the model. The assessment procedure aids in determining which model is most suited for particular environment monitoring task.


*D. Project Measurement Setup and Description*

Accurate data collection and validation depend on system's measurements being accurate. To ensure good data quality, have deployed a variety of sensors and devices as part of measuring system. Use sensors to measure CO2 levels, temperature, humidity, and other pertinent environmental factors. The system is built to last and function reliably even in challenging environmental circumstances. To sum up, implementation phase includes building a robust, scalable, and adaptable system architecture; processing data effectively; precisely training and testing models; conducting thorough performance evaluations; and setting up a reliable measurement system. Together, these components allow to provide an environment monitoring solution that is microservice-based and satisfies the scalability, accuracy, and real-time responsiveness requirements of environmental monitoring applications.

The overall plan and methodology used for creating the microservice application for environment monitoring is de- scribed in the Project Method Description. This part offers an understanding of the practical aspects of the project's conception, planning, and implementation. The microservice application was developed in a gradual and iterative manner. The process started with a thorough requirements analysis phase where the particular requirements for environment monitoring were determined. To make sure the application will meet needs in the real world, these requirements were obtained through discussions with possible end users, environmental scientists, and domain specialists. The design of the system architecture was the next step after the requirements were clearly stated. The application's structure, comprising its four primary microservices—data collection, data storage, data processing, and visualization—was delineated at this phase. Scalability, resilience, modularity, and flexibility were also taken into consideration as essential architectural tenets to guarantee the application's capacity to adjust to shifting requirements and circumstances. The design was followed during the implementation phase, with simultaneous development of each microservice.

A microservices design made this possible by enabling several teams to work independently on distinct services. Were able to deploy and manage microservices in an efficient manner by utilizing orchestration and containerization technologies. Because changes and enhancements to a single microservice could be performed without affecting the operation of the entire program, this strategy also encouraged flexibility. Testing played a pivotal role in the project's methodology. Adopted a combination of unit testing, integration testing, and end-to-end testing to ensure the reliability and accuracy of each microservice. Additionally, a continuous integration and continuous deployment (CI/CD) pipeline was set up to automate the testing and deployment processes, promoting agility and quick adaptation to changes. Additionally, a feedback loop with end users and domain experts was built into the project methodology. At several phases of development, collected input and performed user acceptance testing (UAT). Were able to consistently improve the application's functionality, usability, and performance thanks to this iterative feedback approach. Performance optimization and security considerations were addressed in the project's final stages. To improve the application's performance, used a number of strategies, including database optimization, load balancing, and caching. To secure data and make sure the application complied with regulations, security procedures included authorization, authentication, and encryption.

Predictive Accuracy:

LSTM models generally provided better predictive accuracy due to their ability to capture long-term dependencies in the environmental data.

RNNs were useful for capturing short-term patterns and trends.

Real-time Monitoring:

The models were integrated into the microservice architecture, allowing for real-time monitoring and prediction of environmental parameters.

This enabled timely responses to adverse environmental conditions.

# 4  Results and Discussion

The research results are presented in this section of the paper, along with a comparison of work with relevant research in the field of microservice applications for environment monitoring, as well as an emphasis on the experimental results and their implications.

### A. Presentation of Experimental Results
In this section, Present the outcomes of experiments conducted within the microservice framework for environment monitoring these experiments aimed to evaluate the performance and effectiveness of the proposed system.

(1) System Architecture Evaluation: An essential part of suggested approach is the system architecture. It evaluated its scalability, resilience, modularity, and adaptability through trials. Findings show that the microservice design efficiently grows to handle growing data loads, guaranteeing that environmental data is collected, stored, processed, and visualized without hiccups. The system demonstrated exceptional resilience by continuing to function in the face of data disruptions and node failures. Moreover, the microservices' modular design made it simple to include extra monitoring components. According to research, the suggested system design is quite flexible and can be adjusted to fit a variety of environmental monitoring scenarios.

(2) Data Processing and Machine Learning Performance: To assess the performance of the machine learning and data processing microservices, researchers ran a number of in-depth experiments. The microservice for data processing demonstrated effective capabilities for cleaning and transforming data, guaranteeing that information gathered from diverse sensors was appropriately prepared for additional examination and the flow of the Preprocessing script explained in Fig. 4. Trials with LSTM networks for CO2 emissions prediction showed encouraging outcomes in terms of machine learning. Specifically, Evaluated three scenarios for prediction.

(1) **Single-Step Prediction:** Model accurately predicted CO2 emissions for the next time step, providing real- time insights for monitoring and control.

(2) **Multi-step, Single Shot Prediction:** In this scenario, LSTM network predicted CO2 emissions for multiple time steps in a single prediction, allowing for a broader view of future trends.

(3) **Multi-step, Regressive Prediction:** Evaluated the network's ability to predict CO2 emissions retroactively, providing insights into past environmental conditions.

The experimental results indicated that the LSTM network was effective in all three scenarios, with the multi-step, single shot prediction offering the most valuable insights for environment monitoring.

### B. Discussion of Findings.
In this section, to delve into the implications of experimental results and discuss the significance of findings.

(1) *System Scalability and Resilience:* Two important features of findings are the resilience and scalability of microservice architecture. This system is appropriate

for both small- and large-scale monitoring applications since it can handle a broad range of environmental data loads. The durability of the system guarantees continuous data gathering and processing, which is essential for environmental monitoring decision-making in real time. This is especially crucial in situations like monitoring natural disasters or controlling industrial pollution, where system failures could have far- reaching effects.

(2) *Data Processing and Machine Learning:* machine learning and data processing components operate at a promising level. The study is guaranteed to be founded on clean and trustworthy data thanks to the precise data pretreatment. The LSTM network provides a flexible way to track and forecast CO2 emissions because of its flexibility to provide single-step and multi-step predictions. This has important ramifications for reducing greenhouse gas emissions and opens the door to preventative actions to lessen the impact on the environment.

This system's modularity and adaptability enable it to serve diverse environmental monitoring needs beyond highway trajectory prediction, making it a versatile solution. Test findings show that the microservice application for environment monitoring described in this research provides a practical and adaptable method for gathering, analyzing, and forecasting environmental data. A wide range of monitoring applications can benefit from the system's scalability and reliability, and its machine learning components show promise for precise CO2 emissions prediction. This approach is unique in the field since it can be used to a wide range of environmental circumstances and is more flexible than previous comparable work (Figs. 5 and 6).

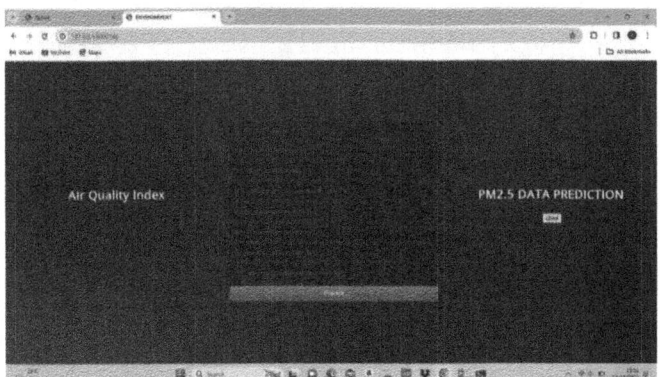

**Fig. 4.** Air Quality index

From the above figures, Measure the air quality index (AQI) in environmental monitoring, specialized sensors data's are deployed to detect various air particles. Common particles include particulate matter (PM10 and PM2.5), ozone (O3), sulfur dioxide (SO2), nitrogen dioxide (NO2), carbon monoxide (CO), and others. These sensors collect data, and the AQI is calculated based on the concentrations of these air particles.

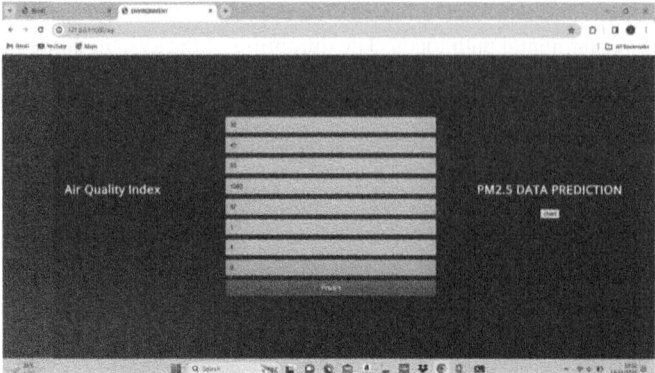

**Fig. 5.** Values of environment

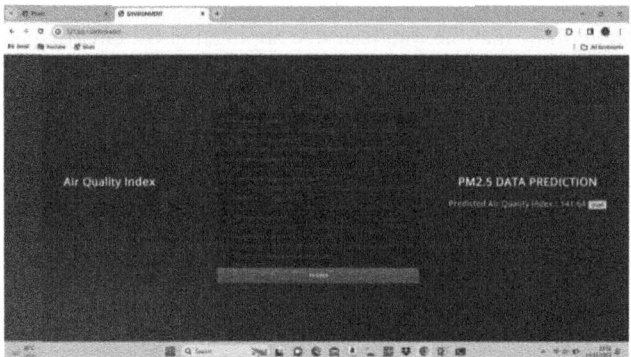

**Fig. 6.** Predicted Air Quality index

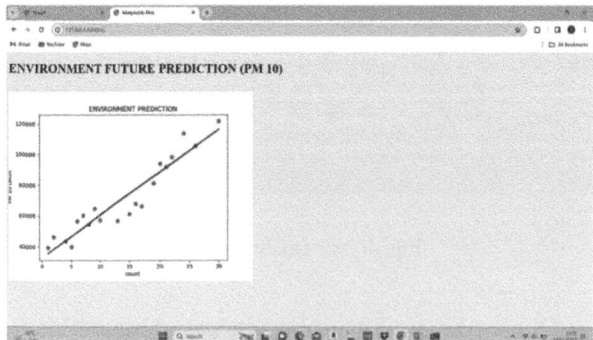

**Fig. 7.** Prediction graph of PM 10

AQI is computed using predefined formulas or standards set by environmental agencies. The AQI is then categorized into different air quality levels, such as good, moderate, unhealthy, etc., to provide a clear understanding of the current air quality. Cities and environmental agencies often have monitoring networks in place to continuously assess air quality and provide real-time information to the public. Access to this information can be through websites, mobile apps, or other communication channels.

From Fig. 7, PM10 (Particulate Matter with a diameter of 10 $\mu$m or smaller) is typically associated with air quality monitoring, while pressure is a meteorological parameter. If you're interested in understanding the impact of air pressure on PM10 levels, you might consider looking at how meteorological conditions influence air quality.

## 5 Conclusion

This research and development efforts in the field of "Microservice Application for Environment Monitoring" have culminated in a deep grasp of how cutting-edge technology and the urgent need to monitor and protect this environment interact. This paper presents strategy in this regard with important highlights the contributions in this area, and suggests future directions for both theoretical and practical applications. In addition to delving into the complexities of machine learning, it focused on RNN and LSTM architecture. The Internet of Things is the cornerstone of environmental data collecting. Microservices rely on these technologies as their brains, which provide precise environmental data processing and prediction. It demonstrated how well microservices predicted and analyzed environmental data. The conversation reaffirmed research goals and emphasized the importance of contributions by monitoring the environment. Finally, work on the Microservice Application for Environment Monitoring serves as a foundation for the development of more sophisticated and comprehensive environmental monitoring systems. Have shown how cutting-edge technologies and machine learning algorithms can improve comprehension of the surrounding world. Development of a resilient, scalable, and modular microservice architecture. As understand that there is still much to learn and accomplish in this area as to move forward. Prospective avenues for investigation encompass the integration of increasingly sophisticated machine learning methodologies, the investigation of novel sensor technologies, and the creation of intuitive user interfaces intended for environmental management decision-makers. Hope that by applying cutting-edge technologies and data-driven insights, work will encourage others to join in the effort to preserve and safeguard planet.

## References

1. Hsu, C.-C., Quang-Thanh, N., Chien, F., Li, L., Mohsin, M.: Evaluating green innovation and performance of financial development: mediating concerns of environmental regulation. Environ. Sci. Pollut. Res. **28**(40), 57386–57397 (2021)
2. Chen, L., et al.: IoT microservice deployment in edge - cloud hybrid environment using reinforcement learning. IEEE Int. Things J. **8**, no. 16, 12610–12622 (2020)
3. Hampton, C., Reeping, D., Ozkan, D.S.: Positionality statements in engineering education research: a look at the hand that guides the methodological tools. Stud. Eng. Educ. **1**, no. 2 (2021)
4. Nelson, M.K., Shilling, D., eds.: Traditional Ecological Knowledge: Learning from Indigenous Practices for Environmental Sustainability. Cambridge University Press (2018)

5. Aminizadeh, S., et al.: The applications of machine learning techniques in medical data processing based on distributed computing and the Internet of Things. Comput. Methods Prog. Biomed. 107745 (2023)
6. Fuller, R., et al.: Pollution and health: a progress update. Lancet Planet. Health **6**, 6, e535–e547 (2022)
7. Patton, C., Sawicki, D., Clark, J.: Basic Methods of Policy Analysis and Planning–Pearson Etext. Routledge (2015)
8. Gibb, R., Browning, E., Glover-Kapfer, P., Jones, K.E.: Emerging opportunities and challenges for passive acoustics in ecological assessment and monitoring. Methods Ecol. Evol. **10**(2), 169–185 (2019)
9. Driss, M., Hasan, D., Boulila, W., Ahmad, J.: Microservices in IoT security: current solutions, research challenges, and future directions. Proc. Comput. Sci. **192**, 2385–2395 (2021)
10. Li, S., et al.: Understanding and addressing quality attributes of microservices architecture: a Systematic literature review. Inform. Softw. Technol. **131**, 106449 (2021)
11. Ajagbe, S.A., Adigun, M.O., Awotunde, J.B., Oladosu, J.B., Oguns, Y.J.: Internet of things enabled convolutional neural networks: applications, techniques, challenges, and prospects. In: Naved, M., et al. IoT-enabled Convolutional Neural Networks: Techniques and Applications. River Publisher, pp. 27–63 (2023)
12. Eziakolamnwa, V. C., Ajayi, S. A., Adekoya, A. M., Adekunle, A. A., Aliyu, S. M.: Optimised Design and Structural Simulation of a Quad Cycle Chassis Using Finite Element Methods. Path of Science. **10**(11), 4016–4023 (2025). http://dx.doi.org/10.22178/pos.111-13
13. Bibri, Elias, S., Krogstie, J.: Environmentally data-driven smart sustainable cities: applied innovative solutions for energy efficiency, pollution reduction, and urban metabolism. Energy Inform. **3**, 1–59 (2020)
14. Aghdam, Nasiri, Z., Masoud Rahmani, A., Hossein – zadeh, M.: The role of the Internet of things in healthcare: future trends and challenges. Comput. Methods Prog. Biomed. **199**, 105903 (2021)
15. Vijarania, M., Gupta, S., Agrawal, A., Adigun, M.O., Ajagbe, S.A., Awotunde, J.B.: Energy Efficient Load-Balancing Mechanism in Integrated IoT–Fog–Cloud Environment. Electronics **12**(11), 2543 (2023)
16. Okafor, N.U., Alghorani, Y., Delaney, D.T.: Improving data quality of low-cost IoT sensors in environmental monitoring networks using data fusion and machine learning approach. ICT Express **6**(3), 220–228 (2020)

# Real-Time Surveillance Network System for Traffic Monitoring and Reporting

Abiodun A. Akanni$^{(\boxtimes)}$ and Wilson Sakpere🆔

Lead City University, Ibadan, Oyo State, Nigeria
abiodunakanni760@gmail.com

**Abstract.** As urban populations continue to surge, the prevalence of traffic-related issues escalates, leading to heightened concerns over public safety, property damage, and various offences posing significant risks to life and assets. Traditional solutions have relied heavily on infrastructure-integrated systems, which are often costly to install and maintain, and lack flexibility and scalability. This study aims to address these challenges by developing a low-cost, real-time vehicular monitoring and reporting system. The system employs readily available technology, built on a foundation of electronic architecture, encompassing a network unit (tunnel server), mobile unit (mobile app), and number plate detection unit. The process involves establishing an HTTP connection between the tunnel server and the mobile app. A tunnelling server, a web application, and a number plate detection unit collaborate to detect license plates in real-time. ML5.js and OpenCV.js are employed to process captured frames, identify objects, and extract license plate numbers. This study marks a significant technological achievement in the realm of web and mobile applications, computer vision, and artificial intelligence. The developed system successfully detects license plate numbers, promising enhanced public safety, property protection, and traffic management. It is recommended that future enhancements, such as expanding its object recognition capabilities and maintaining a robust testing and quality assurance process, should ensure its continued excellence.

**Keywords:** Computer Vision · Infrastructure-Integrated Systems · License Plates · Number Plate Detection · Object Recognition · OpenCV.js · Tunnel Server

## 1 Introduction

The study of road traffic is a multifaceted subject that encompasses the complex interactions among different entities, such as pedestrians, cars, trucks, buses, trams, and bicycles, as they navigate a shared infrastructure. Given the infrastructure limitations and the increase in the vehicular population, effectively managing and controlling traffic has become a highly intricate undertaking. This necessitates using specialised algorithms and accurate historical and current traffic data [1]. The data on vehicle numbers and types can significantly reduce travel times and emissions.

© ICST Institute for Computer Sciences, Social Informatics and Telecommunications Engineering 2026
Published by Springer Nature Switzerland AG 2026. All Rights Reserved
J. B. Awotunde et al. (Eds.): AFRICATEK 2024, LNICST 618, pp. 35–52, 2026.
https://doi.org/10.1007/978-3-031-93557-2_3

Accurate traffic data is crucial for optimising traffic control, adapting management policies to varying conditions, and forecasting infrastructure bottlenecks [2]. For example, Shenzhen, China, has over 2 million vehicles and over 600 traffic surveillance cameras to monitor passing vehicles 24 h a day [3]. On average, over 1,200 vehicles are captured and transmitted per second via the network, with plans to install additional cameras on roadways at some point [3]. The situation worsens when metropolitan areas like Beijing, Shanghai, New York City, and Tokyo are included.

"Automatic vehicle license plate recognition (AVLPR)" is widely used in a range of applications, including highway surveillance, tracking of vehicles, parking, and intelligent transportation systems (ITS) [4]. A license plate (LP) is a metal plate with characters and words attached to a vehicle's exterior and serves the purpose of identification [4]. Based on its unique characteristics and regulations, various methods for AVLPR have been proposed for LP due to its discrimination across different countries. It is challenging to locate a license plate in a complex background. Therefore, several critical factors must be considered to achieve successful LP extraction. They include plate size, image quality, plate styling, illumination condition, plate location, and background specifics [3].

This study focuses on providing interventions to address high-cost and complex vehicular monitoring and reporting systems. It develops a low-cost, real-time vehicular monitoring and reporting system that employs readily available technology, built on a foundation of electronic architecture, encompassing a network unit (tunnel server), mobile unit (mobile app), and number plate detection unit. The study intends to answer the question, "How can a license plate detection system prototype device using a camera (phone) and wireless technology be developed?" The study will serve as a reference point for researchers and practitioners and contribute to the body of knowledge in surveillance systems.

## 2   Related Works

ITS is a collection of technologies integrated into the transportation network and management system. This integration includes processing, control, communication, and electronic components. In addition, it incorporates cutting-edge methods of managing traffic [5]. The technologies incorporated into ITS are part of an effort to save lives, money and time. Also, it encompasses a wide range of fields, including transportation engineering, telecommunications engineering, computer science, finance, electronics, and commerce, among others. Because of the capacity of a computer to eradicate the possibility of error caused by human intervention, ITS may soon be fully dependent on computers. Today, there are navigation technologies that can lead people to their destinations while avoiding traffic jams, and it is expected that this type of technology will continue to advance in the years to come [6, 7].

A region-based convolutional neural network was used to detect vehicle license plates [8, 9] and a novel strategy for solving the license plate detection problem was proposed. This involved treating the license plate vehicle as an object. The study aimed to identify LPs in video sequences, detect partial LPs and detect LPs using moving cameras and vehicles. This work utilised advanced object detection techniques such as

Convolutional Neural Networks with Region proposal (RCNN), Fast-RCNN, Faster-RCNN, and exemplar-SVM. The authors claim that their comprehensive tests yielded better results than traditional methods.

Utilising the YOLO object detector as the foundation for a dependable real-time automatic license plate recognition system [10, 11] resulted in a dependable and productive ALPR system. CNNs undergo rigorous training and fine-tuning at each stage of the ALPR process to ensure their resilience in various settings like camera, lighting, and background variations. A two-stage method was developed for character segmentation and recognition, utilising simple data augmentation techniques like flipped characters and inverted LPs. This allows the segmentation and recognition of characters more accurately. The ALPR approach that was developed achieved remarkable success. First, the system achieved a recognition rate of 93.53% and 47 frames per second (FPS) with the SSIG dataset, consisting of 2,000 frames from 101 vehicle videos. Second, a larger public dataset was used to simulate a situation more representative of the real world. This dataset consists of 150 videos and 4,500 still images. The performance of this system attained a recognition rate of 78.33% and 35 frames per second (FPS) [10].

ALPRNet, a single neural network, was proposed for detecting and recognising mixed-style long plays using different license plates [12]. ALPRNet employed two fully convolutional one-stage object detectors to, simultaneously, detect and classify LPs and characters. ALPRNet treats LPs and characters equally and treats the object detectors' output bounding boxes of LPs and characters with matching labels. Because of this, ALPRNet can bypass the recurrent neural network (RNN) branches in existing optical character recognition (OCR) approaches. ALPRNet was evaluated using a dataset containing mixed LP style examples and two datasets with single LP style examples. The experimental results demonstrate that the proposed network achieved advanced results with a simple one-stage network.

A Generative Adversarial Network (GAN) based approach explored the concept of an automatic parking system that automatically parks a vehicle based on the driver's license plate [13]. The proposed solution will be more efficient and reduce the hassles involved by removing the need for human interaction. It will also enhance vehicle safety by eliminating the need for slips or magnetic cards for parking, which is currently the standard method. Image processing algorithms were utilised to, automatically, input parking spot information into the database. Automatic Vehicle Number Plate Recognition (AVNPR) was used to identify the plates' respective numbers. CNN and RNN could not, accurately, identify the misidentification of vehicle plate numbers due to noise. The GAN algorithm was utilised to solve this issue and produce the desired results. When tested in practice, the proposed method achieved a recognition accuracy of 99.39% for a vehicle number plate.

A novel method was applied for character recognition on license plates featuring a variety of fonts and designs [14]. The project involved designing a novel license plate recognition network that can accurately locate and classify characters and LP regions simultaneously. The study suggests that the proposed method can achieve a recognition rate of 98.57% for multi-style LPs in real-world applications. The authors tested the proposed method for license plate recognition using standard license plate datasets, which contain only single-style LPs.

An automatic license plate recognition system was developed to enhance the license plate recognition accuracy at wide camera angles [15, 16]. The system enables the recognition of images through highly accurate CNN applications. The normalisation and segmentation of a license plate's image were also improved. The goal is to enhance the accuracy of recognition through these enhancements. Mask R-CNN is utilised in both the segmentation and recognition stages. The primary segment-search algorithm was Selective search. The combined loss function is utilised to expedite the training and classification of the network. To solve the problem of interclass segmentation, an additional module was added to the CNN.

A virtual vehicle identification system uses wireless communication interfaces to track vehicles involved in hit-and-run accidents [17], aiding in accident investigation and traffic monitoring. The system utilises vehicle access points and the Vehicular Ad Hoc Network (VANET) to aid in tracking vehicle identities. The Internet of Things development board conducts a thorough scan of all vehicle Wi-Fi access points within the beacon frames. Accurately identifying the offender's vehicle is challenging due to signal strength variations and station distance to the access point. However, specific Wi-Fi access point identities like Service Set Identifier (SSID) and Media Access Control (MAC) addresses can be used as virtual vehicle identities for vehicle tracking and traffic surveillance systems. The system demonstrates the ability to detect and track the suspect vehicle. It can track vehicle access point signals from 45 m away and is operational at speeds exceeding 50 km/h.

To investigate the hardware-software co-simulation of vehicle license plate detection using the ZedBoard system-on-chip (SoC) platform [18], a demonstration of the SoC implementation of the Vehicle License Plate Detection System (VLPDS) was done. VLPDS is a technique for license plate recognition based on a histogram technique of edge processing. Following the completion of the design phase on the Xilinx Zynq-7000 ZedBoard SoC using MATLAB Simulink and Xilinx System Generator (XSG), the system is put into operation. XSG is widely used in image processing, simplifying structural design and enabling hardware-software co-simulation. The algorithm's accuracy was assessed across different input picture sets, revealing significant performance improvements, leading to the best SoC-based hardware implementation of VLPDS [18].

The reviewed license plate detection systems show significant potential and functionality, but it is essential to acknowledge their limitations. A system's reliance on network connectivity can be a limitation, particularly in areas with poor or unreliable internet connections. Also, the license plate detection accuracy heavily relies on the underlying machine learning models (ML5.js and OpenCV.js). If these models are not updated or retrained regularly, the system's ability to detect license plates accurately may decrease over time. While it can identify other objects, it may not be as accurate or versatile in recognising a wide range of objects or scenarios. In addition, the system's resources may be inadequate. Thus, expanding the object recognition capabilities may require additional development efforts. These efforts should address high installation and maintenance costs, system flexibility and complexity, and real-time vehicular monitoring and reporting. However, most development efforts are done in other countries with a dearth of literature and implemented works on license plate recognition in Nigeria. This has left an open issue for this paper's study.

# 3  System Design

This study generates a real-time low-cost highway vehicular monitoring and reporting system having low-cost inputs. The vehicular monitoring system node's prototype is created using a mobile phone (with camera detection capability of 15–20 m at a coverage of 180 degrees and 1200 x 900 pixels resolution) and a laptop computer. A license plate monitoring model software was developed and installed on the mobile phone and the laptop. A mobile app, a tunnelling server, a web application and a number plate detection unit were used in the development process of the model software. A functional HTTPS connection is established between the tunnelling server and the mobile application by the server. The prototype system is developed using an electronic architecture, such as a network unit (tunnel server), a mobile unit (mobile app), and a number plate detection unit.

## 3.1  Requirement Specification

**Hardware Minimum Requirements.**  Hardware specification for the prototype system consists of an Intel® Pentium® CPU processor, 4 GB RAM and 250 GB disk storage. the android phone used for the mobile app is a Kernel Version 4.4.147 +, Android Version 10 with 1 GB RAM.

**Software Requirements.**  The software specification consists of a 64-bit Windows 10 operating system. The Web App is a WAMP Server (Windows, Apache, MySQL, PHP), built on Laravel. The tunnel server is Ngrok.io and the Mobile App is Developed Using Flutter and MATLAB R2015a for OCR.

## 3.2  The Tunnel Server

The tunnel is the software that helps us communicate with the local web server through our phones (mobile app). The tunnel employed for this project is ngrok.io. It is a command-line application that helps generate an active HTTPS link between our server and the mobile app. Ngrok exposes local networked services behind Network Address Translations (NATs) and firewalls to the public internet over a secure tunnel. Ngrok is a cross-platform tool enabling developers to connect a local development server to the Internet swiftly and easily. The software makes the locally hosted webserver seem to be hosted on the ngrok.com subdomain, removing the requirement for the local computer to have a public IP address or domain name [19].

Ngrok uses a safe tunnel to open local networked resources behind NATs and firewalls to the public internet, enabling consumers to build webhooks, self-host services, and share local websites. Ngrok launches a small client process that creates a private connection tunnel to the cloud service to get around access limitations [19]. A remote user can access the localhost development server by mapping it to an 'ngrok.io' subdomain. Ngrok enables a local web server to be connected to the internet. Hence, the command to generate the webhook is "ngrok http 80".

Moreover, the command "ngrok http 8000" was typed on the tunnelling to replace the "http 80". This will then generate two protocols – HTTP and HTTPS. For this study, the secured tunnel (protocol) was used.

### 3.3 The Mobile App

The mobile app for this project was built on Flutter. This is used to capture and send images to a backend API URL. Flutter is Google's mobile app SDK, which includes a platform, widgets, and tools to help developers build and launch visually attractive, fast Android and iOS applications [20]. Flutter simplifies the method of designing cross-platform smartphone software. It is based on Dart, a swift and easy-to-learn object-oriented programming language. Flutter widgets, which are rendered with a high-performance rendering engine, are also supported. They are simple, appealing, and adaptable [20].

The code snippet used in designing the mobile app is shown below.

```
import 'dart:async';
import 'package:flutter/material.dart';
import 'package:flutter_inappwebview/flutter_inappweb-
view.dart';
```

The mobile app consists of two view pages namely, the tunnel url input and the web view, as shown in Fig. 1.

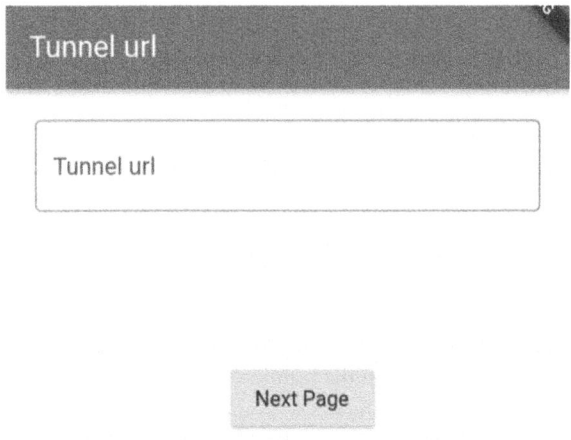

**Fig. 1.** The Tunnel URL

The tunnel url input helps get the dynamically generated tunnel url to be viewed through a web view. With the help of a tunnelling link, the mobile app can access what is on the server as this will entail that both the server and the mobile app must be connected to the internet. A web viewer synchronises the canvas (web browser) and mobile app in such a way that the camera of the mobile app can be used to work as the camera for the mobile detection system using the code snippet below.

```
class InAppWebViewPage extends StatefulWidget {
  final String url;
  InAppWebViewPage(this.url);
  @override
```

### 3.4   The Detection Unit

The detection unit is divided into three:

1. Video Capture Unit
2. ML5.js
3. OpenCV.js

**Video Capture Unit.** The video source capture uses "navigator.getUserMedia" facility in a browser to access the device's camera. Since a browser is used on the app, the app loads a browser on its own. however, since the browser is expected to use a camera, the phone camera now becomes the access camera of the detection unit. Instead of using the system's webcam, the mobile app accesses the mobile phone's camera, which serves as the camera for the detection unit. The camera is initiated with the following code snippet.

```
const videoElement = document.createElement('video');
videoElement.setAttribute("style", "display: none;");
videoElement.width = width;
videoElement.height = height;
document.body.appendChild(videoElement);
```

**ML5.js.** A video element was created to get a navigator device "navigator.mediaDevices.getUserMedia".

```
// Create a webcam capture
const capture = await navigator.mediaDevices.getUserMe-
dia({ video: true })
videoElement.srcObject = capture;
videoElement.play();
return videoElement
```

ML5 examines all the visible video elements. ML5.js is an open-source JavaScript library that provides a high-level interface for machine learning in the browser. It is built on top of TensorFlow.js [5]. ML5.js simplifies tasks like image classification, object detection and text generation using pre-trained machine learning models. In this study, ML5 is used so that every frame the camera is recording is passed through the library "Objectdetector= await ml5. Objectdetector ('cocossd', startDetecting)". When it looks for anything in its library, e.g. a car or person, it will identify it.

**OpenCV.js.** This is used to find the number plate using the find number plate function "Function findPlateNumber(Image)", which will read the image, convert it to greyscale, and detect edges. Then, it finds contours to see if there is a number plate based on the detected characteristics. If there is a number plate, it should provide coordinates (x, y position, width, and height) and display them on the canvas.

OpenCV.js is a JavaScript port of the widely-used OpenCV (Open-Source Computer Vision) Library [21]. OpenCV is a library designed for computer vision tasks. It offers a diverse array of features for image and video analysis, object detection, feature extraction and facial recognition. It extends the accessibility of OpenCV to web applications, making it possible to perform computer vision tasks in web browsers. OpenCV.js is built with performance in mind. It leverages hardware acceleration through WebGL, when available, which can significantly speed up computer vision tasks when running in a web browser [21] (Figs. 2 and 3).

### 3.5  License Plate Capturing

The prototype camera has a resolution of 1200 x 900 pixels and 13 megapixels (with an aperture of f/2.2). However, a field view formula was developed to determine how far the mobile phone and prototype cameras would see. This formula determines the distance at which a license plate can be identified [19].

$$\text{Field View} = \frac{\text{Horizontal Resolution}}{\text{Pixel per feet}} \qquad (1)$$

The entire road network distance will be divided into nodes based on the distance the camera can cover (field view).

Number of Nodes = Total Road Network Length
Field View

### 3.6  License Plate Detection

An HTML file was created to set up the structure of the web application. JavaScript libraries, such as ML5.js and OpenCV.js, were included in the HTML file. HTML5's *"getUserMedia"* API was used to access the user's camera, capture video and display the video stream on an HTML5 ' $< video >$ ' element.

$< video\ id = $ *"videoElement" autoplay* $> \ < $ */video* $>$

ML5.js, which includes pre-trained machine learning models, was used for object detection. Also, a pre-trained object detection model (e.g., COCO-SSD) and the video element were specified as the input source. Thus, detecting objects including license plates in each video frame.

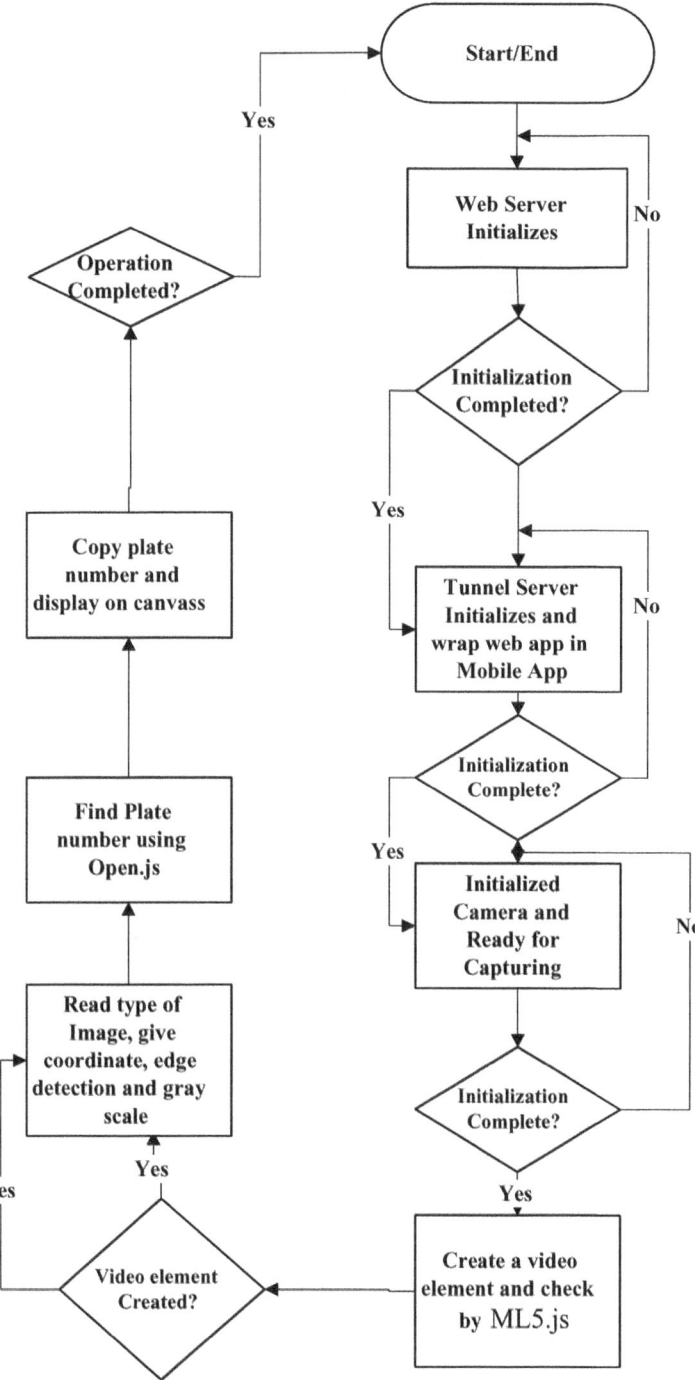

**Fig. 2.** Flowchart of Vehicular Monitoring and Reporting System.

**Fig. 3.** Field view position showing height, capture distance and license plate capture

// Initialise the video capture

```
const videoElement = document.getElementById('videoEle-
ment');
const detector = ml5.objectDetector('cocossd', {}, () =>
{
  console.log('Model is ready');
  detector.detect(videoElement, gotResults);
});
  // Process the detected objects, including license
plates
  // Implement logic to filter license plates from other
objects
}
```

Once the number plate is detected, Optical Character Recognition (OCR) can be performed to recognise the characters on the plate. The image was processed using OpenCV.js for additional image processing tasks such as filtering or perspective transformations to enhance the quality of the license plate.

### 3.7 Performance Evaluation

To accomplish the goals of this study, a form of software testing known as the "black box testing" method was used because it is devoid of any functional aspects. The "black box testing" examines a program's functionality without considering the program's internal structure or the code it was written in. Testing by hand can be carried out in several ways, including black box testing, white box testing and grey box testing. The tester first selects a function to validate that it is operational and then examines the output of the function to determine whether it generates the expected result. On the developed prototype of the system, performance and scalability testing were conducted, as well as usability testing, compatibility testing and reliability testing. The performance and scalability testing measured response time, stability and load capacity with up to 10 concurrent users. Usability testing evaluated the interface's user-friendliness and gathered feedback for improvements. Compatibility testing ensured functionality across different devices, browsers, and network conditions. Reliability testing focused on long-term operation, error handling, and data accuracy, confirming the system's consistent performance and robustness under various conditions. The system demonstrated high reliability and effective operation.

## 4   Implementation and Analysis

### 4.1   The Tunnel Server

To generate a result for the system design, a command "php artisan serve" was written for the "ngrok http port 80" (secure public URL for port 80 web server) highlighted on the tunnelling server, as shown in Fig. 4, and is forwarded to port 8000 as shown in Fig. 5. Hence, starting the laravel development server. The terminal was cleared and showed the status with the two forwarding HTTP and HTTPS addresses. Ngrok initiates an HTTP tunnel, enabling the opening of endpoints for both HTTP and HTTPS traffic.

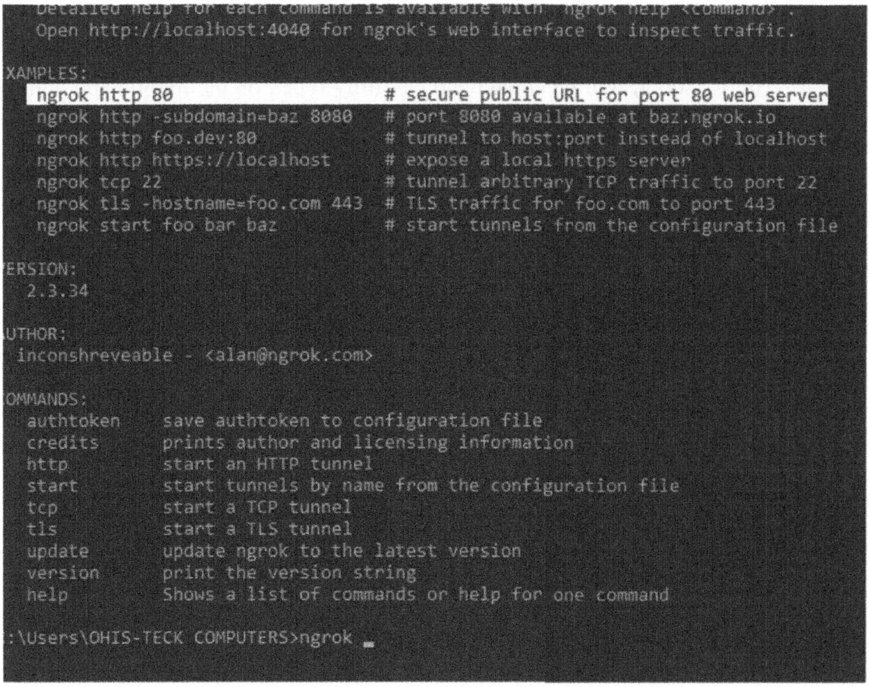

**Fig. 4.** Tunneling Server showing HTTP port 80

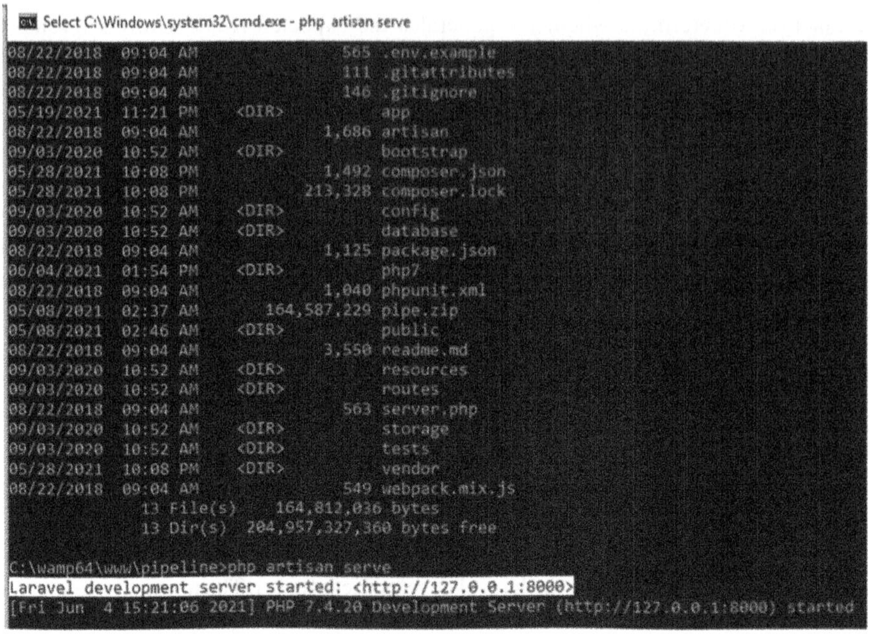

**Fig. 5.** PHP Artisan Serve showing the port 8000

## 4.2  The Mobile App

The newly generated secured tunnel, i.e. http://2d24-185-113-82-229.ngrok-free.app -
> http://localhost:8000/, will be copied and carefully typed on the mobile app built as
shown in Fig. 6. The HTTPS protocol employs TLS (SSL) to encrypt normal HTTP
requests and responses. Thus, HTTPS is significantly more secure than HTTP. Also, the
prototype design can run only on a secured protocol.

## 4.3  The Detection Unit

Immediately the next tab is clicked and processed, it goes to a web browser which is a
canvas. The canvas opens the link to the detection unit where the detection takes place.
A web viewer synchronises the canvas (web browser) and mobile app in such a way that
the camera of the mobile app can be used to work as the camera for the mobile detection
system as shown in Fig. 7.

## 4.4  Discussion

The developed system consists of a web application enclosed within a mobile application
using a tunnelling server. The system can capture license plate numbers using plate
number detection on the mobile application and employing the camera module. The
tunnelling server was configured to use ngrok with the default settings to expose a local
HTTP server. This was done to package the web application into a mobile application.
Consequently, the server for the developed application was successfully initiated.

**Fig. 6.** Snapshot of the tunnel URL input section of the mobile app

**Linsence plate detection**

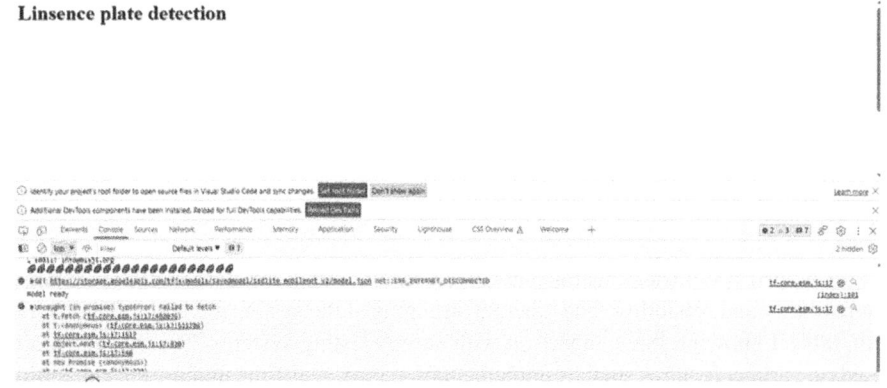

**Fig. 7.** License Plate Detection Canvas (Web Browser)

Furthermore, an HTTP tunnel was established, thereby enabling access to the application from the mobile app. The ML5 library was utilised to process each frame captured by the camera. The system searches inside its library, enabling it to identify various objects such as cars or individuals. After the completion of the initialisation process, the resulting output was transferred to a detect function.

The "find number plate function" (open.js) is used to detect the number plate. This function operates by analysing the image, converting it to grayscale, performing edge detection, and subsequently identifying contours to determine the presence of a number plate based on its distinctive features. If a number plate is detected, the function provides the coordinates (x, y position), and the width and height of the number plate.

**Performance Testing**

**Response Time:** This metric measured the time it took for the system or application to respond to a specific user action or request. It's an essential metric for user experience, as users generally expect quick responses. A lower response time is usually better. The detection process was about 3–5 s showing a good response time of 80%. However, the response time depended on the mobile network used for Internet access.

**Stability:** Stability assesses the reliability of a system or application over time and under varying conditions. A stable system does not crash or produce unexpected errors frequently. High stability is therefore desirable. The design was stable for the load at a response time of 3–5 s. However, this depended on the RAM of the system used. For this study, the stability measure attained was 80%.

**Load:** Load is the system's capacity to handle a specific level of concurrent users or workloads without compromising performance. The system was designed to handle the expected load efficiently. A higher load capacity is generally better. The prototype design was tested with 10 mobile apps running simultaneously. The goal is to respond immediately with the number of users. However, it showed the capacity to be stable with a score of 70%.

**Reliability:** Reliability measures the system's ability to consistently perform its functions accurately without failures. A reliable system can be trusted to work correctly. The design was reliable and had a good network speed with attenuation. Hence, a score of 80% was attained.

## 4.5  Summary

The developed system demonstrated good performance with robust scalability, usability, compatibility and reliability. The inherent strengths of the system are highlighted below with Table 1 showing the comparison with some existing systems. The comparison is based on various features such as implementation cost, real-time monitoring capability, compatibility, scalability, and comprehensive evaluation.

**Low-Cost Implementation:** It utilises readily available hardware (mobile phones and laptops) and open-source software (Flutter, ML5.js, OpenCV.js).

**Real-Time Monitoring:** It can capture and process license plates in real-time.

**High Compatibility:** It is compatible with various devices, browsers, and network conditions.

**Scalability:** It demonstrates the ability to handle multiple concurrent users.

**Comprehensive Evaluation:** The performance, usability, compatibility, and reliability testing ensure robustness.

**Table 1.** Comparison with Related Works

| Feature | Subject of Study | Silva & Jung (2020) | Anandhi et al. (2020) | Shashirangana et al. (2020) |
|---|---|---|---|---|
| Low-Cost Implementation | Utilizes mobile phones, laptops, Flutter, ML5.js, OpenCV.js | Uses deep learning techniques with specialized hardware | Employs GPU-accelerated hardware for YOLOv3 | Surveys various techniques, some using accessible tech while others require more specialized hardware |
| Real-Time Monitoring | Real-time license plate detection with 3–5 s response time | Real-time detection with deep learning, dependent on hardware performance | Achieves real-time detection with YOLOv3, known for speed and accuracy | Discusses real-time and non-real-time systems; real-time performance varies based on technique |
| High Compatibility | Works across different devices, browsers, and network conditions | Focused on specific hardware setup, limiting compatibility | Primarily tested on specific hardware configurations | Covers multiple systems with varying compatibility; does not focus on compatibility as a primary aspect |
| Scalability | Can handle multiple concurrent users, tested with up to 10 users | Scalability not primary focus; performance depends on deep learning model and hardware | Scalable with appropriate hardware; performance may degrade with increased load | Discusses scalability challenges across different systems; specific scalability testing not highlighted |
| Comprehensive Evaluation | Extensive testing for performance, usability, compatibility, and reliability | Evaluation primarily based on detection accuracy and speed | Focuses on detection accuracy and speed, with some mention of real-time performance | Provides broad evaluation of multiple systems, highlighting strengths and weaknesses but does not perform direct tests |

Table 1 shows this study excels in low-cost implementation, real-time monitoring, high compatibility, scalability, and comprehensive evaluation. Unlike other studies, it uses readily available hardware and open-source software, ensuring broader accessibility and adaptability, while maintaining robust performance and reliability in various conditions.

## 5   Conclusion

The developed system was designed to capture license plate numbers using plate number detection on a mobile application with a camera module. A tunnelling server, configured with the ngrok secure tunnelling platform, was used to expose a local HTTP server to package the web application into the mobile application. The server for the application was successfully initiated, enabling communication between the web and mobile components. ML5.js and OpenCV.js frameworks were used to process images captured by the camera. Response time was measured and found to be about 3–5 s, indicating a good response time of 80%. However, it was noted that the response time depends on the network used. Stability was tested and found to be stable with a score of 80%, although it depends on the system's RAM. Load testing with 10 concurrent mobile apps showed that the prototype design was stable with a score of 70%. Reliability was rated at 80% when tested under good network conditions. Also, the system was found to be easy to understand (90%) and easy to access (80%). Faster access received a score of 80%, and navigation was rated at 85% effectiveness. Further, the system was compatible with various operating systems and browsers, achieving a score of 95% for software compatibility. It was also compatible with different hardware configurations (80%). Mobile compatibility was established for iOS and Android platforms, with some restrictions on Android versions (80%). Network compatibility included parameters like operating speed, bandwidth, and capacity, with a score of 80%. The throughput received a score of 85%, indicating good performance in processing tasks. Memory usage was relatively low, with a score of 1.6. The CPU and network usage were moderate, with scores of 2 each. The developed system effectively captures license plate numbers and performs well in terms of response time, stability, and usability. However, some performance aspects may depend on network conditions and system resources. For future research and development, efforts would focus on the following areas:

i. Enhanced Accuracy with Deep Learning: Investigate the use of deep learning techniques, such as Convolutional Neural Networks (CNNs), for license plate detection. These models have shown remarkable accuracy in image recognition tasks and could further improve the precision of plate detection.
ii. Multi-Language Support: Extend the system's capabilities to detect license plates with characters from multiple languages and scripts. This would be particularly valuable for international applications and could involve training models on diverse character sets.

# References

1. Selmi, Z., Ben Halima, M., Pal, U., Alimi, M.A.: DELP-DAR system for license plate detection and recognition. Pattern Recognit. Lett. **129**, 213–223 (2020). https://doi.org/10.1016/j.patrec.2019.11.007
2. Arora, P., Kapse, V.M., Sinha, S., Gera, S.: Number plate recognition system using convolutional neural network. In: 9th International Conference on Reliability, Infocom Technologies and Optimization (Trends and Future Directions) (ICRITO 2021), pp. 1–5. IEEE, Noida (2021). https://doi.org/10.1109/ICRITO51393.2021.9596134
3. Darapaneni, N., et al.: Computer vision based license plate detection for automated vehicle parking management system. In: 11th IEEE Annual Ubiquitous Computing, Electronics and Mobile Communication Conference (UEMCON 2020), pp. 0800–0805. IEEE, New York (2020). https://doi.org/10.1109/UEMCON51285.2020.9298091
4. Badru, R.A., Waheed, A.A., Akinmoluwa, O.A., Obayemi, O.R.: Generation of surveillance networked nodes for oil pipelines' Theft. Int. J. Recent Eng. Sci. **8**(5), 21–26 (2021). https://doi.org/10.14445/23497157/ijres-v8i5p104
5. Lv, Z., Zhang, S., Xiu, W.: Solving the security problem of intelligent transportation system with deep learning. IEEE Trans. Intell. Transp. Syst. **22**(7), 4281–4290 (2021). https://doi.org/10.1109/TITS.2020.2980864
6. Sakpere, W., Adeyeye, M.: Can near field communication solve the limitations in mobile indoor navigation?. In: Lee, I. Ed., RFID Technology Integration for Business Performance Improvement, pp. 52–79. IGI Global, Hershey (2015).https://doi.org/10.4018/978-1-4666-6308-4.ch003
7. Sakpere, W.E., Mlitwa, N.B.W., Oshin, M.A.: Towards an efficient indoor navigation system: a near field communication approach. J. Eng. Des. Technol. **15**(4), 505–527 (2017). https://doi.org/10.1108/JEDT-10-2016-0073
8. Rafique, M.A., Pedrycz, W., Jeon, M.: Vehicle license plate detection using region-based convolutional neural networks. Soft. Comput. **22**, 6429–6440 (2018). https://doi.org/10.1007/s00500-017-2696-2
9. Silva, S.M., Jung, C.R.: Real-time license plate detection and recognition using deep convolutional neural networks. J. Vis. Commun. Image Represent. **71**, 1–9 (2020). https://doi.org/10.1016/j.jvcir.2020.102773
10. Laroca, R., et al.: A robust real-time automatic license plate recognition based on the YOLO detector. In: International Joint Conference on Neural Networks (IJCNN 2018), pp. 1–10. IEEE, Rio de Janeiro (2018). https://doi.org/10.1109/IJCNN.2018.8489629
11. Anandhi, R., Sekar, G., Kalaivani, C., Jayalakshmi, N.: Vehicle detection and system tracking using Yolo V3 model, a computer vision technique. Webology **19**(2), 1066–1073 (2022)
12. Huang, Q., Cai, Z., Lan, T.: A single neural network for mixed style license plate detection and recognition. IEEE Access **9**, 21777–21785 (2021). https://doi.org/10.1109/ACCESS.2021.3055243
13. Kukreja, V., Kumar, D., Kaur, A., Geetanjali, Sakshi: GAN-based synthetic data augmentation for increased CNN performance in vehicle number plate recognition. In: 4th International Conference on Electronics, Communication and Aerospace Technology (ICECA 2020), pp. 1190–1195. IEEE, Coimbatore (2020). https://doi.org/10.1109/ICECA49313.2020.9297625
14. Huang, Q., Cai, Z., Lan, T.: A new approach for character recognition of multi-style vehicle license plates. IEEE Trans. Multimed. **23**, 3768–3777 (2021). https://doi.org/10.1109/TMM.2020.3031074
15. Kuchuk, H., Podorozhniak, A., Liubchenko, N., Onischenko, D.: System of license plate recognition considering large camera shooting angles. Radioelectron. Comput. Syst. **2021**(4), 82–91 (2021). https://doi.org/10.32620/REKS.2021.4.07

16. Shashirangana, J., Padmasiri, H., Meedeniya, D., Perera, C.: Automated license plate recognition: a survey on methods and techniques. IEEE Access **9**, 11203–11225 (2021). https://doi.org/10.1109/ACCESS.2020.3047929

17. Sheng, K.B., Saad, A.A., Ishak, M.K.: Development of a virtual vehicle identification for tracking hit-and-run vehicle. In: 4th IEEE International Conference on Artificial Intelligence in Engineering and Technology (IICAIET 2022), pp. 1–6. IEEE, Kota Kinabalu (2022). https://doi.org/10.1109/IICAIET55139.2022.9936747

18. Chhabra, S., Saini, S., Lata, K.: Hardware–software co-simulation of vehicle license plate detection on the zedboard soc platform. In: Saini, S., Lata, K., Sharma, A., Sinha, G.R. Eds., Advances in Image and Data Processing using VLSI Design, vol. 1, pp. 15-1–15-19. IOP Publishing, Bristol (2021). https://doi.org/10.1088/978-0-7503-3919-3ch15

19. Irunokhai, E.A., Adigun, J.O., Dada, O.S., Irunokhai, B.O., Onihunwa, J.O.: Analysis of traffic light violation on Nigerian roads (A Case Study of Sango T Junction, Ibadan, Oyo State). Int. J. Comput. Appl. **176**(30), 8–13 (2020). https://doi.org/10.5120/ijca2020920299

20. Xu, H., Cai, Z., Li, R., Li, W.: Efficient city cam-to-edge cooperative learning for vehicle counting in ITS. IEEE Trans. Intell. Transp. Syst. **23**(9), 16600–16611 (2022). https://doi.org/10.1109/TITS.2022.3149657

21. Ditcharoen, A., Chhour, B., Traikunwaranon, T., Aphivongpanya, N., Maneerat, K., Ammarapala, V.: Road traffic accidents severity factors: a review paper. In: 5th International Conference on Business and Industrial Research (ICBIR 2018), pp. 339–343. IEEE, Bangkok (2018). https://doi.org/10.1109/ICBIR.2018.8391218

# Curation and Annotation of an Indigenous Bible Corpus for Named Entity Recognition Model

Peace Busola Falola[1,3], Biswajit Brahma[2(✉)], and Solomon Olalekan Akinola[1]

[1] Department of Computer Science, University of Ibadan, Ibadan, Nigeria
[2] McKesson Corporation, Irving, CA, USA
biswajit.brahma@gmail.com
[3] Department of Computer Sciences, Precious Cornerstone University, Ibadan, Nigeria

**Abstract.** This study presents a study on the development of a Yorùbá Bible dataset aimed at enhancing Named Entity Recognition (NER) for Yorùbá, a low-resource language. It outlines the process of manually extracting and annotating phrases from key books of the Bible. The emphasis is on the dataset's importance for future NER and Natural Language Processing (NLP) applications, especially in supporting languages with limited resources. The study covers dataset creation, annotation guidelines, challenges encountered due to the language's tonal nature, and future directions for expanding the dataset and developing a NER model tailored to the Bible domain, with broader implications for indigenous language processing and preservation.

**Keywords:** Named Entity Recognition · Bible · Annotation · low-resource language

## 1 Introduction

One of the primary Information Extraction (IE) tasks is Named Entity Recognition and Classification. It involves recognizing entity mentions in unstructured text as text fragments indicating real-world objects and categorizing them into entity types based on a predetermined classification schema. Knowledge discovery from natural language text depends critically on extracting useful information from user-generated material, such as entity mentions, events, and relations [1].

For some Natural Language Processing applications, such as Information Extraction (IE) and Question Answering (QA), Named Entity Recognition is crucial [2]. Additionally, it is a crucial part of many products, such as conversational agents, speech and dialogue system localization, and spellcheckers [3]. Its goal is to recognize and categorize names of individuals (PER), places (LOC), organizations (ORG), and numerical expressions, such as percentages, dates, and currencies [2].

Most research on named entity recognition is done in languages that are commonly spoken, such as Arabic, Chinese, and English [4]. As such, research that compares and benchmarks named entity recognition in commonly spoken languages may be discovered

© ICST Institute for Computer Sciences, Social Informatics and Telecommunications Engineering 2026
Published by Springer Nature Switzerland AG 2026. All Rights Reserved
J. B. Awotunde et al. (Eds.): AFRICATEK 2024, LNICST 618, pp. 53–63, 2026.
https://doi.org/10.1007/978-3-031-93557-2_4

[4]. However, current Yorùbá research is restricted to a small number of datasets and lacks thorough error analysis [4]. African languages are not well-represented in this important endeavor because there are insufficient datasets, inconsistent findings, and the challenges these languages present for Named Entity Recognition (NER), as recognized by academics [3].

More than 20 million people in Nigeria, Benin, Togo, and other West African countries speak Yorùbá, a tonal language. Yorùbá is a rich, complicated language that is different from other languages in the globe due to its numerous distinctive characteristics [3]. Yorùbá is considered a low-resource language because, despite its popularity among the populace, there is now little linguistic material accessible for it. This is because fewer scholars have focused on studying Yorùbá [5]. Because of this, most natural language processing (NLP) tasks for these low-resource languages—such as Named Entity Recognition (NER), POS tagging, sentiment analysis, question answering, etc.—are still in their infancy and lack adequate language resources, like corpora. In contrast, NLP tasks for languages with abundant resources, like English, French, etc., have advanced significantly as a result of the development of deep learning technologies [5].

The expertise of native speakers participating in the creation of datasets and models would be beneficial for many NLP tasks, including machine translation, text classification, part-of-speech tagging, and named entity identification [3, 21, 22]. When it comes to making movies with indigenous languages and cultural content more real, accurate, and sensitive to cultural differences, NER is essential. It encourages indigenous research and filmmaking, fosters intercultural understanding, and aids in the preservation and promotion of indigenous traditions.

In this research paper, we curated and annotated a corpus of the Yorùbá Bible specifically for Named Entity Recognition (NER). This corpus will support the future studies for various subfields of Natural Language Processing (NLP). The remainder of this work is structured as follows: Sect. 2 gives a review of the literature; Sect. 3 discusses dataset creation; Sect. 4 contains the discussion; and Sect. 5 delivers the study's conclusion.

## 2  Related Works

An unambiguous structure for summarizing the development of seemingly separate datasets that have been available since the named entity identification task was introduced was the focus of Zhang, Y., and Xiao's [6] work. According to their research, these datasets have certain aspects in common, albeit to differing degrees, when one looked more closely at the attributes and the context of each dataset's creation. They examined the evolution of named entity recognition datasets over time and provided descriptions pertaining to the dataset's language, the study topic, the kind of entity, its granularity, and its annotation. Lastly, they offered a concept for further named entity recognition dataset development. The future direction of their work suggested that other domains should be employed especially the ones that are of industrial and commercial value. Additionally, they proposed that the dataset construction aim for entity annotation should be to reduce manual participation while improving the quality and consistency of annotations.

Heng et al. [7] investigated a novel, economical method to use LLMs with low NER capability to generate better NER datasets. By giving LLMs instructions to self-reflect on the particular domain, they deviated from the standard class-conditional prompts and produced domain-relevant attributes (e.g., category and emotions for movie reviews), which are then used to create attribute-rich training data. Moreover, they developed NER context data surrounding these entities after anticipatorily generating entity words, hence avoiding the complicated structural challenges faced by LLMs. Their tests on a variety of broad and specialized domains show notable improvements in performance over traditional data generation techniques, all at a lower cost than current options.

Anandika, Chakravarty & Paikaray [8] created a technique to automatically identify NEs from tourist domain data using a traditional technique, i.e., a rule-based approach. The algorithm evaluated words both with and without repetition, achieving accuracy rates of 83% and 71%, respectively.

By annotating portions of the existing corpora with named elements, Mundotiya et al. [9] concentrated on creating an NER benchmark dataset for machine translation systems designed to translate from these languages to Hindi. 22 entity labels were used to annotate the Bhojpuri, Maithili, and Magahi corpora, which had token counts of 228,373, 157,468, and 56,190, respectively. The tagset utilized in one of the Hindi NER datasets was examined after the coarse-grained annotation labels. Additionally, they disclosed a Deep Learning baseline based on the LSTM-CNNs-CRF model. For Bhojpuri, Maithili, and Magahi, the lower baseline F1-scores using the NER tool generated using Conditional Random Fields models are 70.56%, 73.19%, and 84.18%. The LSTM-CNNs-CRF method, which is based on Deep Learning, produced results of 61.41% for Bhojpuri, 71.38% for Maithili, and 86.39% for Magahi. As the findings demonstrate, in the cases of Bhojpuri and Maithili, when there is more data in terms of token count but not named entity count, LSTM-CNNs-CRF is unable to exceed the lower baseline. Nonetheless, the LSTM-CNNs-CRF cross-lingual model training for Bhojpuri and Maithili exceeded the CRF.

A method for creating a 20,146-sentence Malay NER dataset (MS-NER) using labeled datasets of similar languages and iterative optimization was published by Fu et al. [10]. To better incorporate boundary information for NER, they also suggested a multi-task framework with a bidirectional revision (Bi-revision), called MTBR. They experimented extensively with English, Malay, and Indonesian. According to experimental findings, MTBR is capable of performing competitively and often outperforms several baselines.

Singh, De Clercq & Lefever [11] addressed the issue of the limited number of large multilingual models, such as mBERT and XLM-RoBERTa, that are available for low-resource languages. These models have significant deployment overheads due to their size and inference speeds. To tackle this, the authors developed a unique methodology that can often outperform the instructor model by filtering language-specific information from a huge multilingual model into a compact, fast monolingual model using knowledge distillation techniques. To demonstrate how useful this method is, the authors utilized two downstream tasks for each of the six languages. They also looked into methods to improve the final vocabulary of the reduced models, going further into possible changes to the basic structure for languages with limited resources. Finally, they carried out an extensive ablation investigation to gain a deeper understanding of the various components of the setup and ascertain what works best for the two under-resourced languages, Slovene and Swahili.

Using MuRIL and a conditional random field (CRF) layer, Sharma, Morwal & Agarwal [12] created a Hindi NER system. The model was then refined using the ICON 2013 Hindi NER dataset. Their suggested model beats all other current Hindi NER systems created on the ICON 2013 dataset, achieving state-of-the-art outcomes as high as 87.89% accuracy, 83.74% recall, and 85.77% F1-score. To evaluate the effectiveness of these language models for the Hindi NER job, they also created a comparable Hindi NER system by swapping out the MuRIL language model with the multilingual Bidirectional Encoder Representations from Transformers (mBERT) language model, which is another cutting-edge language model.

Fudholi et al. [13] collected 18,075 phrases from publications produced in Bahasa Indonesia that contained information about drugs. In Indonesian, they provided the CNN-BiLSTM architecture evaluation and the medication NER model. They employed a deep learning architectural model called CNN-BiLSTM, a hybrid Convolutional Neural Network-Bidirectional Long-Short Term Memory model, which can automatically identify characteristics at the word and character levels. To determine the optimal model, they trained the architecture using six alternative sets of hyper-parameters. According to the trials, one of the models achieved the highest F1 score of all. The model makes use of an extra chunk tag-based feature, two layers of CNN with a kernel size of seven, a CNN filter of fifty, and a single LSTM layer with 200 hidden units. With a f1-score of 0.892, a precision of 0.881, and a recall of 0.903, the model performed well.

Ozcelik, & Toraman [4] provided comprehensive research for Turkish named entity identification by contrasting the performances of the state-of-the-art models on datasets with varying domains. This allowed researchers to better understand the models' generalization capabilities and investigate the reasons behind their success or failure in this task. Their experimental results, which were corroborated by statistical testing, demonstrated that Transformer-based language models produce the greatest weighted F1 scores, which range from 80.8% in tweets to 96.1% in news pieces. Additionally, they discovered that, in comparison to traditional models, Transformer-based language models are more resilient to entity types with smaller sample sizes and longer-named entities; nonetheless, all models perform poorly for longer-named entities in social media. Furthermore, they found that there was a greater decline in performance—12% in well-written texts as opposed to 7% in noisy texts—when they shuffled 80% of the words in a phrase to mimic flexible word order in Turkish.

Zhang et al. [14] they developed the LELNER model, which includes an information fusion network and an information interaction module, to address the deficiencies in trigger representation creation, information fusion, and low resource model training. The trigger representation gains additional entity information when the information interaction module recognizes the interaction between the trigger and sentence. The trigger representation and the phrase sequence are flawlessly combined by the information fusion network. Consequently, the network outperforms earlier nonlinear fusion techniques in terms of fusion effect. The two-step training approach utilized in earlier versions was replaced by a one-step training method that they created, which made the training procedure more convenient overall. Based on three publicly available datasets

(BC5CDR, CONLL, and SemEval-lap), experimental findings demonstrated that the suggested LELNER model produced state-of-the-art results.

Adelani et al. [3] created a new benchmark dataset for news subject categorization using MasakhaNEWS, which covers 16 commonly spoken African languages. By refining many language models and training traditional machine learning models, they produced an assessment of baseline models. They also looked into less drastic methods of fine-tuning language models, such as prompting language models, parameter-efficient fine-tuning, and utilizing multilingual transformer embeddings, which are more appropriate for zero-shot and few-shot learning. According to their experimental findings, they were able to get almost 80% of the performance of fully supervised training with just 10 samples per label (92.6 F1 points).

### 2.1 Indigenous Language Preservation

In recent times, there has been a notable surge in interest in the preservation of indigenous languages and cultures through technology. Numerous research, projects, and efforts have been initiated globally to tackle this pressing subject. These initiatives are essential for preserving the rich cultural legacy and linguistic variety of indigenous peoples, which are frequently threatened by assimilation, globalization, and the dominance of major international languages. Here are a few noteworthy instances and methods in this field:

I. Digital Language Documentation: Documenting languages that are in danger of extinction is the main goal of initiatives like DOBES (Documentation of Endangered Languages) and ELAR (Endangered Languages Archive) [15]. They provide thorough recordings of these languages using text, video, and audio annotations, which are very helpful to scholars and the communities themselves.

II. Language Learning Apps: Apps such as Rosetta Stone, Memrise, and Duolingo have begun to offer native language support [16]. For instance, Duolingo expanded the languages it offers by including Navajo and Hawaiian, assisting in the revival and instruction of these tongues among a wider student body [16].

III. Online Dictionaries and Encyclopedias: Online dictionaries, text corpora, and multimedia resources for indigenous languages—especially those spoken in Canada—are provided via initiatives like the FirstVoices site [17]. To guarantee authenticity and consideration for cultural subtleties, these resources are created in partnership with indigenous groups.

IV. Virtual Reality (VR) and Augmented Reality (AR): Immersion language and cultural education is one area in which emerging technologies like VR and AR are being investigated for their potential [18]. To educate indigenous languages and cultures in a captivating and immersive setting, for example, the Virtual Reality Indigenous Language Experience project seeks to develop VR experiences [18].

These illustrations show the variety and creativity with which indigenous languages and traditions are being technologically preserved. Working in tandem with the indigenous communities themselves to ensure that the programs are community-led, culturally sensitive, and suited to their unique needs and goals is frequently the key to their success.

# 3  Dataset Creation

This section presents the process of creating the dataset.

## 3.1  Dataset Collection

The goal of the painstaking process of compiling these sentences was to represent the textual subtleties and grammatical complexity of the Yorùbá language as they appear in biblical literature. After the data-gathering stage, these phrases were carefully copied into a Notepad document, which functioned as the first dataset repository.

An example of the dataset's post-annotation section is shown in Fig. 1, which provides an overview of the sentences' meticulous annotations and well-organized structure.

```
📄 *Bible_Annotate_Paper - Notepad
File  Edit  Format  View  Help
JẸNẸSISI B-Book B-Book B-Book
Orikini 0 0 0

Ìtàn 0 0 0
Bí 0 0 0
A 0 0 0
ṣe 0 0 0
Dá 0 0 0
Ayé 0 0 0

Ní 0 0 0
ìbẹ̀rẹ̀ 0 0 0
, 0 0 0
nígbà 0 0 0
tí 0 0 0
Ọlọrun B-DEITY B-DEITY B-DEITY
dá 0 0 0
ọrun B-LOC B-LOC B-LOC
ati 0 0 0
ayé B-LOC B-LOC B-LOC
, 0 0 0
ayé B-LOC B-LOC B-LOC
rí 0 0 0
júujùu 0 0 0
, 0 0 0
ó 0 0 0
sì 0 0 0
```

**Fig. 1.** Dataset after annotation

## 3.2  Dataset Annotation

The Yorùbá Bible dataset was annotated using guidelines for named entity identification that were influenced by several established standards, including the Universal Named Entity Recognition (NER) annotation guidelines. These guidelines are also influenced by ACE, MUC-6, MUC-7, CONLL NER shared task, and Ontonotes 5 [19]. The process typically involved the following steps:

- Preparation: Before annotation, the Yorùbá Bible dataset was familiarized with, and its language subtleties and peculiarities were understood. It was also understood what the definitions and requirements meant for every type of named entity—Book of the Bible, Person, Place, Deity, and so on.
- Annotation Tool: Named items within the Yorùbá Bible text were identified, labeled, and categorized by an annotator. Annotation was carried out manually.
- Annotation Process: Sentence segmentation was the first step in the annotation process, which divided the Yorùbá Bible text into separate sentences to make annotation simpler. The next step was to tokenize each sentence into words or tokens. The annotator then went on and used predetermined categories to locate and annotate text segments that corresponded to the designated items. The semantic type of these detected things is then used to classify them. Figure 2 shows the processes of annotation.

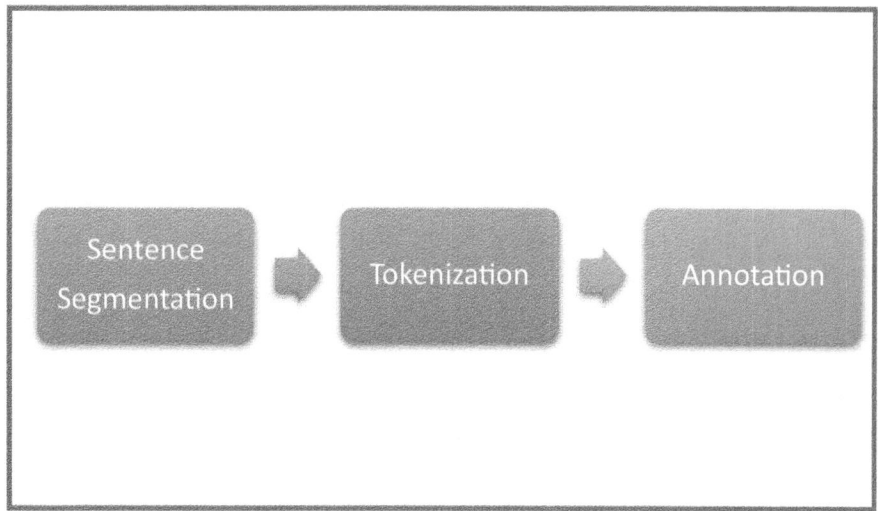

**Fig. 2.** Annotation Process

### 3.3 Dataset Statistics

The study comprised a thorough analysis of the opening chapters of 29 Bible books [20], from which a sizable dataset consisting of 1356 phrases were assembled. 20,010 unique tokens were produced from this extensive collection, demonstrating the great linguistic diversity seen in these texts. To try to make sense of this enormous amount of material, five distinct entities were found to be pertinent to the Bible's setting. These entities include Book, Deity, Location, Person, and Others, each serving to classify the text spans according to their semantic significance within the biblical domain.

A thorough annotation procedure was applied to 222 sentences which gave us 5707 tokens. To gain a better understanding of how these semantic kinds are distributed across the corpus, our procedure attempted to locate and categorize the text spans by the established entities. The outcomes of this meticulous annotation are as follows:

- Book: This category, which encompasses references to the various books within the Bible, accounted for a total of 8 instances within the annotated sentences.
- Deity: References to divine figures or deities were notably prevalent, with 92 instances identified, reflecting the central role of the divine in biblical texts.
- Location: Geographical locations, significant within the biblical narratives, were marked 76 times, highlighting the importance of place in these stories.
- Person: Human figures, whether historical or mythological, were the most frequently annotated entity, with 158 instances. This underscores the Bible's focus on human experiences and interactions with the divine.
- Others: A broad category capturing all other elements within the text, amassed a substantial 5367 instances, indicating a wide range of topics and concepts beyond the specific entities categorized.

The general statistics of the annotated dataset, as summarized in Table 1, underscore the diversity and complexity of the biblical narrative, as seen through the lens of these five entities.

**Table 1.** Statistics of our dataset

| No of sentences | No of annotator | BOOK | DEITY | LOC | PER | OTHERS | % of Entities in Tokens | No of Tokens |
|---|---|---|---|---|---|---|---|---|
| **222** | 1 | 8 | 92 | 76 | 158 | 5367 | 5.85 | 5707 |

## 4  Discussions

The challenges encountered in this research and the future direction are discussed in this section.

### 4.1  Challenges

Several challenging obstacles during our study that had a big influence on the data collection and annotation process were faced. Tonality is a common linguistic trait in many languages, therefore that was one of the main challenges. It was essential to make sure that every word had the appropriate tonal marks highlighted since words inside sentences lose their intended contextual meaning if they are not marked correctly. This aspect of this study was particularly challenging due to the intricate nature of tonal languages, where slight variations in tone can alter the meaning of a word entirely. The meticulous attention required to accurately represent tonal marks thus posed a substantial obstacle in the preparation of our dataset.

Our manual annotation approach was quite labor-intensive, which presented another major problem. It took a lot of time and effort to do this operation, mostly because low-resource languages lack automated annotation tools. The absence of these platforms meant that annotation had to be done manually, which not only delayed our work but also increased the possibility of human mistakes. The annotator had to carefully examine and classify every word or phrase in the dataset as part of the manual process, which required a high degree of focus and skill.

Considering these difficulties, we ardently encourage the creation of automated systems tailored for low-resource language annotation. The invention of such tools would constitute a huge leap in the discipline, enabling researchers to expedite the annotation process and get more accurate findings in a fraction of the time now necessary.

Additionally, there is a pressing need for the development of technological solutions that simplify the process of typing languages with tonal marks. This makes it easier to accurately represent these languages in written form, thereby preserving their richness and nuance, ensuring that they continue to be used and studied for generations to come.

## 4.2  Future Work

In the next phase of our research, we will enhance and expand our methodological approach to annotating biblical texts, aiming to add more value to the dataset specifically focused on the bible. To provide a thorough coverage of the text under investigation, this attempt will entail finishing the annotation process for the sentences that have already been gathered. We have collected 1,000 sentences and are presently engaged in the annotation process, which will be followed by the development of a Named Entity Recognition (NER) model. To get a greater level of accuracy and dependability in the annotations, one or two experts as supplementary annotators will annotate the dataset on their own. this approach should help the annotators reach a consensus more quickly and improve the quality of the annotations by encouraging individual contributions. A high degree of annotation agreement by holding in-depth conversations on the annotated dataset, which will guarantee the production of a dataset of unmatched quality is aimed at.

Additionally, we will be developing a Named Entity Recognition (NER) model that is customized for the dataset that comes from the Bible domain. Using the comprehensive annotations that our team of experts have given, this model will be the basis for locating and classifying named items throughout the biblical texts.

The reach of our study will be extended to include a multi-domain NER system for low-resource languages, looking beyond the current focus of our work. With this large-scale project, the difficulties brought about by linguistic and domain variety and the lack of computational resources for a large number of languages and domains will be tackled. We want to aid in the development of improved NER capabilities that are inclusive and adaptable by including the bible domain as one of the fundamental elements in this multi-domain framework.

## 5 Conclusion

Indigenous languages are frequently underrepresented and under-resourced in digital resources. This work highlights the tremendous potential of computational linguistics in supporting these languages by focusing on the compilation and annotation of a Yorùbá Bible corpus for Named Entity Recognition (NER). This research makes a significant contribution to the area of NER as well as the preservation of cultural heritage by developing a customized dataset and starting the process of developing a NER model specifically for the Yorùbá Bible.

The thorough annotation procedure described in this study not only improves the dataset's quality and usefulness but also establishes a standard for research of a similar nature in other low-resource languages. This dataset may be used for more than just language preservation; it can help develop natural language processing (NLP) systems that are contextually and culturally sensitive.

Furthermore, this study establishes the foundation for further research into the creation of a multi-domain NER system. This approach aims to close the gap between models that are limited to a particular domain and those that can function well in a variety of language and cultural situations. Anticipated multi-domain NER model is intended to improve NER systems' performance and flexibility, allowing them to better handle the linguistic diversity present in global languages. These developments are essential for both academic study and real-world technological applications, such as boosting information accessibility for a range of demographics and refining AI interfaces.

In conclusion, the Yorùbá Bible NER dataset's successful implementation marks a major advancement in the fields of computational linguistics, language preservation, and technology. It contributes to the preservation of a priceless cultural legacy while simultaneously advancing the technological capacities required for the wider implementation of NER systems in a variety of areas and languages, opening the door to more inclusive and culturally sensitive AI technologies.

## References

1. Nozza, D., Manchanda, P., Fersini, E., Palmonari, M., Messina, E.: LearningToAdapt with word embeddings: domain adaptation of Named Entity Recognition systems. Inf. Process. Manage. **58**(3), 102537 (2021). https://doi.org/10.1016/j.ipm.2021.102537
2. Sun, P., Yang, X., Zhao, X., Wang, Z.: An overview of named entity recognition. In: Proceedings of the 2018 International Conference on Asian Language Processing, IALP 2018, pp. 273–278 (2019). https://doi.org/10.1109/IALP.2018.8629225
3. Adelani, D.I., et al.: Masakhaner: named entity recognition for African languages. Trans. Assoc. Comput. Linguist. **9**, 1116–1131 (2021). https://doi.org/10.1162/tacl_a_00416
4. Ozcelik, O., Toraman, C.: Named entity recognition in Turkish: a comparative study with detailed error analysis. Inf. Process. Manage. **59**(6), 103065 (2022). https://doi.org/10.1016/j.ipm.2022.103065
5. ohannes, H.M., Amagasa, T.: Named-entity recognition for a low-resource language using pre-trained language model. In: Proceedings of the ACM Symposium on Applied Computing, pp. 837–844 (2022).. https://doi.org/10.1145/3477314.3507066
6. Zhang, Y., Xiao, G.: Named entity recognition datasets: a classification framework. Int. J. Comput. Intell. Syst. **17**, 71 (2024). https://doi.org/10.1007/s44196-024-00456-1

7. Heng, Y., et al.: ProgGen: Generating Named Entity Recognition Datasets Step-by-step with Self-Reflexive Large Language Models. arXiv preprint arXiv:2403.11103 (2024)

8. Anandika, A., Chakravarty, S., Paikaray, B.K.: Named entity recognition in Odia language: a rule-based approach. Int. J. Reason.-Based Intell. Syst. **15**(1), 15–21 (2023). https://doi.org/10.1504/IJRIS.2023.128379

9. Mundotiya, R., et al.: Development of a dataset and a deep learning baseline named entity recognizer for three low resource languages: Bhojpuri, Maithili, and Magahi. ACM Trans. Asian Low-Resour. Lang. Inform. Process. **22**(1), 1–20 (2023). https://doi.org/10.1145/353 3428

10. Fu, Y., Lin, N., Yang, Z., Jiang, S.: Towards Malay named entity recognition: an open-source dataset and a multi-task framework. Conn. Sci. **35**(1) (2023). https://doi.org/10.1080/095 40091.2022.2159014

11. Singh, P., De Clercq, O., Lefever, E.: Distilling monolingual models from large multilingual transformers. Electronics **12** (2023). https://doi.org/10.3390/electronics12041022

12. Sharma, R., Morwal, S., Agarwal, B.: Named entity recognition using neural language model and CRF for Hindi language. Comput. Speech Lang. **74**, 101356 (2022), (2021). https://doi.org/10.1016/j.csl.2022.101356

13. Fudholi, D.H., Nayoan, R.A.N., Hidayatullah, A.F., Arianto, D.B.: A Hybrid CNN-Bilstm model for drug named entity recognition. J. Eng. Sci. Technol. **17**(1), 730–744 (2022)

14. Zhang, Z., Zhang, H., Wan, Q., Liu, J.: LELNER: a lightweight and effective low-resource named entity recognition model. Knowl.-Based Syst. **251**, 109178 (2022). https://doi.org/10.1016/j.knosys.2022.109178

15. Sallabank, J., Austin, P.K.: Endangered Languages. In: The Routledge Handbook of Applied Linguistics. Taylor &Francis Group (2023)

16. Chew, K.A.B., Calls Him, M., Dormer, J., Tennell, C.: Learning in relation: a guide to creating online indigenous language courses that center indigenous ways of knowing and being. UVivSpaceHome (2022). http://hdl.handle.net/1828/14403

17. Pankratz, E., Arppe, A., Lachler, J.: Low hanging fruit and the Boasian trilogy in digital lexicography of morphologically rich languages. Septentrio Academic Publishing, vol. 46, Issue 1, (2022). https://doi.org/10.7557/12.6441

18. Wallis, K., Ross, M.: Fourth VR: indigenous virtual reality practice. Sage J. **27**(2) (2020). https://doi.org/10.1177/1354856520943083

19. Mayhew, S.: Annotation Guidelines (2023). https://www.universalner.org/guidelines/. Accessed 15 October 2023

20. YouVersion (2023). https://www.bible.com/bible/207/GEN.1.YCE. Accessed 2 December 2023

21. Brahma, B., Bhuyan, H.K.: Soft computing and machine learning techniques for e-Health data analytics. In: Mishra, S., González-Briones, A., Bhoi, A.K., Mallick, P.K., Corchado, J.M. (eds.) Connected e-Health. Studies in Computational Intelligence, vol. 1021. Springer, Cham (2022). https://doi.org/10.1007/978-3-030-97929-4_4

22. Brahma, B., et al.: Mathematical model for analysis of COVID-19 outbreak using VON Berta-lanffy Growth Function (VBGF). Turkish J. Comput. Math. Educ. (TURCOMAT), **12**(11), 6063–6075 (2021). https://doi.org/10.17762/turcomat.v12i11.6925

# Selected Applications of Artificial Intelligence in Pursuing the Sustainable Development Goals

Mobayode O. Akinsolu[1,2](✉) ⓘ, Chekwube Ezechi[2](✉) ⓘ, Wilson Sakpere[2] ⓘ, and Mingwei Sun[3] ⓘ

[1] Faculty of Arts, Computing and Engineering, Wrexham University, Wrexham LL11 2AW, UK
`mobayode.akinsolu@wrexham.ac.uk`
[2] Faculty of Natural and Applied Sciences, Lead City University, Ibadan, Oyo State, Nigeria
`chekwube.ezechi@lcu.edu.ng`
[3] College of Computer Science, Tongua Normal University, Tonghua 134000, China

**Abstract.** This paper presents an exploratory study to provide a broad outline of how AI-facilitated strategies are advancing or aiding in the accomplishment of the Sustainable Development Goals (SDGs), serving as an introduction to such a prospective analysis. In particular, this paper highlights the advancements in areas such as (1) AI-powered medical diagnostics and disease forecasting for enhanced health and well-being, (2) AI-mediated educational interactions for enriched learning experiences in tertiary institutions, (3) AI-supported prompt detection of oil spills to mitigate pollution, and (4) AI-informed predictions of urban land use and cover changes, along with other modern AI applications. These examples are briefly examined and demonstrate that AI-driven methods surpass conventional approaches in accuracy, efficiency, optimization, decision-making, and predictive capabilities. Concentrating on the SDGs, the insights provided in this paper support the data-backed claim that AI-centric paradigms are closely linked with intelligent decision-making, which can, in turn, contribute to the effective and resilient design, implementation, and strategizing of our planet's future sustainability.

**Keywords:** Artificial Intelligence · Sustainability · Sustainable Development Goals (SDGs)

## 1 Introduction

With the rise of Artificial Intelligence (AI) and its expanding influence across various societal sectors, it is crucial to identify AI applications that support or propel the attainment of the Sustainable Development Goals (SDGs). The introduction of AI-driven systems is anticipated to have significant effects on environmental sustainability, global productivity, healthcare, and other areas, both in the immediate and distant future concerning the SDGs. AI is expected to play a multitude of roles in supporting the global effort to meet the United Nations SDGs by 2030. The 2030 Agenda for Sustainable Development comprises 17 goals and 169 targets that have been internationally ratified [1]. Various studies indicate that AI strategies could have both beneficial and detrimental impacts on sustainable development [2].

J. B. Awotunde et al. (Eds.): AFRICATEK 2024, LNICST 618, pp. 64–85, 2026.
https://doi.org/10.1007/978-3-031-93557-2_5

The advent of Artificial Intelligence (AI) is fundamentally altering numerous sectors of society, necessitating a broad understanding of its role in fostering sustainable development. AI is defined as a computer system capable of learning and making decisions based on accumulated experience [3]. As a field within computational science, AI aims to enable computers to undertake complex tasks with little or no human oversight. Essentially, AI strives to emulate intelligent human behaviour in computers and machines. While there is no universally accepted definition of AI, All software technology that can perform tasks like interactive communication (social robots or chatbots), perception (facial recognition), prediction (like weather forecasting), decision-making (like medical diagnostic systems), data-driven knowledge extraction and pattern identification (like identifying fake news on social media), and logical reasoning (like creating theories based on preexisting premises) is generally considered to fall under this category [3]. AI's applications span various domains, including business, healthcare, and the environment. Additionally, it has the potential to drastically alter consumer behavior, business structures, sales procedures, customer service methods, and marketing strategies [4]. According to a recent survey, AI is projected to be the most adopted technology by marketer soon [4]. Companies such as Birchbox, Stitch Fix, and Trendy Butler are already leveraging AI to anticipate customer preferences, achieving mixed results.

A targeted approach that is more closely aligned with the SDGs involves AI applications in environmental monitoring and healthcare. The healthcare sector inundated with vast amounts of data including test results, diagnoses, treatments, medical histories, and wellness metrics, necessitates computational tools for enhanced precision and efficiency [1]. AI also plays a role in projecting changes in global average temperatures and in forecasting severe weather events like floods, tsunamis, and wildfires [5]. Given the ongoing need for better predictive and evaluative methods to address these issues and promote urban sustainability, AI emerges as a crucial resource for the effective development and advancement of sustainability measures. Sustainability is about making positive contributions to the future, improving the collective well-being of humanity and the planet, and eschewing practices that exhaust natural resources [6, 7]. It is based on respect for nature, human rights, economic fairness, and a culture of peace. Similarly, sustainable development refers to the application of sustainability principles [6, 7]. Originating from the 1987 Brundtland Commission [7], "development that satisfies current needs without jeopardizing the ability of future generations to meet their own needs" is defined as sustainable development.

The SDGs are instrumental in eradicating global poverty and hunger, and they contribute to the worldwide pursuit of peace, equality, and prosperity, fostering a more unified and healthier global community. As previously mentioned, the primary aim of the SDGs is to shield the planet from degradation through sustainable practices in consumption and production, and by managing natural resources to meet the needs of both present and future generations. The SDGs also focus on addressing the requirements of the poorest and most vulnerable groups across all nations [8–10]. The 17 SDGs that have received international consensus are outlined in Table 1. To summarize the overall impact of AI as both a facilitator and a barrier to the SDGs, the objectives of sustainable development can be divided into three primary categories: the environment, the economy, and society [1]. The effect of AI on the SDGs has been extensively discussed in

[1], where it is demonstrated that AI has both direct and indirect influences on achieving the SDGs, with particular attention to societal, economic, and environmental aspects, as determined through a consensus-based expert elicitation process. Thus, forging a partnership between AI and sustainable development is deemed essential.

**Table 1.** The sustainable development goals (SDGs) [2].

| Goal | Description |
| --- | --- |
| Goal 1 | Eradicate poverty in every form across the globe |
| Goal 2 | Eliminate hunger, secure food availability, enhance nutrition, and advance sustainable farming |
| Goal 3 | Guarantee healthy living and foster well-being for individuals of all ages |
| Goal 4 | Ensure universal and fair quality education and encourage continuous learning opportunities for everyone |
| Goal 5 | Attain gender parity and empower females worldwide |
| Goal 6 | Ensure that everyone has access to safe drinking water and sanitary facilities through sustainable governance |
| Goal 7 | Make affordable, dependable, modern, environmentally friendly energy more accessible to everyone |
| Goal 8 | Promote sustained economic growth that is inclusive, environmentally sustainable, full and productive employment, and decent work for all |
| Goal 9 | Encourage inclusive and sustainable industrialization, build resilient infrastructure, and foster innovation |
| Goal 10 | Reduce the differences between and within countries |
| Goal 11 | Build rural and urban communities that are sustainable, safe, resilient, and inclusive |
| Goal 12 | Encourage sustainable manufacturing and consumption practices |
| Goal 13 | Take immediate action to mitigate the effects of climate change |
| Goal 14 | Seas, oceans, and marine resources should be preserved and used responsibly for development |
| Goal 15 | Preserve, restore, and promote the sustainable use of land ecosystems; manage forests responsibly, oppose desertification, halt biodiversity loss, and reverse land degradation |
| Goal 16 | To ensure sustainable growth, promote an inclusive, and peaceful society |
| Goal 17 | Establishing inclusive, dependable, and successful institutions at all levels will guarantee justice for all |

AI methodologies have revolutionized human interactions and environmental engagement, promising enduring effects on societal, economic, and ecological sustainability at various temporal scales. This research seeks to shed light on the recent AI innovations that support the United Nations Sustainable Development Goals (UN SDGs), with a focus on public health, climate action, sustainable urban development, and land ecosystems. It's important to clarify that this work doesn't aim to cover every existing and potential AI application related to the UN SDGs comprehensively. Instead, our objective is to offer a broad perspective on specific sectors where AI strategies are facilitating progress towards achieving the UN SDGs. The study makes the following key contributions:

- A broad discussion on the implementation of state-of-the-art AI algorithms and methods in achieving the UN SDGs within certain domains.
- Emphasis on modern real-life examples where AI methods are applied.
- Association of specific AI methods with their corresponding SDGs that they most directly impact.

While quantitative analysis and data visualization are commonly associated with scoping studies and similar scholarly endeavors [11], it should be noted that this research incorporates a limited number of such analyses and visual representations. This study aims to offer a general overview of how AI methods are contributing to the pursuit of sustainability in specific sectors, as documented in existing literature. The main goal is to equip researchers with a foundational guide and a comprehensible reference to aid further exploration in this field. Given the dynamic and expansive nature of AI, it is anticipated that future developments will yield numerous additional possibilities and wider applications beyond those discussed in this study.

The structure of this paper is as follows: Sect. 2 reviews relevant literature, examining the use of k-nearest neighbors (k-NN) algorithm on large datasets for accurately classifying diabetes mellitus (DM) patients, exploring advancements in addressing excessive climate pollution through an AI-powered disaster monitoring framework, discussing AI's role in designing sustainable urban environments and waste management with the aid of Big Data and cloud computing technology, and detailing the application of the Internet of Things (IoT) and AI in enhancing agricultural practices for better soil utilization and plant disease detection. Section 3 consolidates and emphasizes the principal discoveries of this research across seven key areas, including health data categorization, prediction of wind energy production, identification of oil spills, and forecasting changes in urban land use and cover. The paper concludes with a summary of insights in Sect. 4.

## 2  AI Advancing Sustainability

In this section, the key domains where AI is contributing to the pursuit of SDGs are explored using six primary areas.

### 2.1  Good Health and Well-Being

The United Nations established the SDGs (refer to Table 1) as part of a global initiative to envision and create a more prosperous future for all by the year 2030. Within these goals, the third objective identifies the importance of ensuring robust health and wellness. Diabetes mellitus (DM) features among the leading causes of mortality worldwide, positioned as the ninth leading cause of death according to the World Health Organization (WHO) [12]. The year 2017 saw a global diabetic population of 451 million individuals as reported by the International Diabetes Federation, with projections indicating a potential increase to 693 million within the following 26 years [13]. DM is known to precipitate the failure of multiple organs in affected individuals. The extensive data requirements for diagnosing and treating DM make it an ideal candidate for the application of AI to improve outcomes and foster the development of novel strategies. AI methodologies have proven beneficial in the detection, diagnosis, and categorization of DM among patients. For instance, [14] demonstrates that the Type 2 Machine Learning (T2ML) hybrid model, which utilizes algorithms like random forest, XGBoost (extreme gradient boosting), - means clustering, and logistic regression, achieves a detection and classification accuracy of 97.5% for DM, surpassing other machine learning techniques such as naive Bayes, support vector machine, and multi-layer perceptron (MLP) classifiers. Additionally, a k-NN-based AI model cited in [15] has attained an accuracy exceeding 90% in the detection and classification of DM.

While the above-discussed methods have shown high accuracy rates in classifying DM, their effectiveness diminishes when dealing with extensive, disorderly medical datasets, commonly referred to as big data. To address this, an enhancement to the k-NN algorithm is suggested in [16], which clusters to eliminate noise and accelerate the neighbor search process in large-scale health data, without compromising algorithmic precision. Additional practical instances of AI-driven technologies fostering health and wellness include robotic-assisted surgeries and virtual nursing assistants, both utilizing a model-based intelligent algorithm known as active relative motion cancelling (ARMC). These innovations are already operational; for instance, Cedars-Sinai Hospital in Los Angeles, United States, employs them to execute complex surgeries with remarkable accuracy, control, and adaptability [17]. However, it's important to recognize that such cutting-edge digital solutions are not widely accessible in economically disadvantaged or less developed regions, largely due to the sluggish pace of technology transfer (TT) and acquisition (TA) [18]. Consequently, there is a pressing need for concerted efforts to enhance TT and TA within the international health domain to ensure equitable access across all demographics and age groups.

A recent study has shown that approximately 90% of hospitals in the United States have implemented an AI strategy [19]. This pattern is mirrored in China's healthcare sector, which is forecasted to reach a market value of nearly 12 billion USD by 2030 due to AI integration [20]. The United Kingdom is also progressing with initiatives like the National Health Service AI Laboratory (NHS AI Lab), among others, which are dedicated to facilitating the understanding and adoption of AI within healthcare [21]. While the advantages of embracing AI are acknowledged in developing nations (for example, the Philippines and Nigeria), the substantial financial investments required for effective deployment and adoption are hindered by more immediate societal, economic, and welfare challenges these countries face [22, 23]. As a result, the incorporation of AI technologies to enhance health and well-being may advance more gradually in these developing regions compared to their more affluent and technologically advanced counterparts.

## 2.2 Climate Action

Addressing climate change is the thirteenth objective among the SDGs (refer to Table 1), and it is recognized as a primary driver of extensive population displacement throughout Africa, prompting the United Nations to label it a "threat-multiplier" that exacerbates social, political, and international tensions [24]. The IPCC's (Intergovernmental Panel on Climate Change) 2018 special report on limiting global warming to 1.5 °C suggests that achieving this target could "significantly reduce the number of individuals at risk of climate-related threats and poverty by potentially several hundred million by 2050," while also mitigating severe effects on ecosystems, human health, and well-being [25].

Urban areas contribute a substantial portion of the world's total $CO_2$ emissions (ranging from 60% to 80%) and are anticipated to spearhead the implementation of climate change goals outlined in the Paris Agreement [26]. [27] proposes that the application of information and communication technologies (ICT), particularly AI, can diminish environmental pollution in urban settings. For instance, artificial neural networks (ANNs) have been utilized to enhance the daily prediction of the hazardous air pollutant PM2.5 in China [28], and an AI-powered disaster monitoring system has been devised to detect floods and abnormal air pollution levels [29].

Currently, policymakers spearhead renewable energy as a key strategy to counteract climate change threats [30]. Photovoltaic (PV) farms and wind farms stand as the leading renewable energy sources for economic sustainability and development objectives [31]. Nonetheless, the challenge of intermittency still constrains modern renewable energy systems. Therefore, enhanced prediction and modelling of these energy sources are crucial for their practicality. For instance, [31] details the use of three AI-driven predictive models—response surface methodology (RSM), artificial neural network (ANN), and adaptive neuro-fuzzy inference system (ANFIS)—to estimate power output and performance ratio for a two-megawatt peak (MWp) solar PV farm in Kerala, India. The application of AI in renewable energy facilities, as shown in [31], aids in managing and optimizing energy loads and selecting diverse renewable resources to meet demand based on their availability. AI is also utilized for forecasting PV production, as mentioned in [32]. Consequently, AI-facilitated methods are instrumental for decision-makers in achieving SDGs, especially the seventh and thirteenth goals. Supporting this, the findings from the study in [33] (illustrated in Fig. 1) indicate that the adoption of AI technologies significantly enhances progress toward fulfilling the thirteenth SDG. This is supported by the fact that the majority of respondents concur with this view, while a minimal percentage dissent, as depicted in Fig. 1.

## 2.3 Sustainable Cities and Communities

The eleventh SDG focuses on transforming urban areas, communities, and settlements into sustainable entities (refer to Table 1). This goal aims to restructure societies for sustainability by employing smart, eco-friendly planning strategies for development [34]. The United Nations reports that the world population has reached 8 billion and is trending towards greater urbanization [35]. Since 2007, more than half of humanity has resided in urban centres, a figure expected to climb to 60% by 2030 [36, 37]. The concept of smart cities, synonymous with sustainable cities, emerges from leveraging

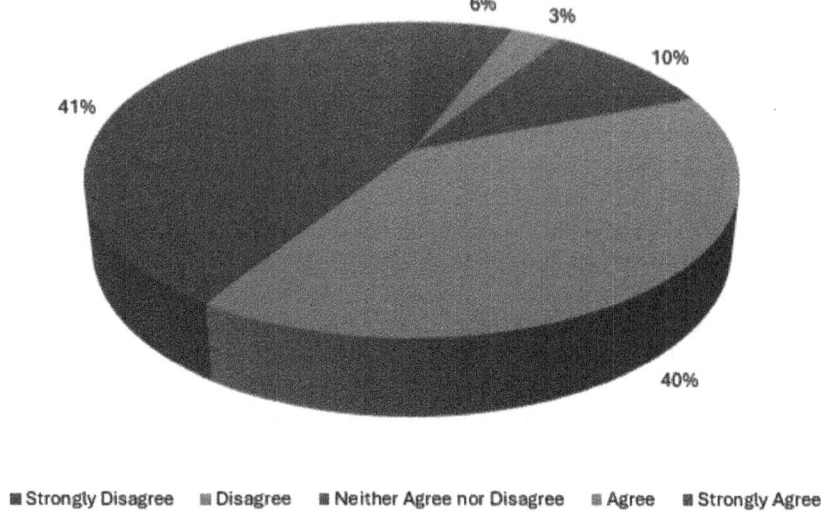

■ Strongly Disagree     ▨ Disagree     ■ Neither Agree nor Disagree     ▨ Agree     ■ Strongly Agree

**Fig. 1.** The impact of AI on climate initiatives [33].

ICT to enhance the quality of life for city dwellers [38]. These cities boast advanced energy management and transportation systems, along with efficient governance, all contributing to reduced carbon emissions and the adoption of clean technology for a healthier urban environment.

Urban planning and decision-making processes increasingly rely on cloud computing and predictive analytics for the diverse collection, storage, and real-time analysis of essential data [39]. In Barcelona, for instance, sensor-equipped waste bins connected to the cloud notify authorities when they need emptying, and AI algorithms optimize collection routes to minimize transportation expenses [40]. Currently, real-time data aids in mapping routes and scheduling trips for public transportation, with AI-powered tools like Waze and Google Maps enhancing efficiency, and Internet of Things (IoT)-enabled parking systems directing drivers to the nearest available parking spot [38]. In the realm of sustainable urban mobility, particularly bus transit management, a three-tiered management system utilizing big data has been implemented [41]. In Fortaleza, Brazil's fifth-largest city, they trialed this system, applying big data methods to effectively and cost-efficiently calculate bus travel times and passenger demand. It also analyzed passenger travel patterns and provided decision support through interactive visualizations. Systems like these are invaluable to urban planners for evaluating policy impact and advancing smart transportation infrastructures. Additionally, technologies like fog computing, IoT, and big data analytics are proving to be key enablers in the development of sustainable, smart transportation solutions for congestion management and route optimization [42].

Furthermore, the research on AI's role in smart cities for enhanced decision-making [43], as detailed in Table 2, indicates a robust positive correlation between AI and smart decision-making (SDM) in smart city development. This conclusion is drawn from the statistical findings where (B = 1.276) and (Beta = 0.811) with a p-value of (0.000), signifying a substantial and affirmative link between AI and SDM. Therefore, this data substantiates the previously mentioned point that AI, through big data analytics and ML, can significantly contribute to informed decision-making processes in the evolution of sustainable cities, aligning with the eleventh SDG.

**Table 2.** Multiple regression, AI, and SDM [43].

| Coefficients [a] | | | | | | |
|---|---|---|---|---|---|---|
| | Model | Unstandardized Coefficients | | Standardized Coefficients | t | Sig |
| | | B | Std. Error | Beta | | |
| 1 | (Constant) | 1.619 | 0.174 | | 9.298 | 0.000 |
| AI | | 1.276 | 0.044 | 0.811 | 28.861 | 0.000 |

[a] Dependent Variable: SDM

## 2.4 Industry, Innovation, and Infrastructure

The ninth SD is centered on establishing dependable infrastructure, encouraging inclusive and sustainable industrial growth, and nurturing innovation. The construction industry noted for its substantial energy consumption and reliance on natural resources, is also a significant source of greenhouse gas emissions and waste [44]. To counteract these impacts, using AI-driven techniques for material optimization and energy forecasting is crucial to lowering carbon emissions [45]. AI's application within the construction sector is diverse, with a focus on sustainable materials and energy management being particularly prominent. Adapting to environmental changes is crucial for the construction industry to thrive and align with the SDGs, leading to a worldwide demand for sustainable materials and energy-saving practices [46].

Advancements in sustainable construction materials have been achieved through AI technologies [47]. For instance, an ANN-based methodology is suggested in [48] to predict the mechanical characteristics of eco-friendly concrete. Similarly, after being exposed to high temperatures, the residual strength of concrete has been evaluated using ANN-based models that take thermal effects into consideration [49]. ANNs have also been employed to analyze the performance of lightweight concrete made from recycled aggregates [50]. It has been reported that the building and operating phases in the construction sector account for 39% of $CO_2$ emissions connected to energy and 36% of world energy use [51], posing challenges to the attainment of the thirteenth SDG. The focus on energy conservation and $CO_2$ emission reduction is central to sustainability discussions. AI techniques, such as ANN for load forecasting, are instrumental in devising efficient energy management systems [52], and for the predictive analysis and maintenance of renewable energy systems in buildings, like wind and solar power [53].

## 2.5  Zero Hunger

The second SDG, Zero Hunger, is intended to put an end to hunger, ensure food security, enhance nutrition, and advocate for sustainable agricultural practices [54]. Approximately 4.4% of the population in Europe is directly employed in the agriculture sector, which generates over $181 billion in gross value added (GVA) [55]. In India, agriculture is a lifeline for at least 60% of the populace, offering employment and sustenance [56]. As the global population grows and climate change intensifies, the need for sustainable food production and water-efficient agricultural practices becomes more pressing. Agriculture has developed through four phases, culminating in Agriculture 4.0, also termed smart or precision agriculture [57, 58]. This advanced stage represents the seamless fusion of contemporary science and technology with traditional farming methods, leading to autonomous, automated, and intelligent agricultural processes [57, 58]. Smart agriculture involves the use of IoT and AI to implement intelligent farming techniques, such as embedding sensors in plants and soil to monitor vital parameters like chlorophyll content, humidity, moisture, and the presence of chemicals, aiding in decision-making and the prevention of diseases, pests, erosion, and drought [59].

Supporting the previously mentioned points, a novel irrigation system utilizing IoT technology has been developed to gather environmental data from farmlands, such as humidity and moisture levels [60]. This system, integrated with an ANN, analyzes these parameters to determine optimal irrigation times, offering potential water savings over conventional methods. Additionally, a designed sensor network employs AI to monitor and interpret soil conditions, aiding farmers in assessing land suitability for crop cultivation, thereby promoting efficient land use [61]. Beyond these advancements, the management of crop pests and diseases remains a critical issue for sustainable agriculture. The South American tomato pinworm's impact on crops exemplified the detrimental effects of pests in Almería, Spain [62]. Ineffective pest control can lead to significant yield losses [63]. AI's role extends to smart greenhouses and precision agriculture, incorporating ecological algorithms like ANFIS-PSO (adaptive neuro-fuzzy inference system with particle swarm optimization), ANFIS-GA (adaptive neuro-fuzzy inference system with genetic algorithm), and ANFIS-ACO (adaptive neuro-fuzzy inference system with ant colony optimization), along with swarm intelligence algorithms for advanced pest management [64]. These algorithms, combined with unmanned aerial vehicles (UAVs), enhance the efficiency of pest control measures and pesticide application [64, 65]. Furthermore, AI systems have been instrumental in creating intelligent pest management strategies that can detect early infestations of pests such as whiteflies and thrips [66].

While the aforementioned studies offer valuable perspectives on how AI technologies are enhancing agricultural efficiency to boost food production, it's important to recognize that further comprehensive research, including detailed surveys and field studies, is necessary to fully assess the effectiveness and impact of these AI methodologies. Conducting such in-depth investigations, which extend beyond the general overview provided here, would greatly benefit governmental bodies, agencies, and organizations dedicated to achieving maximum food productivity through sustainable farming methods.

## 2.6  Affordable and Clean Energy

The seventh SDG focuses on providing access to affordable, reliable, sustainable, and modern energy. Electricity is particularly vital for elevating living standards. With escalating demand and energy supply, the importance of energy efficiency is amplified. Buildings account for nearly half of global energy usage, with heating, ventilation, and air conditioning (HVAC) systems consuming about 40% of a building's total energy [67]. An AI-driven, occupant-focused HVAC control system for cooling has been introduced to enhance energy efficiency in multi-zone commercial buildings [68]. This innovation is crucial for both economic and environmental sustainability.

Traditional HVAC systems rely on sensors to regulate thermal comfort within buildings, typically using proportional-integral-derivative (PID) controllers [69]. Yet, these systems often fall short in responding to abrupt shifts in occupancy and environmental factors like outside air temperature, humidity, and airflow, leading to energy inefficiency, particularly in multi-zone commercial structures [69]. To address this, A cooling system based on AI and occupant-centric HVAC control has been created [68]. This AI model operates in three phases: forecasting hourly occupancy, creating an AI-driven HVAC control system, and conducting a comparative analysis of traditional and AI-based controls through simulation. The AI technology significantly enhances occupancy accuracy and energy efficiency, achieving at least a 10% reduction in energy use compared to conventional automated systems [68]. Thus, the adoption and advancement of AI-powered building energy control systems are imperative for achieving economic and environmental sustainability.

Table 3 and Fig. 2 offer a synopsis of how AI applications correspond to the SDGs. The subsequent section will delve into current AI applications relevant to SDGs.

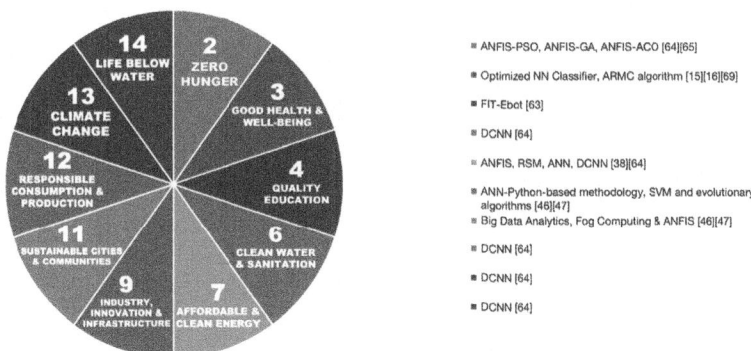

**Fig. 2.** Overview of AI methods relevant to selected SDGs.

**Table 3.** Selected AI methods promoting sustainable development goals (SDGs).

| Method | SDGs | Reference |
|---|---|---|
| Optimized - NN classifier with noise removal and optimal hyperparameter | SDG 3: Enhancing patient categorization | [15, 16] |
| Artificial neural network (ANN), Adaptive neuro-fuzzy interference system (ANFIS), and Response surface methodology (RSM) | SDGs 7, 13: Analytical model for predicting clean energy output from solar farms | [38] |
| Big data Analytics, fog computing, and adaptive neuro-fuzzy interference system (ANFIS) | SDG 11: Traffic flow optimization and strategic route planning for smart urban mobility | [46, 48] |
| ANN-Python-based methodology, support vector machines and evolutionary algorithms | SDG 9: Analytical model to predict the properties of eco-friendly construction materials | [46, 48] |
| FIT-Ebot (a chatbot using natural language processing (NLP) to classify, predict, and generate text and speech | SDG 4: Smart assistants for administrative and educational support in tertiary institutions | [64] |
| Deep convolutional neural network (DCNN) classification technique: Oil spill convolutional neural network (OSCNet) | SDGs 6, 7, 12, 13, and 14: Precise identification of oil spill incidents | [65] |
| ANFIS with Genetic Algorithm, ANFIS with Ant Colony Optimization and Adaptive Neuro-Fuzzy Inference System – Particle Swarm Optimization (ANFIS-PSO), | SDG 2: Advanced intelligent integrated pest management (IPM) systems for early detection of pest infestations | [65, 66] |
| Model-based intelligent active relative motion cancelling (ARMC) algorithm | SDG 3: Surgery facilitated by robotic technologies | [70] |

## 3   Some Contemporary AI Techniques Promoting SDGs

The rapid accumulation of medical data from wearable technology, smartphones, and other peripheral devices has necessitated the precise categorization of health data for accurate disease prediction, detection, diagnosis, treatment, and pharmaceutical development [71]. The k-NN algorithm is highly regarded for its accuracy and low computational demands in these contexts. Nonetheless, its performance is lessened when applied to voluminous health datasets with intricate attributes [72]. An enhanced version of the k-NN algorithm has been introduced to address this issue [16]. This refined method employs a coefficient designed to cluster and trim noisy data within large datasets, thereby preserving valuable information in less dense areas and reducing data in denser regions to expedite training. This results in a more efficient k-NN operation, improving its test data classification capabilities. However, this enhancement is generally confined to single-class classification, while many real-world scenarios necessitate the use of multi-label or multi-category classification. Future research is anticipated to concentrate on these broader classification types and the procurement of high-quality medical data for precise categorization.

In recent years, AI has significantly transformed the landscape of healthcare, particularly in nursing efficiency and hospital management. One notable area of advancement is in robotic-assisted surgery, where AI-driven innovations have revolutionized the field by enhancing precision, control, and adaptability in complex surgical procedures. These AI-powered systems, such as the da Vinci Surgical System, have enabled surgeons to perform intricate operations with unprecedented accuracy and minimal invasiveness, ultimately leading to improved patient outcomes and reduced recovery times [73]. Additionally, virtual nursing assistance powered by AI has emerged as a valuable tool in hospital management. These systems utilize ML algorithms to monitor patients' vital signs, track medication schedules, and provide real-time support to healthcare professionals, thereby optimizing workflow efficiency and enhancing patient care [74]. By integrating AI-driven technologies into nursing practice and hospital management, healthcare institutions can streamline processes, minimize errors, and ultimately improve the overall quality of care.

Digital and emerging technologies, particularly those based on AI, are also revolutionizing education and learning. This technological shift has seen learning platforms evolve from e-learning and mobile learning to intelligent learning environments. These AI-powered environments enhance flexibility, content customization, learners' engagement, and motivation [75]. They also offer a superior user experience that bolsters learning outcomes and minimizes discouragement among learners. An illustration of this is the FIT-EBot, an AI-driven chatbot designed to support the administrative and academic needs of students at the Faculty of Information Technology, Ho Chi Minh City University of Science, Vietnam (FIT-HCMUS) [76]. Developed using the Dialogflow framework, which incorporates natural language processing, FIT-EBot processes various forms of student inputs—ranging from text and audio to video and images—in both administrative and academic contexts, generating accurate responses with little to no human intervention. Trained on FIT-HCMUS's historical data, FIT-EBot can engage in intelligent dialogue and providing informed answers. Integrated with Facebook Messenger, it offers a convenient communication channel for students. This system aims to streamline the often-bureaucratic communication processes in higher education, thereby enhancing the educational experience and efficiency of students' learning time.

In the quest to safeguard, rejuvenate, and sustainably manage terrestrial ecosystems, aligning with the fifteenth SDG, a novel AI-based method known as the oil spill convolutional neural network (OSCNet) has been developed to identify oil spills in petroleum-producing nations [77]. The research carried out in [77] utilized a substantial collection of synthetic aperture radar (SAR) imagery featuring dark spots indicative of oil. SAR sensors can measure the roughness of the sea's surface, facilitating the detection of oil spills. OSCNet underwent fine-tuning, enhancing its efficacy markedly over conventional ML algorithms like support vector machine (SVM), decision tree (DT), and k-NN. Notably, its accuracy and precision rose from 92.50% and 80.95% to 94.01% and 85.70%, respectively. It's important to note that convolutional neural networks (CNNs) belong to the deep learning category, which involves training neural networks with multiple hidden layers [78]. Thus, OSCNet is rooted in deep learning. For an AI-driven oil spill monitoring system to be sustainable and functional, it's imperative to enlarge the SAR dataset, which is currently scarce. To enhance CNN's learning capabilities, data augmentation is proposed as an innovative solution to enrich the SAR dataset. Data augmentation is a strategy that enhances the generalization of convolutional networks by creating new data points from existing training samples [79]. Introducing these new samples adds variability to the training data, smoothing the input SAR data distribution and simplifying the learning process for the network, thereby bolstering its robustness.

The sustainable management of land ecosystems, central to the fifteenth SDG, is increasingly emphasized in discussions on terrestrial conservation [80]. Additionally, there's a growing focus on global land use and land cover (LULC) changes, which serve as indicators of ecological shifts [81]. Urban LULC planning is crucial for addressing the physical attributes of city landscapes to foster sustainable urban growth, aligning with the eleventh SDG, and ensuring cities are inclusive, safe, and sustainable. A novel AI method known as self-adaptive cellular-based deep learning (SaCDL) has been introduced to predict urban LULC changes with high efficiency [82]. This approach utilizes a variety of data, including remote sensing, real estate, meteorological, and economic data. For precise prediction targets, urban land cover is segmented into impervious, green, and water spaces. Research indicates that SaCDL can accurately forecast LULC alterations with an average accuracy of 93.1% for the period between 2010 and 2016, as evidenced by ground-level data from Wuhan, China [82]. Remarkably, SaCDL surpasses leading algorithm like the greedy algorithm by 29.95% and big data analysis methods by 8.27%. While SaCDL's global application is pending, it's worth noting that, like all deep learning methods, it demands significant computational resources and may necessitate cloud computing for effective deployment.

In the area of renewable energy, the synergy of AI, sensor networks, and IoT plays a pivotal role in harmonizing various renewable energy sources with the current power grid [83]. This integration is a critical step in addressing climate change and its consequences, as well as in ensuring the provision of energy that is affordable, dependable, sustainable, and modern. The hybridization and storage solutions for renewable energy are vital for stabilizing power grids amidst the variability and unpredictability of renewable sources [84]. Accurate forecasting of wind and solar PV farms' outputs is essential for the global management of electricity demand and supply. Presently, solar PV farms stand as the primary renewable energy source for the generation of clean energy [30, 31]. The previously mentioned predictive model designed to estimate the annual energy yield and performance ratio (PR) of a two MWp solar PV system, utilizing environmental factors such as solar irradiance, wind speed, and ambient temperature, exemplifies AI's application in this sector [31]. The model incorporated three techniques: ANFIS, RSM, and ANN. Through statistical analysis, ANFIS was determined to be the most accurate in predicting the PR [31]. Such precise forecasting of solar energy production via AI can significantly aid load dispatch centres and the scheduling of power from various sources for electricity generation.

Moreover, the literature abounds with real-world instances that reinforce the general insights discussed above. For instance, numerous practical applications of AI and related data-driven approaches have been documented in support of smart agriculture, including smart irrigation, pest management, and crop protection [85]. In the healthcare domain, AI-based technologies have been effectively implemented for tasks such as screening, diagnosis, risk assessment, and treatment of conditions like breast cancer and diabetic retinopathy [86]. Additionally, AI has been actively employed in conservation efforts, aiding in the protection and promotion of land and wildlife conservation [87].

Large language models (LLMs) are also playing an important key role in recent times to promote sustainable practices. For example, in climate modeling, LLMs are increasingly proving to be invaluable. They can harness their prowess in parsing and making sense of extensive datasets, which encompass atmospheric dynamics, emissions of greenhouse gases, and records of historical climate patterns. By amalgamating climate-related data from a multitude of sources, LLMs can efficiently discern complex patterns and connections, thereby contributing to the development of advanced climate models. Recent research endeavors, such as the work carried out in [88], have focused on evaluating the efficacy of LLMs in communicating climate change information. In [88], the role of LLMs in bridging the gap between complex scientific data and the general populace is revealed, thus empowering individuals and communities to engage proactively in climate change adaptation and mitigation measures. Similar studies have also underscored the significance of LLMs, including Chat Generative Pre-Trained Transformer (ChatGPT), in collating information and enhancing public consciousness about climate change [like the one referred to as [89]. As a results, it can be said that LLMs are becoming increasingly pivotal in facilitating the dissemination of climate change knowledge, which in turn accelerates more informed and prompt decision-making and initiatives.

## 4 Benefits, Challenges, and Future Prospects of AI in Achieving the SDGs

AI holds significant potential in advancing the United Nations' SDGs, a set of 17 global goals aimed at addressing critical challenges such as poverty, inequality, climate change, and health. However, while AI can be a powerful tool for progress, it also presents unique challenges and prospects that need careful consideration.

### 4.1 Benefits of AI in Achieving the SDGs

AI can revolutionize healthcare (SDG 3: Good Health and Well-being) through early diagnosis, personalized medicine, and efficient management of health systems. Machine learning (ML) algorithms can analyze large datasets to predict disease outbreaks, identify risk factors, and optimize treatment plans. For instance, AI-driven diagnostic tools have been instrumental in detecting diseases like cancer at early stages, significantly improving patient outcomes [90]. AI-powered educational platforms (SDG 4: Quality Education) provide personalized learning experiences, bridging gaps in education quality and accessibility [91]. Intelligent tutoring systems adapt to individual learning paces and styles, offering tailored content and real-time feedback, thus enhancing the learning experience and outcomes [91]. In agriculture (SDG 2: Zero Hunger), AI applications can potentially improve methods of farming, boost crop yields, and lessen their negative effects on the environment [92]. Precision agriculture, powered by AI, uses data from various sources to optimize planting schedules, irrigation, and pest control, ensuring sustainable food production [92]. AI also aids in climate action (SDG 13: Climate Action) by contributing to climate modeling, predicting environmental changes, and developing strategies for mitigation and adaptation [93]. AI algorithms analyze vast amounts of climate data to provide accurate forecasts and identify trends, helping policymakers implement effective climate action plans [93].

### 4.2   Challenges of AI in Achieving the SDGs

The widespread use of AI involves the collection and processing of massive amounts of data, raising concerns about data privacy and security [94]. Ensuring that data is handled responsibly and ethically is crucial to maintain public trust and protect individuals' rights [94]. Additionally, AI systems can perpetuate and even exacerbate existing biases if not properly designed and trained, leading to unfair outcomes that particularly affect marginalized communities [95]. Therefore, it is essential to develop AI systems that are transparent, fair, and inclusive [95]. The benefits of AI are not evenly distributed, with significant disparities in infrastructure and technological access between developed and developing regions. Bridging this digital divide is necessary to ensure that all countries can benefit from AI advancements [96]. Furthermore, the rapid development of AI technologies poses ethical dilemmas and governance challenges, making it essential to establish robust frameworks for AI ethics, regulation, and accountability to ensure that AI is used for the common good [97].

### 4.3   Future Prospect of AI in Achieving the SDGs

The future prospect of AI in achieving the SDGs lies in collaborative innovation involving governments, the private sector, academia, and civil society. Multi-stakeholder partnerships can drive the development of AI solutions that address global challenges effectively [98]. Developing comprehensive policies and regulatory frameworks will be crucial in guiding the ethical deployment of AI, with policies promoting transparency, accountability, and inclusiveness in AI development and application [99]. Investing in education and capacity building is essential to equip individuals and institutions with the skills needed to leverage AI for sustainable development, ensuring widespread AI literacy through accessible training programs and resources [100]. Additionally, the future of AI should prioritize sustainability, focusing on reducing the environmental impact of AI technologies. Efforts to develop energy-efficient AI systems and promote green computing practices will be vital in the future prospect of AI in achieving the SDGs [101].

## 5   Conclusion

Faced with growing demands for a more livable planet, communities worldwide are turning to digital and innovative technologies like AI to drive sustainable development across various sectors. This paper has delved into AI's role in enhancing medical health data analysis and patient classification, particularly in disease diagnosis and prognosis, as well as transforming educational experiences through automated interactions. Additionally, it has explored AI's contributions to smart urban mobility, addressing environmental hazards such as oil spills, and predicting land use and cover changes—key factors in designing intelligent ecosystems with efficient natural resource management. Serving as an introduction to potential in-depth studies in these areas, this paper underscores AI's pivotal role in rapidly achieving the SDGs. Despite AI's current nascent stage, marked by challenges in transparency, safety, and interpretability, it is poised for progressive refinement. Future research will likely address these challenges, further unlocking AI's potential across various applications.

# References

1. Vinuesa, R., et al.: The role of artificial intelligence in achieving the sustainable development goals. Nat. Commun. **11**(233), 1 (2020). https://doi.org/10.1038/s41467-019-14108-y
2. United Nations Department of Economic and Social Affairs, "The 17 Goals," Sustainable Development. Accessed 18 July 2024. https://sdgs.un.org/goals
3. Weiss, S.M., Kulikowski, C.A.: Computer Systems that Learn: Classification and Prediction Methods from Statistics Nets, Machine Learning, and Expert Systems. Morgan Kaufmann Publishers Inc., San Francisco (1991)
4. Battina, D.S.: A systematic review on how artificial intelligence will change the future of marketing. Int. J. Res. Eng. Appl. Sci. **7**(2), 116–120 (2017)
5. Cowls, J., Tsamados, A., Taddeo, M., Floridi, L.: The AI gambit: leveraging artificial intelligence to combat climate change — opportunities, challenges, and recommendations. AI Soc. **38**, 283–307 (2023). https://doi.org/10.1007/s00146-021-01294-x
6. Stuart, O.: Psychology of promoting environmentalism: psychological contributions to achieving an ecologically sustainable future for humanity. J. Soc. Issues **56**(3), 373–390 (2000). https://doi.org/10.1111/0022-4537.00173
7. Calder, W., Clugston, R.M.: Education for a sustainable future. J. Geogr. High. Educ. **29**(1), 7–12 (2005). https://doi.org/10.1080/03098260500030231
8. Chams, N., García-Blandón, J.: On the importance of sustainable human resource management for the adoption of sustainable development goals. Resour. Conserv. Recycl. **141**, 109–122 (2019). https://doi.org/10.1016/j.resconrec.2018.10.006
9. Özsoy, V.: Arts and design education for sustainable development. New Trends Issues Proc Humanit. Soc. Sci. **2**(1), 487–497 (2016). https://doi.org/10.18844/prosoc.v2i1.335
10. Biermann, F., Kanie, N., Kim, R.E.: Global governance by goal-setting: the novel approach of the UN Sustainable Development Goals. Curr. Opin. Environ. Sustain. **26–27**, 26–31 (2017). https://doi.org/10.1016/j.cosust.2017.01.010
11. Raikes, A., Yoshikawa, H., Britto, P.R., Iruka, I.: Children, youth and developmental science in the 2015–2030 global sustainable development goals. Soc. Policy Rep. **30**(3), 1–23 (2017). https://doi.org/10.1002/j.2379-3988.2017.tb00088.x
12. World Health Organization, "The top 10 causes of death," Newsroom Fact Sheets. Accessed 05 January 2024. https://www.who.int/news-room/fact-sheets/detail/the-top-10-causes-of-death
13. Cho, N.H., et al.: IDF Diabetes Atlas: global estimates of diabetes prevalence for 2017 and projections for 2045. Diabetes Res. Clin. Pract. **138**, 271–281 (2018). https://doi.org/10.1016/j.diabres.2018.02.023

14. Albahli, S.: Type 2 machine learning: an effective hybrid prediction model for early type 2 diabetes detection. J. Med. Imaging Heal. Informatics **10**(5), 1069–1075 (2020). https://doi.org/10.1166/jmihi.2020.3000

15. Ali, A., Alrubei, M.A.T., Hassan, L.F.M., Al-Ja'afari, M.A.M., Abdulwahed, S.H.: Diabetes diagnosis based on kNN. IIUM Eng. J. **21**(1,) 175–181 (2020). https://doi.org/10.31436/iiu mej.v21i1.1206

16. Xing, W., Bei, Y.: Medical health big data classification based on KNN classification algorithm. IEEE Access **8**, 28808–28819 (2020). https://doi.org/10.1109/ACCESS.2019.295 5754

17. Ramzy, D., et al.: Three hundred robotic-assisted mitral valve repairs: the Cedars-Sinai experience. J. Thorac. Cardiovasc. Surg. **147**(1), 228–235 (2014). https://doi.org/10.1016/j.jtcvs.2013.09.035

18. Goralski, M.A., Tan, T.K.: Artificial intelligence and sustainable development. Int. J. Manag. Educ. **18**(1), 1–9 (2020). https://doi.org/10.1016/j.ijme.2019.100330

19. Olive, "New Report Finds 90 Percent of Hospitals Have an AI Strategy; Up 37 Percent from 2019," PR Newswire. Accessed 08 May 2024. https://www.prnewswire.com/news-rel eases/new-report-finds-90-percent-of-hospitals-have-an-ai-strategy-up-37-percent-from-2019-301242756.html

20. Shen, K., Tong, X., Wu, T., Zhang, F.: The next frontier for AI in China could add $600 billion to its economy (2022). 08 May 2024. https://www.mckinsey.com/capabilities/quantumbl ack/our-insights/the-next-frontier-for-ai-in-china-could-add-600-billion-to-its-economy

21. NHS England, "NHS AI Lab," Transformation Directorate. Accessed 08 May 2024. https://transform.england.nhs.uk/ai-lab/

22. Mohammed, K., Shehu, A.: A review of Artificial Intelligence (AI) challenges and future prospects of explainable AI in major fields: a case study of Nigeria. Open J. Phys. Sci. **4**(1), 1–18 (2023). https://doi.org/10.52417/ojps.v4i1.458

23. Concepcion, R.S., Bedruz, R.A.R., Culaba, A.B., Dadios, E.P., Pascua, A.R.A.R.: The technology adoption and governance of artificial intelligence in the Philippines. In: IEEE 11th International Conference on Humanoid, Nanotechnology, Information Technology, Communication and Control, Environment, and Management, Laoag, Philippines, pp. 1–10. IEEE (2019). https://doi.org/10.1109/HNICEM48295.2019.9072725

24. Scheffran, J., Battaglini, A.: Climate and conflicts: the security risks of global warming. Reg. Environ. Chang. **11**, 27–39 (2011). https://doi.org/10.1007/s10113-010-0175-8

25. Bazaz, A., et al.: Summary for urban policymakers: what the IPCC special report on global warming of 1.5°C means for cities, Bengaluru. India (2018). https://doi.org/10.24943/SCPM.2018

26. Warren, R., Price, J., VanDerWal, J., Cornelius, S., Sohl, H.: The implications of the United Nations Paris Agreement on climate change for globally significant biodiversity areas. Clim. Change **147**, 395–409 (2018). https://doi.org/10.1007/s10584-018-2158-6

27. Zawieska, J., Obracht-Prondzyńska, H., Duda, E., Uryga, D., Romanowska, M.: In search of the innovative digital solutions enhancing social pro-environmental engagement. Energies **15**(14), 1–18 (2022). https://doi.org/10.3390/en15145191

28. Feng, X., Li, Q., Zhu, Y., Hou, J., Jin, L., Wang, J.: Artificial neural networks forecasting of PM2.5 pollution using air mass trajectory based geographic model and wavelet transformation. Atmos. Environ. **107**, 118–128 (2015). https://doi.org/10.1016/j.atmosenv.2015.02.030

29. Krzhizhanovskaya, V.V., et al.: Flood early warning system: design, implementation and computational modules. Proc. Comput. Sci. **4**, 106–115 (2011). https://doi.org/10.1016/j.procs.2011.04.012

30. Bishoyi, D., Sudhakar, K.: Modeling and performance simulation of 100 MW LFR based solar thermal power plant in Udaipur India. Resour. Technol. **3**(4), 365–377 (2017). https://doi.org/10.1016/j.reffit.2017.02.002

31. Gopi, A., Sharma, P., Sudhakar, K., Ngui, W.K., Kirpichnikova, I., Cuce, E.: Weather impact on solar farm performance: a comparative analysis of machine learning techniques. Sustainability **15**(1), 1–28 (2023). https://doi.org/10.3390/su15010439

32. Moreira, M.O., Balestrassi, P.P., Paiva, A.P., Ribeiro, P.F., Bonatto, B.D.: Design of experiments using artificial neural network ensemble for photovoltaic generation forecasting. Renew. Sustain. Energy Rev. **135**, 1–14 (2021). https://doi.org/10.1016/j.rser.2020.110450

33. Leal Filho, W., et al.: Deploying artificial intelligence for climate change adaptation. Technol. Forecast. Soc. Change **180** (2022). https://doi.org/10.1016/j.techfore.2022.121662

34. Song, J., Lee, E.W.: Goal 11: sustainable city and communities. In: Jung, T.Y. Ed., Sustainable Development Goals in the Republic of Korea, pp. 110–137. Routledge, London (2018). https://doi.org/10.4324/9781351067478-7

35. United Nations, "Population," Global Issues. Accessed 05 January 2024. https://www.un.org/en/global-issues/population

36. Zarocostas, J.: The UN reports global asymmetries in population growth. Lancet **400**(10347), 148 (2022). https://doi.org/10.1016/S0140-6736(22)01323-X

37. Syed, A.S., Sierra-Sosa, D., Kumar, A., Elmaghraby, A.: IoT in smart cities: a survey of technologies, practices and challenges. Smart Cities **4**(2), 429–475 (2021). https://doi.org/10.3390/smartcities4020024

38. Khan, Z., Anjum, A., Soomro, K., Tahir, M.A.: Towards cloud based big data analytics for smart future cities. J. Cloud Comput. **4**(2), 1–11 (2015). https://doi.org/10.1186/s13677-015-0026-8

39. Pardini, K., Rodrigues, J.J.P.C., Kozlov, S.A., Kumar, N., Furtado, V.: IoT-based solid waste management solutions: a survey. J. Sens. Actuator Netw. **8**(1), 1–25 (2019). https://doi.org/10.3390/jsan8010005

40. Wang, Y., Ram, S., Currim, F., Dantas, E., Sabóia, L.A.: A big data approach for smart transportation management on bus network. In: IEEE International Smart Cities Conference (ISC2), pp. 1–6. IEEE, Trento (2016). https://doi.org/10.1109/ISC2.2016.7580839

41. Verba, N., Chao, K.-M., Linford, S., Anoyrkati, E.: Smart transportation platform for big data analytics and interconnectivity. In: 4th International Conference on Traffic and Transport Engineering, pp. 232–238. City Net Scientific Research Center Ltd., Belgrade (2018)

42. Bokhari, S.A.A., Myeong, S.: Use of artificial intelligence in smart cities for smart decision-making: a social innovation perspective. Sustainability **14**(2), 1–17 (2022). https://doi.org/10.3390/su14020620

43. Ahmed, M., Qureshi, M.N., Mallick, J., Ben Kahla, N.: Selection of sustainable supplementary concrete materials using OSM-AHP-TOPSIS approach. Adv. Mater. Sci. Eng. Article ID 2850480, pp. 1–12 (2019). https://doi.org/10.1155/2019/2850480

44. Bhatnagar, V., Sharma, S., Bhatnagar, A., Kumar, L.: Role of machine learning in sustainable engineering: a review. IOP Conf. Ser. Mater. Sci. Eng. **1099**(012036), 1–20 (2021). https://doi.org/10.1088/1757-899x/1099/1/012036

45. Adel, H., Ghazaan, M.I., Korayem, A.H.: Machine learning applications for developing sustainable construction materials. In: Asadnia, M., Razmjou, A., Beheshti, A., Eds., Artificial Intelligence and Data Science in Environmental Sensing, pp. 179–210. Elsevier (2022). https://doi.org/10.1016/B978-0-323-90508-4.00002-2

46. Mater, Y., Kamel, M., Karam, A., Bakhoum, E.: ANN-python prediction model for the compressive strength of green concrete. Constr. Innov. **23**(2), 340–359 (2023). https://doi.org/10.1108/CI-08-2021-0145

47. Adediran, E., Salami, A., Ogunyinka, T., Sakpere, W.: Artificial intelligence: a computational and linear programming approach. Int. J. Innov. Sci. Res. Technol. **8**(11), 184–189 (2023). https://doi.org/10.5281/zenodo.10212686

48. Abbas, H., Al-Salloum, Y.A., Elsanadedy, H.M., Almusallam, T.H.: ANN models for prediction of residual strength of HSC after exposure to elevated temperature. Fire Saf. J. **106**, 13–28 (2019). https://doi.org/10.1016/j.firesaf.2019.03.011

49. Kurpinska, M., Kułak, L.: Predicting performance of lightweight concrete with granulated expanded Glass and Ash aggregate by means of using Artificial Neural Networks. Materials (Basel) **12**(12), 1–16 (2019). https://doi.org/10.3390/ma12122002

50. International Energy Agency, "IEA World Energy Statistics and Balances," OECD iLibrary. https://www.oecd-ilibrary.org/energy/data/iea-world-energy-statistics-and-balances_enestats-data-en

51. The United Nations Department of Economic and Social Affairs, "The Sustainable Development Goals Report 2023: Special edition," New York, NY (2023). https://unstats.un.org/sdgs/report/2023/The-Sustainable-Development-Goals-Report-2023.pdf

52. Moon, J., Park, S., Rho, S., Hwang, E.: A comparative analysis of artificial neural network architectures for building energy consumption forecasting. Int. J. Distrib. Sens. Networks **15**(9), 1–19 (2019). https://doi.org/10.1177/1550147719877616

53. Kalogirou, S.A.: Artificial neural networks in energy applications in buildings. Int. J. Low-Carbon Technol. **1**(3), 201–216 (2006). https://doi.org/10.1093/ijlct/1.3.201

54. Mugambiwa, S.S., Tirivangasi, H.M.: Climate change: a threat towards achieving 'sustainable development goal number two' (end hunger, achieve food security and improved nutrition and promote sustainable agriculture) in South Africa. Jamba J. Disaster Risk Stud. **9**(1), 1–6 (2017). https://doi.org/10.4102/jamba.v9i1.350

55. European Economic and Social Committee, "Boosting the Use of Artificial Intelligence in Europe's Micro, Small and Medium-Sized Enterprises," (2021). https://doi.org/10.2864/08775

56. Aggarwal, N., Singh, D.: Technology assisted farming: implications of IoT and AI. IOP Conf. Ser. Mater. Sci. Eng. **1022**(012080), 1–11 (2021). https://doi.org/10.1088/1757-899X/1022/1/012080

57. Abbasi, R., Martinez, P., Ahmad, R.: The digitization of agricultural industry – a systematic literature review on agriculture 4.0. Smart Agric. Technol. **2**, 1–24 (2022). https://doi.org/10.1016/j.atech.2022.100042

58. Gagliardi, G., Cosma, A.I.M., Marasco, F.: A decision support system for sustainable agriculture: the case study of coconut oil extraction process. Agronomy **12**(1), 1–21 (2022). https://doi.org/10.3390/agronomy12010177

59. Yang, X., et al.: A survey on smart agriculture: development modes, technologies, and security and privacy challenges. IEEE/CAA J. Autom. Sin. **8**(2), 273–302 (2021). https://doi.org/10.1109/JAS.2020.1003536

60. Al-Faydi, S.N.M., Al-Talb, H.N.Y.: IoT and artificial neural network-based water control for farming irrigation system. In: 2nd International Conference on Computing and Machine Intelligence (ICMI), pp. 1–5. IEEE, Istanbul (2022). https://doi.org/10.1109/ICMI55296.2022.9873650

61. Vincent, D.R., Deepa, N., Elavarasan, D., Srinivasan, K., Chauhdary, S.H., Iwendi, C.: Sensors driven AI-based agriculture recommendation model for assessing land suitability. Sensors **19**(17), 1–16 (2019). https://doi.org/10.3390/s19173667

62. Dáder, B., Colomer, I., Adán, Á., Medina, P., Viñuela, E.: Compatibility of early natural enemy introductions in commercial pepper and tomato greenhouses with repeated pesticide applications. Insect Sci. **27**(5), 1111–1124 (2020). https://doi.org/10.1111/1744-7917.12723

63. Oerke, E.C., Dehne, H.W.: Safeguarding production - losses in major crops and the role of crop protection. Crop Prot. **23**(4), 275–285 (2004). https://doi.org/10.1016/j.cropro.2003. 10.001

64. Tang, J., Liu, G., Pan, Q.: A review on representative swarm intelligence algorithms for solving optimization problems: applications and trends. IEEE/CAA J. Autom. Sin. **8**(10), 1627–1643 (2021). https://doi.org/10.1109/JAS.2021.1004129

65. Maraveas, C., Asteris, P.G., Arvanitis, K.G., Bartzanas, T., Loukatos, D.: Application of bio and nature-inspired algorithms in agricultural engineering. Arch. Comput. Methods Eng. **30**, 1979–2012 (2023). https://doi.org/10.1007/s11831-022-09857-x

66. Rustia, D.J.A., et al.: Towards intelligent and integrated pest management through an AIoT-based monitoring system. Pest Manag. Sci. **78**(10), 4288–4302 (2022). https://doi.org/10. 1002/ps.7048

67. Yang, L., Yan, H., Lam, J.C.: Thermal comfort and building energy consumption implications - a review. Appl. Energy **115**, 164–173 (2014). https://doi.org/10.1016/j.apenergy. 2013.10.062

68. Yayla, A., et al.: Artificial Intelligence (AI)-based occupant-centric Heating Ventilation and Air Conditioning (HVAC) control system for multi-zone commercial buildings. Sustainability **14**(23), 1–29 (2022). https://doi.org/10.3390/su142316107

69. Gholamzadehmir, M., Del Pero, C., Buffa, S., Fedrizzi, R., Aste, N.: Adaptive-predictive control strategy for HVAC systems in smart buildings – a review. Sustain. Cities Soc. **63**, 1–14 (2020). https://doi.org/10.1016/j.scs.2020.102480

70. Bebek, Ö., Çavuşoğlu, M.C.: Intelligent control algorithms for robotic-assisted beating heart surgery. IEEE Trans. Robot. **23**(3), 468–480 (2007). https://doi.org/10.1109/TRO. 2007.895077

71. Olyanasab, A., Annabestani, M.: Leveraging machine learning for personalized wearable biomedical devices: a review. J. Pers. Med. **14**(2), 1–21 (2024). https://doi.org/10.3390/jpm 14020203

72. Khamis, H.S., Cheruiyot, K.W., Kimani, S.: Application of k-nearest neighbour classification in medical data mining. Int. J. Inf. Commun. Technol. Res. **4**(4), 121–128 (2014)

73. Chatterjee, S., Das, S., Ganguly, K., Mandal, D.: Advancements in robotic surgery: innovations, challenges and future prospects. J. Robot. Surg. **18**(28), 1–11 (2024). https://doi.org/ 10.1007/s11701-023-01801-w

74. Shaikh, A., Ck, H., Mullick, A., Gadia, V.: Enhancing patient care with AI Chatbots and virtual assistants. Int. J. Pharm. Sci. **2**(2), 10–13 (2024). https://doi.org/10.5281/zenodo.106 03065

75. Spector, J.M.: Conceptualizing the emerging field of smart learning environments. Smart Learn. Environ. **1**(2), 1 (2014). https://doi.org/10.1186/s40561-014-0002-7

76. Hien, H.T., Cuong, P.N., Nam, L.N.H., Nhung, H.L.T.K., Thang, L.D.: Intelligent assistants in higher-education environments: The FIT-EBot, a chatbot for administrative and learning support. In: 9th International Symposium on Information and Communication Technology (SoICT), pp. 69–76. ACM, Danang (2018). https://doi.org/10.1145/3287921.3287937

77. Zeng, K., Wang, Y.: A deep convolutional neural network for oil spill detection from spaceborne SAR images. Remote Sens. **12**(6), 1–23 (2020). https://doi.org/10.3390/rs1206 1015

78. Burkov, A.: Neural networks and deep learning. In: The Hundred-Page Machine Learning Book, Quebec, pp. 1–14 (2019)

79. Wang, J., Perez, L.: The effectiveness of data augmentation in image classification using deep learning. Comput. Vis. Pattern Recognit. pp. 1–8 (2017). https://doi.org/10.48550/ arXiv.1712.04621

80. Arana, C., Franco, I.B., Joshi, A., Sedhai, J.: SDG 15 Life on land - a review of sustainable fashion design processes: upcycling waste organic yarns. In: Franco, I.B., Chatterji, T., Derbyshire, E., Tracey, J., Eds., Actioning the Global Goals for Local Impact: Towards Sustainability Science, Policy, Education and Practice, pp. 247–264. Springer, Singapore (2020). https://doi.org/10.1007/978-981-32-9927-6_16

81. Independent Group of Scientists appointed by the UN Secretary-General, "Global Sustainable Development Report 2019: The Future is Now – Science for Achieving Sustainable Development," New York, NY (2019). https://doi.org/10.18356/5d04ad97-en

82. Mu, L., Wang, L., Wang, Y., Chen, X., Han, W.: Urban land use and land cover change prediction via self-adaptive cellular based deep learning with multisourced data. IEEE J. Sel. Top. Appl. Earth Obs. Remote Sens. **12**(12), 5233–5247 (2019). https://doi.org/10.1109/JSTARS.2019.2956318

83. Kanase-Patil, A.B., Kaldate, A.P., Lokhande, S.D., Panchal, H., Suresh, M., Priya, V.: A review of artificial intelligence-based optimization techniques for the sizing of integrated renewable energy systems in smart cities. Environ. Technol. Rev. **9**(1), 111–136 (2020). https://doi.org/10.1080/21622515.2020.1836035

84. Gupta, S.K., Srivastava, R.K.: A novel hybrid solar-wind energy conversion system for remote area electrification. Rec. Adv. Electr. Electron. Eng. **13**(6), 906–917 (2020). https://doi.org/10.2174/2213111607666191204151926

85. Qazi, S., Khawaja, B.A., Farooq, Q.U.: IoT-equipped and AI-enabled next generation smart agriculture: a critical review, current challenges and future trends. IEEE Access **10**, 21219–21235 (2022). https://doi.org/10.1109/ACCESS.2022.3152544

86. Yin, J., Ngiam, K.Y., Teo, H.H.: Role of artificial intelligence applications in real-life clinical practice: systematic review. J. Med. Internet Res. **23**(4), 1–17 (2021). https://doi.org/10.2196/25759

87. Isabelle, D.A., Westerlund, M.: A review and categorization of artificial intelligence-based opportunities in wildlife, ocean and land conservation. Sustainability **14**(4), 1–22 (2022). https://doi.org/10.3390/su14041979

88. Bulian, J., et al.: Assessing large language models on climate information. Comput. Lang. 1–52 (2023). https://doi.org/10.48550/arXiv.2310.02932

89. Rane, N.L., Tawde, A., Choudhary, S.P., Rane, J.: Contribution and performance of ChatGPT and other Large Language Models (LLM) for scientific and research advancements: a double-edged sword. Int. Res. J. Mod. Eng. Technol. Sci. **5**(10), 875–899 (2023). https://doi.org/10.56726/irjmets45213

90. Esteva, A., et al.: Dermatologist-level classification of skin cancer with deep neural networks. Nature **542**, 115–118 (2017). https://doi.org/10.1038/nature21056

91. Holmes, W., Bialik, M., Fadel, C.: Artificial Intelligence in Education: Promises and Implications for Teaching and Learning. Centre for Curriculum Redesign, Boston (2019)

92. Kamilaris, A., Kartakoullis, A., Prenafeta-Boldú, F.X.: A review on the practice of big data analysis in agriculture. Comput. Electron. Agric. **143**, 23–37 (2017). https://doi.org/10.1016/j.compag.2017.09.037

93. Rolnick, D., et al.: Tackling climate change with machine learning. ACM Comput. Surv. **55**(2), 1–96 (2023). https://doi.org/10.1145/3485128

94. Floridi, L., Cowls, J., King, T.C., Taddeo, M.: How to design AI for social good: seven essential factors. Sci. Eng. Ethics **26**(3), 1771–1796 (2020). https://doi.org/10.1007/s11948-020-00213-5

95. Buolamwini, J., Gebru, T.: Gender shades: intersectional accuracy disparities in commercial gender classification. In: 1st Conference on Fairness, Accountability and Transparency, In: Friedler, S.A., Wilson, C. Eds. Proceedings of Machine Learning Research (PMLR), New York, NY, pp. 77–91 (2018)

96. United Nations, "The Age of Digital Interdependence: Report of the UN Secretary-General's High-level Panel on Digital Cooperation," Brussels (2019). https://www.un.org/en/pdfs/Dig italCooperation-report-forweb.pdf

97. Cath, C., Wachter, S., Mittelstadt, B., Taddeo, M., Floridi, L.: Artificial Intelligence and the 'Good Society': the US, EU, and UK approach. Sci. Eng. Ethics **24**(2), 505–528 (2018). https://doi.org/10.1007/s11948-017-9901-7

98. Miao, F., Holmes, W., Huang, R., Zhang, H.: "AI and education: guidance for policy-makers", UNESCO. Paris (2021). https://doi.org/10.54675/pcsp7350

99. European Commission, "White Paper on Artificial Intelligence: A European approach to excellence and trust," Brussels (2020). https://eur-lex.europa.eu/legal-content/EN/TXT/ PDF/?uri=CELEX:52020DC0065

100. International Telecommunication Union, "Assessing the Economic Impact of Artificial Intelligence," Geneva (2018). https://www.itu.int/dms_pub/itu-s/opb/gen/S-GEN-ISSUEP APER-2018-1-PDF-E.pdf

101. Strubell, E., Ganesh, A., McCallum, A.: Energy and policy considerations for deep learning in NLP. In: 57th Annual Meeting of the Association for Computational Linguistics (ACL), pp. 3645–3650. Association for Computational Linguistics, Florence (2019). https://doi.org/ 10.18653/v1/P19-1355

# Innovation in Healthcare Systems

# Early Detection of Pregnancy Complications Using Deep Learning Techniques

Aman Mudgal[1], Manav Dewan[1], Oluwatobi Akinlade[2] (ORCID),
Sunday Adeola Ajagbe[3,4](✉) (ORCID), Payushi Tyagi[1], Swati Gupta[5], Meenu Vijarania[5],
and Matthew O. Adigun[3] (ORCID)

[1] Department of CSE, KR Mangalam University, Gurugram, Haryana, India
[2] Department of Computer Science, Birmingham City University, Birmingham, UK
oluwatobi.akinlade@mail.bcu.ac.uk
[3] Department of Computer Science, University of Zululand, Kwadlangezwa 3886, South Africa
saajagbe@pgschool.lectech.edu.ng, adigunm@unizulu.ac.za
[4] Department of Computer Engineering, First Technical University, Ibadan, Nigeria
[5] Department of Computer Science, Member of Centre of Excellence, KR Mangalam
University, Gurugram, Haryana, India

**Abstract.** The research presents a deep learning approach for detecting complications like preterm birth and endometriosis using machine learning techniques using two datasets: a dataset of ultrasound images which consists of various parts of the fetus and mother, and another dataset of histopathological image samples which are microscopic photos of the endometrium tissue present in the uterus lining. These images capture maternal-fetal development for monitoring parts of fetus and maternal cervix at different weeks of the prenatal period and provide valuable insights. The model uses convolutional neural networks (CNNs) architecture based on Densely Connected Convolutional Networks and Efficient Nets to analyze these images, classifying ultrasound images into features such as Fetal Abdomen, Fetal Brain, Fetal Femur, Fetal Thorax and Maternal Cervix. By training on the Maternal fetal ultrasound dataset of 12400 images, the model achieves a 94.40% accuracy, assisting healthcare professionals in early interventions and improved neonatal outcomes. The second dataset of microscopic image samples contains photos of endometrial specimens stained with hematoxylin and eosin (H&E) for better understanding. The accuracy achieved by the model trained on this dataset is 82.40%. Endometriosis is a painful condition which affects growth of endometrium tissue present at the uterine lining. Ideally, laparoscopy is required to check for endometriosis, but for cases of endometriosis during pregnancy, it was found that analysis of endometrium tissue samples can also be done to detect endometriosis. The approach used in this study is based on transfer learning, which involves fine-tuning pre-trained models like Dense Net and Efficient Net, to classify endometrium tissue samples.

**Keywords:** Deep Learning (DL) · Machine Learning (ML) · Disease Detection · Preterm Birth · Ultrasound Images · Histopathological Samples · Convolutional Neural Networks (CNNs)

© ICST Institute for Computer Sciences, Social Informatics and Telecommunications Engineering 2026
Published by Springer Nature Switzerland AG 2026. All Rights Reserved
J. B. Awotunde et al. (Eds.): AFRICATEK 2024, LNICST 618, pp. 89–104, 2026.
https://doi.org/10.1007/978-3-031-93557-2_6

# 1  Introduction

During pregnancy, the body goes through some of the most intense changes it will ever experience, especially when it comes to hormone levels. These changes are important for supporting the growth and development of the baby.

Better care during pregnancy increases the likelihood of a healthy birth. This vital care can and should start even before conception with a pre-pregnancy care visit to a healthcare provider. Complications can be categorized based on the time of their occurrence which are, before, during or after pregnancy complications. Before pregnancy complications make it either harder to conceive or result in unhealthy pregnancies if conception occurs. Complications like preterm birth are examples of complications that arise during pregnancy which have their hazardous aftereffects post-delivery as well [1]. Gestational diabetes is an example of after pregnancy complications.

A thorough analysis of previous literature reveals that the mother's body is highly vulnerable to exposures or infections during pregnancy. This period is more prone to complications than the periods before conception or after birth. These complications can increase the risk of long-term health issues for both the mother and the fetus. For example, women with a history of adverse pregnancy outcomes are at an increased risk of cardiovascular and metabolic diseases later in life. This emphasizes the importance of prenatal care and the necessity for further research to try predicting these risks.

To understand the reason behind the vulnerability it is important to consider that during pregnancy, the development of the fetus is a uniform process managed by the body with complete attention to a lot of details, with each part of the body forming during its own time. This critical time, known as the "critical period of development," is when that part of the fetus is most susceptible to external influences. These influences can range from medications and alcohol to infections and other substances [2]. The vulnerability during this period means that various exposures can impact the development of various body parts. Every pregnancy brings a 3–5% risk of defects or failure [2]. This is known as background risk. However, if a problem occurs during a critical period, it can increase the probability of birth defects, depending on which body part is undergoing development at that time.

The main objective of this research is to prove that machine learning can be used in medical image analysis and assist medical professionals in taking more efficient decisions. With this work, machine learning models can classify distinct types of endometrioses such as normal, hyperplasia, pre-cancerous polyps, and adenocarcinomas(cancer).

## 1.1  Pregnancy

Pregnancy refers to the duration during which the fetus develops inside the mother's womb or uterus. It takes around 40 weeks (about 9 months) or over nine months for the baby to fully mature. This duration is calculated from the last menstrual period to delivery. The period of pregnancy is categorized by healthcare professionals into three trimesters, each defined by different developmental stages of the fetus [3]. These stages also contain critical periods of development.

The first step after conception is fertilization, where a sperm cell successfully penetrates the ovum. This results in the formation of a fertilized egg, scientifically known as the zygote. The zygote travels through the fallopian tube and implants itself inside the wall of the uterus which is lined with endometrium tissue and mucous membrane for supporting the initial stages of pregnancy. From a cluster of cells, the zygote undergoes transformation to form two different structures - the fetus and the placenta. The placenta acts as a barrier between the mother and the fetus for the transfer of nutrients and oxygen from the mother to the developing fetus. All these processes occur during the first trimester of pregnancy which lasts from the first week to the 12th week of pregnancy [3].

The 13th week of pregnancy until the 28th week of pregnancy is the second trimester. During this period, significant fetal development occurs. Between the 18th and 20th weeks, an ultrasound is commonly performed to check for congenital abnormalities. This can also determine the baby's sex. By the 20th week, fetal movements may be detectable, signaling the formation of fetal brain. By the 24th week, fingerprints and footprints are formed, and the fetus starts to show regular sleep-wake cycles. Research by the NICHD Neonatal Research Network shows that 92% of infants born at 28 weeks (about 6 and a half months) can survive [3]. However, these premature births are bound to an increased risk of respiratory and neurological complications.

The third trimester of pregnancy spans from the 29th to the 40th week. During the 32nd week, fetal bones are nearing full formation via Endochondral ossification, and the infant's eyes gain the ability to open and close. Births prior to the 37th week are categorized as preterm, placing infants at a heightened risk for developmental complications, including auditory and visual impairments, as well as cerebral palsy. The period between the 34th and 36th weeks is specifically termed "late preterm."

## 1.2 Preterm Birth

Birth of babies alive before thirty-seven weeks of pregnancy is referred to as preterm. It is also defined as the delivery of an infant before thirty-seven weeks of gestation, and it remains a global health challenge [4]. This complication accounts for approximately eleven percent of all births worldwide. Numerous factors contribute to preterm birth, including maternal age, maternal health conditions such as hypertension and diabetes or exposure to external influences during the critical period of development throughout the prenatal period.

The forty weeks which the fetus takes to develop inside the womb are necessary as it is the time required for all the organs and parts to form, ideally, promoting a healthy birth. Preterm birth causes the infant to skip this important developmental process which is a cause of potential disorders or disabilities which can be lifetime including brain development issues, visual issues, and hearing problems [1]. This disease is the leading cause of death in children under the age of five years. Infertility and discomfort are the two main symptoms of endometriosis. It is widely acknowledged that endometriosis patients have abnormal endometrium. Furthermore, improper placentation and decidual damage during pregnancy are brought on by these abnormal endometria. Therefore, these procedures could negatively affect the results of pregnancies. One of those negative impacts is preterm birth.

Healthcare professionals use cervical observation to predict preterm birth through ultrasounds during pregnancy. As ultrasound evaluation makes it easier for them to observe the cervix without any need of surgical procedures [5]. Pregnancy is a uniform process managed by the body with complete attention to a lot of details, surgical processes during pregnancy are risky as they can lead to more complications. Therefore, instead of surgical procedures, transvaginal ultrasounds, or TVU's are used to monitor the growth of fetus throughout pregnancy [5]. Here's how TVU's can be utilized by monitoring the cervix through ultrasound based to three features:

**Cervical Length (CL)**
A CL is considered short if the length is less than 25 mm and increases the risk of preterm birth. TVU can be used for accurate measurement of CL, and it can be used with other results of tests on the maternal cervix to predict preterm birth [6].

**Anterior Cervical Angle (ACA)**
The ACA, measured between the cervix and the anterior uterine wall, can be an important predictor of preterm birth. A wider ACA has been associated with an increased risk of preterm delivery. Studies suggest that a cutoff value of approximately 90 degrees can serve as a threshold for increased risk, and when combined with CL measurements, it can improve the predictive accuracy [6].

**Cervical Consistency Index (CCI)**
CCI is calculated by measuring the anteroposterior cervical diameter before and after applying pressure with the transvaginal probe. A higher CCI indicates a softer cervix, which is more likely to dilate prematurely [6]. The CCI has shown to be a reproducible and effective predictor of spontaneous preterm birth, potentially offering better prediction than CL alone.

### 1.3 Endometriosis

Well, most pregnancy complications occur during pregnancy, endometriosis is one of those conditions which can occur before or even after pregnancy as well. Endometriosis affects pregnancy in a very peculiar way. To understand endometriosis, it is important to understand the concept behind endometrium first. Endometrium is an essential tissue in the female anatomy. It is present inside the wall of the uterus along with the mucus membrane [7]. Ideally, it is formed on the inside wall of the uterus before the menstrual cycle and is shed during the menstrual cycle. On fertilization, where zygote gets planted inside the uterus, the endometrium is used to support the early stages of pregnancy. Endometriosis is a condition in which endometrial tissue grows irregularly or grows outside the uterus. The tissue itself is benign in nature but it is the way this tissue grows that makes it a complication [8].

Shedding this irregularly grown tissue during the menstrual cycle causes extreme pain to the patient. It also makes it hard for the patient to conceive. Although, people with endometriosis still do get pregnant. Getting pregnant with endometriosis relieves the patient from pain and discomfort, since there are no menstrual cycles during pregnancy, but it comes with its own set of complications, which are miscarriage, preterm birth, and placenta previa [7]. In this research, four categories of endometriosis are covered according to the dataset. First is normal endometrium which is the ideal case where no disease is present. Second is endometrial polyp, where millions of endometrium tissue accumulate at a single spot in the uterus forming a stroma or organ, third is when overgrowth of endometrium tissue occurs inside the uterus walls known as endometrial hyperplasia, this causes the uterus walls to grow thick [8]. Endometrial hyperplasia, if left untreated, can cause the development of endometrial cancer cells inside the uterus, which describes the last case, known as endometrial adenocarcinoma [8].

Endometriosis causes irregular bleeding and menstruation, which can be an indication of the disease. Although concrete test of endometriosis involves performing laparoscopy by observing the endometrial tissue inside the uterus with the help of a camera on a needle, this study suggests that microscopic observation of menstrual samples can also help in detecting endometriosis as results from the model applied on the dataset achieved an accuracy of 82.4%.

## 2   Literature Review

With recent advancements, machine learning is a technique used widely to shift the landscape of healthcare. It has a lot of applications in patient care ranging from predictive analytics, medical imaging to diagnostic advancements. It is that branch of artificial intelligence which uses algorithms to allow a model to perform one task as closely as a human would [9]. Depending on the dataset on which a machine learning model is trained on, the performance varies from model to model, but a model can simply be trained to analyze complex medical data, identify trends, or even predict disease progression. Recent reports suggest that some implementations of machine learning solutions are often used by healthcare organizations constituting approximately eighty six percent of them. Almost eighty percent of these healthcare organizations have some artificial intelligence interventions [9].

Diagnostic advantages from machine learning can be utilized for providing better care during pregnancy. This project aims to set up a milestone in prenatal care using predictive analysis done in artificial intelligence from datasets. The project does not aim to make prenatal care completely dependent on artificial intelligence, but to assist healthcare professionals in taking the right decisions and to learn and apply new things learned from the research aspect of the project making it easier for them to identify new trends.

Medical image monitoring for predicting pregnancy complications was addressed in Burgos-Artizzu et al. (2020). The models exhibited comparable performance to human research technicians in classifying common fetal planes. However, the study highlighted the need for further research to enhance results, particularly in the fine-grained categorization of fetal anatomical planes [10]. The proposed models achieved and increased accuracy without applying PCA and boosting.

He et al. (2016) presented a breakthrough in training deeper neural networks with a residual learning framework. By reformulating layers as residual functions with reference to layer inputs, improved optimization and accuracy was demonstrated for networks up to 152 layers [11]. The study focused on the vital importance of depth in representations for visual recognition tasks, resulting in twenty eight percent relative improvement on the object detection dataset. Proposed models used data augmentation to improve the dataset and allow the residual networks to perform more efficiently.

A modularized network architecture called ResNext designed for image classification was also used. The network's structure is composed of a repeating building block that aggregates transformations with the same network topology that introduces the concept of "cardinality". The study proved that increasing cardinality could enhance classification accuracy on the dataset, proving more effective than increasing depth or width while maintaining complexity. ResNeXt secured 2nd place in the ILSVRC 2015 classification task, outperforming its ResNet counterpart on various datasets [11]. Future work may involve exploring variations or extensions of the ResNeXt architecture in specific applications or domains, optimizing hyperparameters, or adapting the approach for different datasets. The proposed model EfficientNet-B7 used the latest bottleneck residual networks which combines the attributes of two models that is ResNet and DenseNet (Tables 1, 2 and 3).

**Table 1.** Performance comparison (Maternal Fetal Ultrasound Dataset)

| Reference | Dataset Used | Model Used | Accuracy (%) |
|---|---|---|---|
| [10] | Maternal-fetal US | Baseline1 (PCA + Boosting) | 54.7 |
| [10] | Maternal-fetal US | Baseline2 (Hog + Boosting) | 68.6 |
| [11] | Maternal-fetal US | ResNet-101 | 93.4 |
| [12] | Maternal-fetal US | DenseNet-121 | 92.9 |
| [13] | Maternal-fetal US | ResNeXt-50 | 92.7 |
| Proposed | Maternal-fetal US | ResNet-50 | 93.02 |
| Proposed | Maternal-fetal US | DenseNet-169 | 93.42 |
| Proposed | Maternal-fetal US | DenseNet-201 | 93.90 |
| Proposed | Maternal-fetal US | EfficientNet-B7 | 94.40 |

Medical image analysis for predicting endometriosis is not a widely researched area in terms of applying deep learning analysis. Although according to the wide amount of research explaining the anatomy of the endometrium. The results from this research suggest that the disease can be detected from the images of microscopic tissue samples of the endometrium.

Medical professionals use laparoscopy as a concrete test for determining endometriosis which is a mildly invasive surgical procedure. Although machine learning cannot be a concrete procedure for the detection of endometriosis, the analysis can provide more clarity to the healthcare professionals and assist them in taking the right decisions through this non-invasive and cost-effective method [7]. The insights achieved from more improved datasets can further improve the accuracy of the model and the prediction can be closer to humans.

**Table 2.** Performance Comparison (Histopathological image dataset)

| Reference | Dataset Used | Model Used | Accuracy (%) |
|---|---|---|---|
| [8] | Histopathological Image Dataset | ResNet-50 | 73.3% |
| Proposed | Histopathological Image Dataset | DenseNet-121 | 76.1% |
| Proposed | Histopathological Image Dataset | DenseNet-169 | 77.2% |
| Proposed | Histopathological Image Dataset | DenseNet-201 | 77.4% |
| Proposed | Histopathological Image Dataset | EfficientNet-B7 | 82.4% |

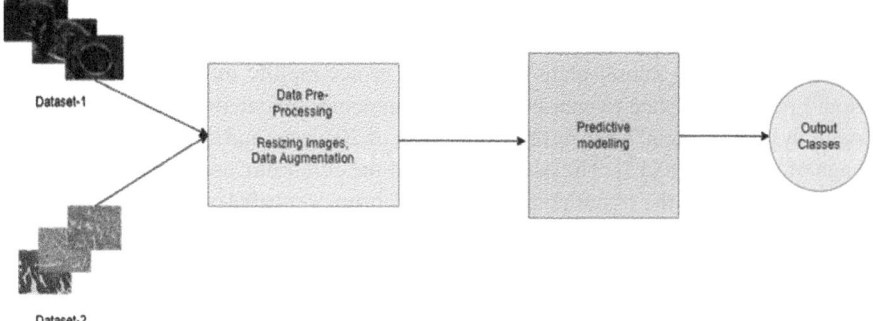

**Fig. 1.** Proposed Methodology

## 3 Proposed Methodology

### 3.1 Datasets

**Maternal Fetal Ultrasound Dataset**

The dataset is a collection of fetus images throughout the pregnancy. These are ultrasounds taken from patients during their pregnancy journey, the images were taken from almost eighteen hundred pregnant women with each image depicting the important features of dataset used to monitor growth of the fetus, the model was trained in such a way that it will be able to classify ultrasound images into these features which will in turn help in monitoring the growth of fetus throughout the pregnancy potentially detecting complications if present [10] (Fig. 1).

The features included in the images are fetal abdomen, which is basically abdomen of the developing fetus, fetal brain, which is the brain of the fetus, fetal femur which is the thigh bone of the fetus, fetal thorax which is the chest region of the fetus, and last is the part of the mother which is the maternal cervix, it is the structure located at the lower end of the uterus.

Following will be the detailed breakdown on how these features can assist in monitoring pregnancy:

Fetal Abdomen: Fetal abdomen is the largest cavity in the body of the fetus, and it consists of many organs and vessels [14]. The organs present in the fetal abdomen are the stomach, liver, the intestines, the kidneys, and the bladders (urinary bladder and gallbladder). The stomach is present at the upper left side of the abdomen. Whereas the liver is present at the upper right side of the abdomen [13]. The middle part of the abdomen is occupied by the small and large intestines. At the sides of the spine kidneys are present connected to the ureters which eventually connect to the urinary bladder present at the bottom of the abdomen. Gall bladder is found right below the liver. The size of the abdomen and the correct position of the organs present in the abdomen are measured as parameters to figure out the growth of the fetus. Dataset contains 711 numbers of ultrasound images taken from 595 patients which clearly represent the Fetal abdomen [10].

Fetal Brain: The brain of the fetus starts to develop the earliest. Within a few weeks after fertilization the neural plate forms and it grows rapidly throughout the prenatal period. From neural plate to neural tube and from neural tube to the brain and the entire nervous system, the fetal brain develops in a span of 20 weeks and keeps developing until the age of twenty-five [15]. The brain consists of the cerebrum, cerebellum, brain stem, pituitary gland, and the hypothalamus. The cerebrum contributes to memory storage, thought, and feeling. The cerebellum is responsible for any kind of movement related abilities also known as motor skills which involves stuff like movement of arms and legs or grabbing something [15]. The important mechanisms that sustain life in the body are managed by the brain stem. Most of them are involuntary systems, such as respiration, blood pressure, and heart rate. Though signals of hunger originate elsewhere, it also regulates the digestive system. The pituitary gland is responsible for secreting most of the hormones in the body that regulate growth, ovulation, metabolism, and other processes [15]. The hypothalamus controls emotions, sleep, hunger and thirst signals, and body temperature. Dataset consists of 3092 images of fetal brain taken from 1082 patients [10].

Fetal Femur: The growing thigh bone of a fetus is known as the fetal femur. It is an important measurement made during ultrasound exams to determine the size and growth of the fetus. The distal and proximal ossification centres of the femoral diaphysis are the starting points for measuring the femur length [16]. Endochondral ossification is the process by which soft tendon-like skeletal structures get converted into bones [16]. Femur length is used to assess fetal weight together with additional measurements such as head circumference, circumference of the abdomen, and biparietal diameter [14, 21]. These measurements in the second trimester can be used to determine the age of the fetus and to get an estimate of the approximate due date [3]. When an ultrasound reveals a small femur length, it may be necessary to do further testing to rule out disorders such Down syndrome, growth restriction or other chromosomal problems. However, the child remains healthy 73% of the time in such cases. Dataset consists of 1040 images taken from 754 patients which represent fetal femur clearly [10, 22].

Fetal Thorax: Fetal thorax is the chest area of the fetus. It consists of organs like the heart and the lungs, the heart is present at the left anterior half of the chest. At the left and right border of the heart, lung tissue is present. The measurement of fetal cardiac and thoracic/chest wall abnormalities can be done using the fetal cardiothoracic

(C/T) circumference ratio [17, 23]. Abnormalities in the fetal thorax cause conditions like fetal hydrothorax, where the chest cavity gets filled with fluid and that fluid compresses the lungs and shifts the heart from its position eventually disrupting their normal development.

Dataset consists of 1718 images taken from 755 patients which represent the fetal thorax clearly [10]. Maternal Cervix: The maternal cervix is an organ present in the mother which connects the uterus and the vagina, it ensures the transfer of fluids between the uterus and the vagina. It plays an important role in predicting preterm birth. Dataset consists of 1626 ultrasound images taken from 734 pregnant women which clearly represent the maternal cervix [10].

## 3.2 Histopathological Image Dataset

The dataset is a collection of histopathological images, which are basically microscopic photographs of tissue samples stained to highlight various cellular components and structures. In this context, the endometrium refers to the inner lining of the uterus, which undergoes changes throughout the menstrual cycle. The staining technique used, haematoxylin and eosin (H&E), is a common method in histology that differentiates between the acidic and basic components of cells—haematoxylin stains the nuclei blue (basophilic structures), while eosin stains the cytoplasm and extracellular matrix pink (acidophilic structures) [8]. This contrast helps in the examination of tissue architecture and cellular details and helps in differentiating between endometrium and disease cells in those microscopic photos.

The dataset includes images of normal endometrium (NE), which is the ideal state of the endometrial lining during a regular menstrual cycle. Endometrial polyp (EP) is a benign overgrowth of endometrial tissue that can cause irregular bleeding [8]. Endometrial hyperplasia (EH) is a condition where the endometrium becomes excessively thick, often due to hormonal imbalances, and can be a precursor to cancer if left untreated. Lastly, endometrioid adenocarcinoma (EA) is a type of cancer that originates from the glandular cells of the endometrium. It's the most common form of endometrial cancer [7].

**Table 3.** Maternal-Fetal Ultrasound Data Set [10]

| Image Labels | Number of Patients | Number of Images | Development |
|---|---|---|---|
| Fetal Abdomen | 595 | 711 | 12 weeks |
| Fetal Brain | 1082 | 3092 | 20 weeks |
| Fetal Femur | 754 | 1040 | 40 weeks |
| Fetal Thorax | 755 | 1718 | 24 weeks |
| Maternal Cervix | 917 | 1626 | 20 weeks |
| Other | 734 | 4213 | - |
| **Total** | **1792** | **12400** | - |

The features present in the dataset are as follows:

Normal Endometrium (NE): The endometrium is the inner lining of the uterus, which changes throughout the menstrual cycle. During the early part of the cycle, the endometrium thickens in preparation for supporting potential pregnancy [8]. If fertilization does not occur, the lining is shed during menstruation.

Endometrial Polyp (EP): Endometrial polyps are benign (non-cancerous) growths that arise from the endometrial lining. They can vary in size and may cause symptoms such as irregular menstrual bleeding or infertility [8]. While most polyps are benign, a small percentage may contain precancerous cells or cancer.

Endometrial Hyperplasia (EH): This condition involves the thickening of the endometrium due to an excess of oestrogen relative to progesterone. It can present in various forms, from simple hyperplasia without atypia, which has a very low risk of progressing to cancer, to complex atypical hyperplasia, which has a higher risk of developing into endometrial cancer [8].

Endometrioid Adenocarcinoma (EA): Endometrioid adenocarcinoma is the most common type of endometrial cancer. It arises from the glandular cells of the endometrium and can have different grades of severity, with some forms being more aggressive than others [8, 24]. The main symptom is abnormal vaginal bleeding, especially postmenopausal bleeding. Early detection and treatment are crucial for a better prognosis.

### 3.3  Data Pre-processing

**Resizing Images**

Resizing images is a very common data preprocessing technique used to convert all the images in a dataset to one uniform size or resolution. It is important for the algorithm to function properly, as the algorithm can't work with different sized input images. Larger images contain more pixels which increases the computational complexity [18].

### 3.4  Data Augmentation

The process of artificially increasing the amount of data used in machine learning is called data augmentation. It includes copying the same data by making small changes to it using deep learning to generate new data points [9]. Data augmentation helps in improving the performance of models as new diverse data points now exist for the model to train from. Although pre-trained models have layers to prevent overfitting, data augmentation also makes it so that the model is not overfitted. Overfitting is when the model learns the training data too well during the training process. Because of using data augmentation, both the models will be able to perform better on new or unseen images. Since the initial datasets used for this research were already too small, augmenting the data saved the cost and time of collecting and labelling new data, as it can be an exhausting process. Rotation range parameter randomly rotates the images present in both the datasets from the range of 0 to 360 degrees. Width shift range basically shifts the image randomly to left or right by 20 percent. Height shift range shifts the image randomly upwards or downwards by 20 percent. Zoom range randomly zooms the image or adds some pixels around the image to enlarge it. Horizontal and vertical flips flips the image horizontally or vertically by 90 degrees.

## 3.5  Predictive Modelling

**Dense Net**

Densely Connected Convolutional Networks are pre-trained architectures based on deep learning and are recognised because they can increase the efficiency and accuracy of a variety of tasks like computer vision or tasks in which text is classified [9]. Dense net model works by forming dense connections between layers used in it. In a dense net, every layer receives extra information from the layer that comes before it, this layer sends its own feature maps to every layer that comes afterwards. This differentiates the model from traditional neural networks where the outputs of these layers are directly connected to the next layer. Since each layer is sending its own feature maps outputs as inputs to the next layer, it enhances the network's ability to learn more efficiently via feature reuse, by guaranteeing efficient information (and gradient) flow. One more advantage of using dense net architecture is that fewer parameters are required for training in comparison to traditional CNNs as feature maps aren't required to be trained repeatedly as they are sent to the next layer as inputs every time [12]. DenseNet was first used in the year 2017. DenseNet architectures which are DenseNet-121, DenseNet-169, DenseNet-201 are widely used and are distinguished from each other by number of layers, and number of trainable and non-trainable parameters [12]. Number of trainable parameters for DenseNet-121 used in this study is 7.29 million and the number of non-trainable parameters is 86 thousand. Number of trainable parameters for the DenseNet-169 model is 12.9 million and the number of non-trainable parameters are 162 thousand respectively. 18.5 million trainable parameters are used in the DenseNet-201 model and 233 thousand non-trainable parameters are used.

**Efficient Net**

EfficientNet models are CNN architecture based pre-trained models first introduced in 2019 for their effective scaling method which is a differentiating factor from traditional CNNs.

This effective scaling method allows the models to utilise the computational resources more efficiently decreasing the time taken for training the models. The EfficientNet family of models contains architectures labelled from B0 to B7, where B defines the bottleneck residual and the number from 0 to 7 represent the increasing number of layers and parameters present in the model for training [19]. The model uniformly and optimally scales all the dimensions in the dataset by using compound coefficients which basically represent feature engineering, hyperparameter tuning. These data preprocessing coefficients are built in the EfficientNet family of models.

The scaling method scales the network width, depth, and resolution with the scaling coefficients of a fixed set where the main parameters are width scaling, which involves scaling the number of channels, depth scaling, this involves manipulating the number of layers present in the model and last is resolution scaling which randomly increases or decreases the resolution of the images in the dataset applying a form of data augmentation by default [19].

The technique invert bottleneck residual which is used in this architecture is derived from the predecessor architecture which is ResNet where residual networks are used to fix the problem where the gradient descent would select the data point which represents the least loss and the best parameter which eventually slows down the learning process [11]. The original block layer is inverted during this technique and as explained earlier bottleneck layer is added to reduce the number of channels [20]. Number of trainable parameters for this model is 64.4 million and the number of non-trainable parameters are 316 thousand respectively.

## 4    Results and Discussion

### 4.1    Maternal Fetal Ultrasound

Figure 2 is a performance comparison graph which represents the accuracies of a total of seven models which have been trained on the maternal fetal ultrasound dataset, which are Baseline-2, DenseNet-121, DenseNet-169, DenseNet-201, ResNet-50, EfficientNet-B7 and ResNeXt-50, out of these models DenseNet-121, DenseNet-169, DenseNet-201 are of the same families of models which are densely connected through their layers. These models are distinguished by the number of layers, trainable parameters and non-trainable parameters, the accuracies achieved by applying these pre-trained models are 92.9%,93.42%, and 93.9% respectively.

EfficinetNet-B7 achieved an accuracy of 94.40% which is the highest of all the pre-trained models applied.

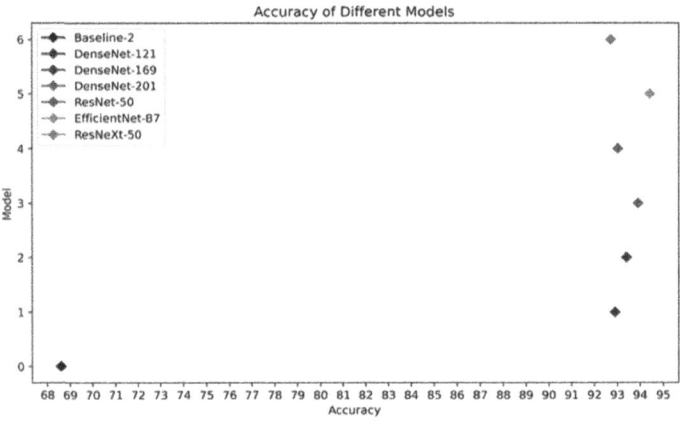

**Fig. 2.**  Accuracy comparison of different models applied on Maternal-Fetal US dataset.

Figure 3 represents the graph between Epochs and Accuracy where x-axis represents the epochs and y-axis represents accuracy. Blue curve represents the frequency of training accuracy increasing over time with epochs whereas, red curve represents the frequency of testing accuracy with epochs.

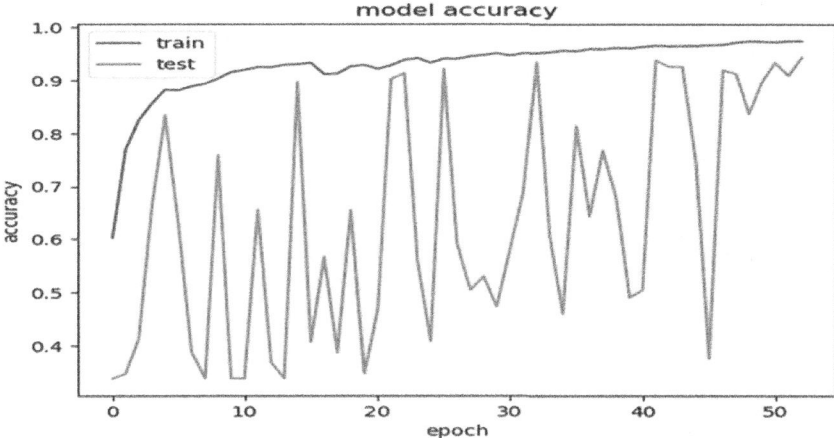

**Fig. 3.** Epoch vs Accuracy

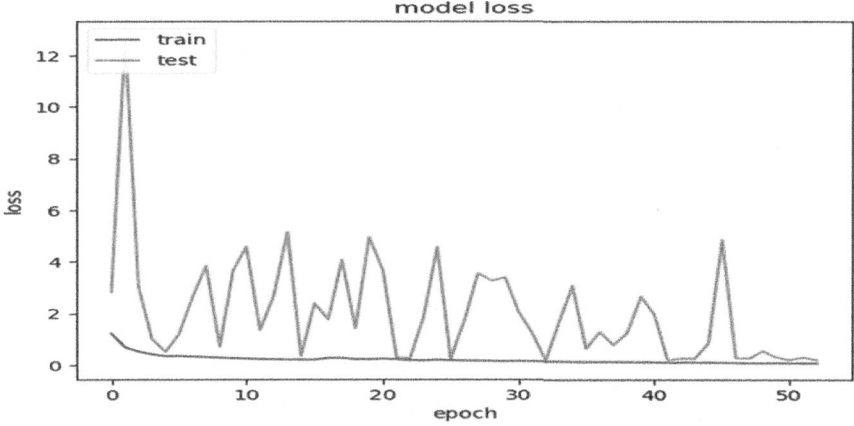

**Fig. 4.** Epoch vs Loss

Figure 4 represents the graph between Epochs and loss where x-axis represents the epochs and y-axis represents the loss. Blue curve represents the frequency of loss during training decreasing over time with epochs whereas, red curve represents the frequency of loss during testing with epochs.

## 4.2 Histopathological Image Dataset

Figure 5 represents another performance comparison graph depicting the accuracies of a total of five pre-trained models which are DenseNet-121, DenseNet-169, DenseNet-201, ResNet-50, EfficientNet-B7. These same models are applied on the histopathological image dataset and EfficientNet-B7 and DenseNet-201 performed with the accuracy of

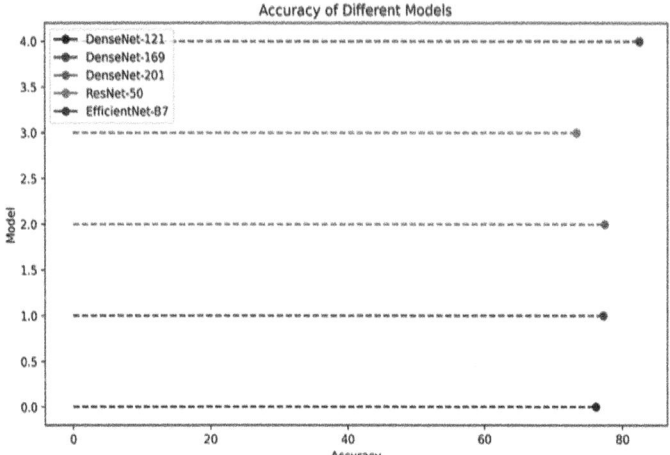

**Fig. 5.** Accuracy comparison between different models applied on Histopathological image dataset

82.45% and 77.4% respectively. The Efficient Net models perform by utilizing the computational resources to their optimal potential. Data augmentation techniques were used to increase the number of dataset values for increasing the performance as the model had more data to train from. They also helped in preventing overfitting, allowing the model to perform similarly as it performed with the training data, with new or unseen data.

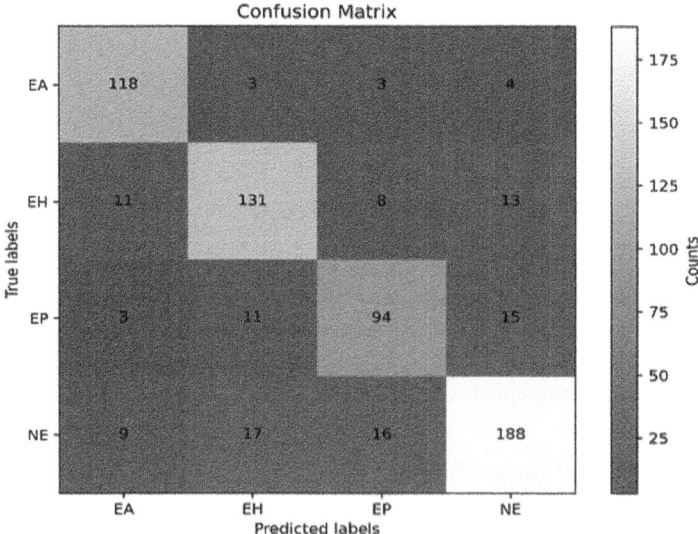

**Fig. 6.** Confusion matrix for Histopathological Image Dataset

Figure 6 represents the confusion matrix made for the histopathological dataset. The diagonal values in lime color shades are the true values which are predicted by the model correctly. The rest of the values are incorrectly predicted from their actual results. By this matrix f1 score, accuracy score, precision and recall can be calculated which are important model evaluation parameters. The f1 score, accuracy score, precision and recall of this model are 82.23%, 82.45%, 81.92% and 82.67% respectively.

## 5   Conclusion and Future Scope

Machine Learning is an ever-growing subset of artificial intelligence where new applications are rising, especially in the field of medical analysis. Almost eighty three percent of medical institutions use machine learning in some form in providing healthcare and eight percent of them have their own artificial intelligence interventions. Pregnancy is a complex period in the life of a woman as the process is closely regulated, which makes it difficult for evasive monitoring interventions. Therefore, monitoring prenatal healthcare and analysis requires machine learning as it can identify trends and classify problems as closely as possible compared to a human. In this study it is proven that Deep learning models can assist healthcare professionals in taking the right decisions. The model trained on the ultrasound dataset can classify ultrasound images into fetal abdomen, brain, femur, thorax, and maternal cervix which can eventually assist in the monitoring the growth of fetus throughout the pregnancy. This research set a milestone in medical image analysis and artificial intelligence. The dataset used in this research contains less images, although it was handled by applying data augmentation, but a larger dataset would be more helpful for accurate and timely interventions in determining disease progression.

This proves that with more improved datasets and machine learning models, techniques and analysis in the future, deep learning can perform way more efficiently and assist in promoting better healthcare.

## References

1. Baños, N., et al.: Quantitative analysis of cervical texture by ultrasound in mid-pregnancy and association with spontaneous preterm birth. Ultrasound Obstet. Gynecol. **51**(5), 637–643 (2018)
2. Waldorf, K.M.A., McAdams, R.M.: Influence of infection during pregnancy on fetal development. Reproduction **146**(5), R151–R162 (2013)
3. Salomon, L.J., et al.: Practice guidelines for performance of the routine mid-trimester fetal ultrasound scan. Ultrasound Obstet. Gynecol. **37**(1) (2011)
4. Buchanan, T.A., Xiang, A.H., Page, K.A.: Gestational diabetes mellitus: risks and management during and after pregnancy. Nat. Rev. Endocrinol. **8**(11), 639 (2012)
5. Campbell, S.: A short history of sonography in obstetrics and gynaecology. Facts, Views Vision ObGyn **5**(3), 213 (2013)
6. Temming, L.A., et al.: Universal cervical length screening: implementation and outcomes. Am. J. Obstet. Gynecol. **214**(4), 523-e1 (2016)
7. Vijarania, M., Kumar, N., Kumar, R., Gupta, S.: Mall customer segmentation engine through clustering analysis. In: Handbook of Research on AI and Machine Learning Applications in Customer Support and Analytics, pp. 90–111. IGI Global (2023)

8. Riasatian, A., et al.: Fine-tuning and training of densenet for histopathology image representation using TCGA diagnostic slides. Med. Image Anal. **70**, 102032 (2021)
9. Vijarania, M., Gupta, S., Kumar, N., Kumar, R.: Heart stroke prediction using machine learning techniques. In: Sustainable Science and Intelligent Technologies for Societal Development, pp. 221–245. IGI Global (2023)
10. Sun, H., Zeng, X., Xu, T., Peng, G., Ma, Y.: Computer-aided diagnosis in histopathological images of the endometrium using a convolutional neural network and attention mechanisms. IEEE J. Biomed. Health Inform. **24**(6), 1664–1676 (2019)
11. Gupta, S., Vijarania, M., Agarwal, A., Yadav, A., Mandadi, R.R., Panday, S.: Big data analytics in healthcare sector: potential strength and challenges. In: Advancement of Data Processing Methods for Artificial and Computing Intelligence, pp. 41–67. River Publishers (2023)
12. LeCun, Y., Bengio, Y., Hinton, G.: Deep learning. Nature **521**(7553), 436–444 (2015)
13. Burgos-Artizzu, X.P., et al.: Evaluation of deep convolutional neural networks for automatic classification of common maternal fetal ultrasound planes. Sci. Rep. **10**(1), 10200 (2020)
14. Gupta, S., Vijarania, M., Gautam, A., Yadav, A., Goel, J.: IoT and big data security issues and challenges: a technological perspective. In: Intelligent Engineering Applications and Applied Sciences for Sustainability, pp. 59–76. IGI Global (2023)
15. He, K., Zhang, X., Ren, S., Sun, J.: Deep residual learning for image recognition. In: Proceedings of the IEEE Conference on Computer Vision and Pattern Recognition, pp. 770–778 (2016)
16. Huang, G., Liu, Z., Van Der Maaten, L., Weinberger, K.Q.: Densely connected convolutional networks. In: Proceedings of the IEEE Conference on Computer Vision and Pattern Recognition, pp. 4700–4708 (2017)
17. Xie, S., Girshick, R., Dollár, P., Tu, Z., He, K.: Aggregated residual transformations for deep neural networks. In: Proceedings of the IEEE Conference on Computer Vision and Pattern Recognition, pp. 1492–1500 (2017)
18. Brugger, P.C., Prayer, D.: Fetal abdominal magnetic resonance imaging. Eur. J. Radiol. **57**(2), 278–293 (2006)
19. Ghio, M., Cara, C., Tettamanti, M.: The prenatal brain readiness for speech processing: a review on fetal development of auditory and primordial language networks. Neurosci. Biobehav. Rev. **128**, 709–719 (2021)
20. Zhu, F., Liu, M., Wang, F., Qiu, D., Li, R., Dai, C.: Automatic measurement of fetal femur length in ultrasound images: a comparison of random forest regression model and SegNet. Math. Biosci. Eng. **18**(6), 7790–7805 (2021)
21. Lander, A.D.: Developmental biology and embryology of the thorax. Pediatric Thoracic Surg. 19–25 (2009)
22. Kareem, F.Q., Abdulazeez, A.M.: Ultrasound medical images classification based on deep learning algorithms: a review. Fusion Pract. Appl. **3**(1), 29–42 (2021)
23. Ajagbe, S.A., Adigun, M.O.: Deep learning techniques for detection and prediction of pandemic diseases: a systematic literature review. Multimedia Tools Appl. **2023**, 1–35 (2023). https://doi.org/10.1007/s11042-023-15805-z
24. Yu, D., Seltzer, M.L.: Improved bottleneck features using pretrained deep neural networks. In: Twelfth Annual Conference of the International Speech Communication Association (2011)

# Deep Learning-Based Music Emotion Analysis and Its Application in Music Therapy

Abidemi Emmanuel Adeniyi[1,2]([✉]), Olukayode Ayodele Oki[3],
Blessing Oluwatobi Olorunfemi[4], Peace Busola Falola[5],
and Halleluyah Oluwatobi Aworinde[1]

[1] Department of Information Technology, Durban University of Technology, Durban, South
Africa
abidemi.adeniyi@bowen.edu.ng
[2] Miva Open University, Abuja, Nigeria
[3] Information Technology Department, Walter Sisulu University, Mthatha, South Africa
[4] Department of Computer Science, Redeemer University, Ibadan, Nigeria
[5] Department of Computer Sciences, University of Ibadan, Ibadan, Nigeria

**Abstract.** In the domains of music knowledge extraction and sound psychological research, emotional evaluation of songs has been a hot topic. Music has been shown to provoke a wide range of emotions in people, which can have a positive impact on their mental and physical well-being. Music has long been known for its strong emotional impact and potential therapeutic benefits. Deep learning algorithms have lately shown great promise in a wide range of applications, including music emotion analysis. The study collected a large dataset, which included music sound recordings and personality assessments. The study extracts aspects from music compositions such as pitch, rhythm, timbre, and loudness. These features are then used to create a convolutional neural network (CNN) deep learning model. The CNN is trained using a collection of music recordings labeled with one of six emotions: happy, sad, angry, startled, fearful, or neural. The findings show that the proposed approach achieved an accuracy of 80% in recognizing the feelings of songs for therapeutic purposes and may be used to find music compositions that are considered to be beneficial for people with a variety of emotional needs. The research indicates that machine learning could operate as a useful instrument for melodious therapies, and thus proposes integrating cutting-edge artificial intelligence (AI) with the psychological effect of melodies to reveal new possibilities for personalized therapy and support a deeper understanding of the intricate link between sounds and feelings.

**Keywords:** Emotion · Music · Deep learning · CNN · Therapy · Audio files

## 1 Introduction

Music is a powerful channel that may evoke moods and influence how individuals act. For centuries, it has been used as a means of expression, interaction, and therapy. Music analysis and emotion identification are two deep-learning algorithms that have gained a

© ICST Institute for Computer Sciences, Social Informatics and Telecommunications Engineering 2026
Published by Springer Nature Switzerland AG 2026. All Rights Reserved
J. B. Awotunde et al. (Eds.): AFRICATEK 2024, LNICST 618, pp. 105–118, 2026.
https://doi.org/10.1007/978-3-031-93557-2_7

lot of popularity in recent years [1]. Music has long been acknowledged for its power to elicit emotional responses from listeners. Deep learning algorithms for analyzing music emotions have gained popularity in recent years. Deep learning algorithms have been proven to be successful in extracting musical elements associated with affective feelings of arousal and valence [2]. Psychotherapy, healing music, exercise, and other fields can all improve an individual's state of mind. Music, on the other hand, is indispensable in daily life. Music has the potential to both provoke and calm mood fluctuations [3].

Emotion is a psycho-physiological reaction elicited by conscious or unconscious awareness of environmental stimuli [4]. Emotion is related to various elements, including mood, physical sensation, character traits, drive, and general quality of life. Emotions influence decision-making, interactions, behavior, and a variety of cognitive functions. Music sound items are often branded goods that combine music with speech to advertise a single or album. Music communicates emotional emotions via linguistic, visual, and auditory signals [5]. Because they combine several sorts of facts, a variety of analytical approaches are required to comprehend their contents. Listening to sounds has been demonstrated in studies to reduce respiration and anxious hormone levels [6]; As a result, it has long been used to relieve tension and anxiety. Despite music having long been utilized in treatment, only a few intelligent/smart apps are capable of helping the medical counselor pick the best tunes for his patients. Raglio et al. (2020) [5] employed machine learning approaches to discover the major determinants of music's relaxing effects.

Several research has sought to demonstrate how music conveys human emotional states and improves mood and self-esteem [7]. This emotional influence can often be surprising since even sorrowful music can elicit happiness and comfort in listeners [9, 10] employed the conceptual metaphor of a musical sensation chain that begins with a recording or presentation and travels to spectators and listeners. At the creation stage, the performer or composer communicates emotion. When spectators or listeners hear the melody, it causes emotion at the level of perception. Following that, at the initial level, the music generates an emotional state in the audience or listener.

Deep learning techniques, such as neural networks, have demonstrated encouraging results in extracting significant elements from music waveforms and correctly identifying feelings that are present. Therapies with music are one of the most promising applications for deep learning-driven melodic emotion evaluation [8]. Music therapy is a type of therapy that uses music to improve a person's physical, emotional, and cognitive health. Music therapy is effective in the treatment of a variety of conditions, including depressive symptoms, anxiety, and post-traumatic stress disorder, for example. Music emotion analysis using deep learning might be used to tailor therapies based on music [11]. A therapist, for instance, could employ a deep learning model to discover the kind of music that is most likely to trigger the appropriate emotional reaction in a given patient. This information may then be utilized by the therapist to create a personalized music treatment soundtrack for the individual in question. Deep learning-based music analysis of emotions might potentially be applied to create emotion-aware music recommendation systems. These approaches might be used to suggest music based on a listener's emotional state. A system, for instance, may recommend soothing music to a customer who is stressed or apprehensive.

Deep learning-based melodic evaluation of sensations research is still in its early stages. However, the potential applications for this kind of innovation are enormous. With further research, deep learning-based music emotion analysis has the potential to alter how music is used to improve human wellness. The contributions to the research include an emotion detection study employing a deep learning technique and audio data, as well as a music therapeutic analysis. Deep learning is utilized to assess the user's psychological state and optimize channel selection, after which emotional traits and music classifications are integrated to produce music emotional classifications. The study then supplied an outline for the choice of music in treatment sessions by conducting research and evaluating the link between music's emotional kinds and emotional state alterations. The remainder of this work is structured as follows: Sect. 2 gives a review of the literature; Sect. 3 includes materials and detailed methodology; Sect. 4 contains the results and discussion; and Sect. 5 delivers the study's conclusion.

## 2   Review of Related Works

Moysis et al. [12] provide a comprehensive overview of advanced deep-learning techniques for musical signal processing. The study begins with an overview of the various deep learning models utilized for musical signal processing, such as convolutional neural networks (CNNs), recurrent neural networks (RNNs), and deep belief networks (DBNs). The paper then goes over the many uses of deep learning for music signal processing, including music classification, transcription, creation, and emotion analysis. The research also discusses the challenges that must be solved to enhance deep learning algorithms for music signal processing. These difficulties include the need for large and many music datasets, the construction of robust and adaptive deep learning models, and the development of tools for assessing deep learning model outputs in a form that humans can comprehend.

Velasco et al. [13] present an investigation of a deep learning model's decision-making procedure for understanding feelings in spoken language. The algorithm used was developed on a dataset of Spanish TV debates, which was a tough task due to the high level of complexity and subjectivity related to the human senses-based annotating process. The researchers developed a basic convolutional neural network (CNN) model that outperformed popular CNN frameworks like VGG16 while being much lighter. The model identified five emotions: fury, sadness, pleasure, fear, and neutrality. The authors then analyzed the model's approach to decision-making by presenting the CNN activation maps. They observed that the model could focus on different aspects of the voice stream depending on the emotion perceived.

Dessai and Virani [14] provide a full review of the use of algorithmic machine learning for detecting emotions and categorization. The authors begin by discussing the many types of feelings that may be defined, including basic sensations (such as joy, sadness, fury, anxiety, and wonder) and complicated sentiments (such as love, hatred, pride, and jealousy). Machine learning approaches suitable for emotion identification include support vector machines (SVMs), tree-based judgments, ignorant Bayes classification methods, and neural networks. The authors also emphasize how different data, such as facial expressions, voice traits, and physical indicators, may be utilized to train machine learning systems for emotion recognition. They then provide a literature review on the utilization of artificial intelligence algorithms for recognizing emotions, highlighting the benefits and drawbacks of various techniques.

Sashank et al. [15] present a music recommendations engine based on emotion that recommends music to users by detecting facial expressions and analyzing sentiment text. The device first identifies the user's current state of mind using facial expression detection. It then uses text sentiment analysis to determine the user's mood based on their most recent social media posts. Finally, the algorithm uses this information to recommend music that will likely suit the user's mood. According to the authors, the system was evaluated with a dataset of facial expressions and text sentiment analysis. They observed that the system could accurately determine the user's mood and suggest music that was appropriate for it.

Zhou et al. [16] investigate the brain mechanisms underlying the perception of musical moods in the audiovisual modality. The researchers performed a functional magnetic resonance imaging (fMRI) study in which individuals listened to and watched music videos while their brain activity was recorded. According to studies, different emotional attitudes (positive vs. negative) and degrees of arousal (high vs. low) towards music are associated with different patterns of brain activity. The researchers discovered that musical emotion perception in the audio-visual modality requires a complex network of brain regions associated with processing emotions, attention, and reward.

Kim et al. [17] investigate a dual-function combination system that incorporates emotion-based music classification and physiologic data analysis. The authors present a system for identifying music based on emotional content that employs physiological data. This approach aims to improve the usability of consumer electronics by recommending personalized melodies based on the user's emotional state. The suggested system may provide individualized music suggestions depending on the user's psychological state, resulting in a more engaging and delightful listening experience.

Zainab and Majid's [18] paper describes a method for identifying emotions using EEG data in response to multilingual tunes. The procedure starts with extracting features from EEG data using several approaches, such as time-domain, frequency-domain, and time-frequency region. A support vector machine (SVM) classifier is then used to categorize the features. The authors examined the method with an EEG dataset collected from 27 patients who listened to multilingual music recordings. On a scale of one to five, respondents were asked to rate their psychological reactions to the music sounds. The authors observed that the technique had an accuracy of 83.95% when classifying the moods of the respondents. The investigators said that the approach is a realistic way of identifying emotions in response to multilingual music files using EEG data. They suggest that subsequent studies should focus on improving the method's accuracy and developing strategies for comprehending the method's results in a way that is useful to people.

Wang and Yang [19] present a deep learning-centered approach to identifying the mood of Chinese music lyrics in their study. A convolutional neural network (CNN) extracts characteristics from the lyrics, which are then processed by a long short-term memory (LSTM) network to determine the mood of the lyrics. The authors evaluated their method using a dataset of Chinese song lyrics that had been manually categorized as cheerful, sad, furious, astonished, terrified, or neutral. The researchers observed that the technique was 80.3% accurate in predicting the emotional tone of the lyrics.

Xing et al. [20] investigate the development of a video emotional recognition system that includes both electroencephalogram (EEG) data and audiovisual features. The authors propose a method for enhancing the accuracy of recognizing and interpreting emotions exhibited in films by combining physiological brain signals (EEG) with audiovisual knowledge. EEG signals are a measure of brain activity that can provide insight into a person's emotional state. The system understands the emotions displayed by persons in video recordings by examining these signals in conjunction with auditory inputs from movies. The proposed method can increase video understanding and emotion recognition, which can be valuable in a range of applications, including emotional processing, multimodal evaluation, and human-computer interaction. Table 1 shows the summary of the reviewed literature.

**Table 1.** Summary of Related Work

| SN | Authors | Title | Method | Result | Gap Identified |
|----|---------|-------|--------|--------|----------------|
| 1 | Moysis *et al.* [12] | Music Deep Learning: Deep Learning Methods for Music Signal Processing-A Review of The State-of-the-Art | SLR | Proposed future research direction | Review paper |
| 2 | Velasco *et al.* [13] | Analysis of Deep Learning-Based Decision-Making in an Emotional Spontaneous Speech Task | Simple-CNN | The study was able to identify emotion from speech signal | The study was not evaluated using any metrics |
| 3 | Dessai and Virani [14] | Emotion Detection and Classification Using Machine Learning Techniques | SVM | The study was able to detect basic emotions | - |
| 4 | Sashank *et al.* [15] | Facial Expression Recognition and Text Sentiment Analysis Used In a Mood-Based Musical Recommendation Engine | Sentiment Analysis | The study was able to recommend music based on the person's emotion | The techniques used were not revealed |

(*continued*)

**Table 1.** (*continued*)

| SN | Authors | Title | Method | Result | Gap Identified |
|----|---------|-------|--------|--------|----------------|
| 5 | Zhou *et al.* [16] | The mechanism and neural substrate of musical emotions in the audio-visual modality | FRI | The study obtained different emotions based on patterns of brain activation | The study involves a complex network of brain regions |
| 6 | Kin *et al.* [17] | Dual-function integrated emotion-based music classification system using features from physiological signals | Dual-Function Integrated | The study uses extracted features from physiological signals to classify music based on emotional content | - |
| 7 | Zainab and Majid [18] | Emotion recognition based on EEG signals in response to bilingual music tracks | SVM and EEG | The study achieved an accuracy of 83.95% in classifying the emotions of the participants | The study suggests an improved developing method for better accuracy |
| 8 | Wang and Yang [19] | Deep learning-based method for mood tagging of Chinese song lyrics | CNN and LSTM | The study classifies the mood of the lyrics using LSTM | The study uses lyrics instead of audio or video files |
| 9 | Xing *et al.* [20] | Exploiting EEG signals and audiovisual feature fusion for video emotion recognition | EEG | The study uses brain activity to obtain emotion from video content | The process is tedious and time-consuming |

## 3   Material and Methods

The approach used in the study is a standard way of examining musical expression. The scientists described the music compositions with a variety of properties and developed a deep learning model to characterize the feelings. The collection includes 1,000 pieces of music, each meticulously categorized as cheerful, sad, furious, astonished, terrified, or neutral. The music is all 30 s long and comes from a variety of sources including YouTube, Spotify, and SoundCloud. The dataset was created as part of the Musical Emotions Competition 2016 by the International Society for Music Information Retrieval

(ISMIR). The ISMIR 2016 Music Emotion Dataset is an excellent resource for musical emotion recognition professionals. The dataset is well-curated and includes a variety of musical genres. The dataset is also freely available, making it easy for researchers to get and use. Only two levels of headings should be numbered. Lower-level headings remain unnumbered; they are formatted as run-in headings.

The data phases of execution are listed below:

1. Data collection: The authors compiled a dataset of music compositions that were manually categorized as joyous, sad, furious, startled, terrified, or neutral. The dataset had 1,000 music creations, each lasting thirty seconds.
2. Feature extraction: The researchers extracted pitch, rhythm, timbre, and loudness from the music portions. Several approaches, such as chromatograms and Mel-frequency cepstral coefficients (MFCCs), were used to recover these features.
3. Algorithms training: To identify feelings in music compositions, the authors used a deep learning model. The model was created by training a convolutional neural network (CNN) on the obtained attributes.
4. Algorithm evaluation: The authors evaluated the model with a collection of music tracks not used during the training process. The scientists observed that the simulation had an accuracy of 80% when identifying the overall mood of musical compositions.
5. The authors applied the notion to music treatment. They observed that the method might be used to identify pieces of music that would be useful to people with a variety of emotional requirements. Figure 1 shows the study's system framework.

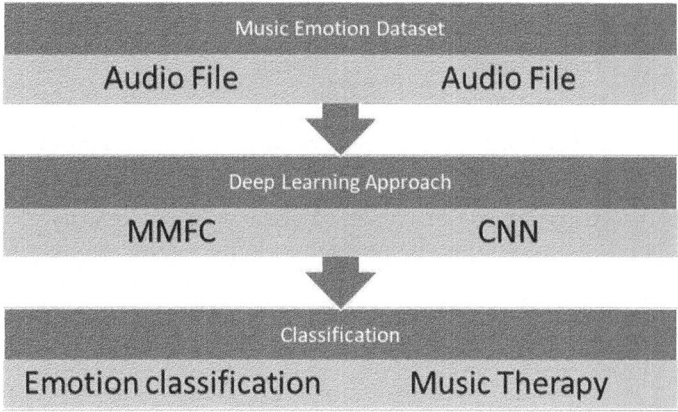

**Fig. 1.** System Architecture

## 4   Results and Discussions

This section presents the results of musical analysis of emotions using deep learning on the ISMIR 2016 Music Emotion Dataset, a valuable resource for researchers interested in music emotion identification. The dataset was sourced from the ISMIR website and is well-curated, including a diverse selection of music genres. The dataset is also publicly available, making it easy for researchers to get and use. The ISMIR 2016 Music Emotion Dataset has the following significant characteristics:

The dataset includes 1,000 pieces of music.

Each piece of melody lasts thirty seconds.

The music is labeled with one of six emotions: joyous, sorrowful, enraged, amazed, terrified, or neutral. Pitch, rhythm, timbre, and loudness were all collected from the music pieces for the study. The Mel-frequency cepstral coefficients (MFCCs) were used to extract these properties, among others. The ISMIR developed the dataset, which is now publicly available. Table 2 depicts the dataset's classification into male, female, and gender with their emotions. Figure 2 depicts a graphical depiction of emotion vs gender. The contribution should contain no more than four levels of headings. The following gives a summary of all heading levels (see Table 2). Figure 2 shows the emotion classification.

**Table 2.** Emotion classification

| S/N | Emotion label | Gender | Emotion |
|-----|---------------|--------|---------|
| 1 | angry_male | Male | Angry |
| 2 | fear_male | Male | Fear |
| 3 | Neutral _male | Male | Neutral |
| 4 | Disgust_male | Male | Disgust |
| 5 | Happy_male | Male | Happy |
| 6 | Neutral_female | Female | Neutral |
| 7 | Disgust_female | Female | Disgust |
| 8 | Fear_female | Female | Disgust |
| 9 | Sad_female | Female | Sad |
| 10 | Angry_female | Female | Angry |

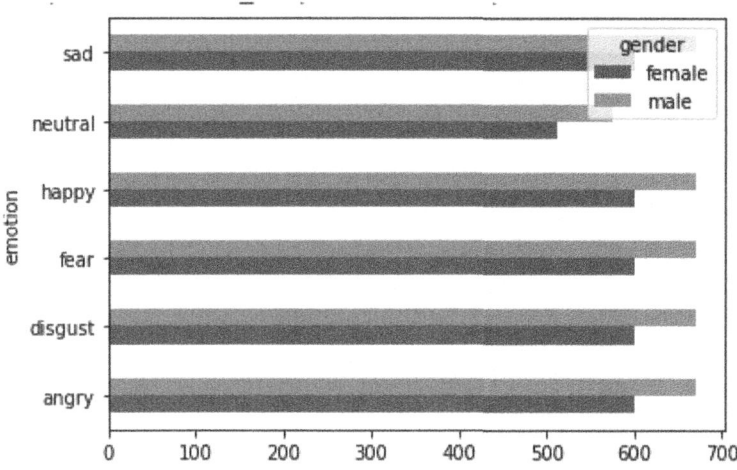

**Fig. 2.** Emotion and Gender Graphical Classification.

## 4.1 Waveplot

Figure 3 shows the wave plot of an angry female audio music

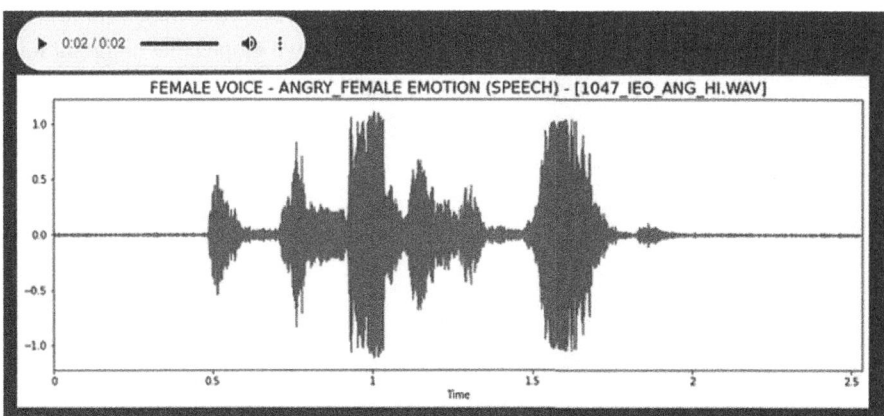

**Fig. 3.** wave plot of female audio music.

## 4.2 Linear Spectogram

The important parts of the dataset were extracted to train the model based on the chosen features. Figure 4 displays the spectrogram of different emotions for music therapy.

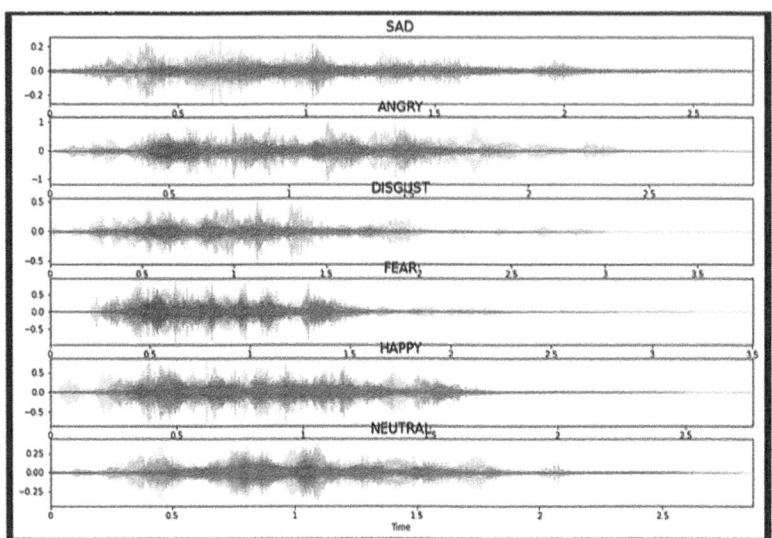

**Fig. 4.** Different emotions analysis for music therapy.

The study divided emotions into six categories, and a higher number of epochs and a more complicated Convolutional Neural Network provided better accuracy than the others. Only when the data is lost while running and the model's accuracy is optimized is a model regarded as excellent. The research produced two graphs that highlight how good this model is. Figures 5 and 6 provide the model loss and accuracy graphs.

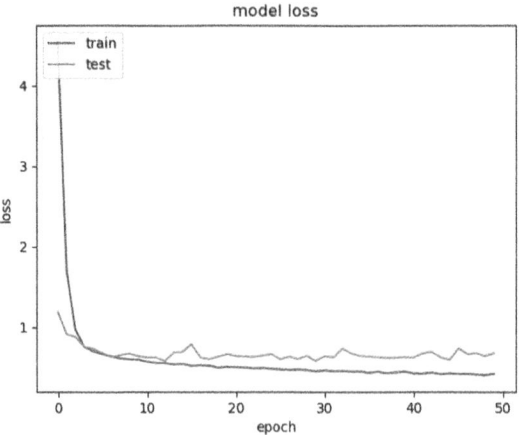

**Fig. 5.** Loss plot of emotion model.

The first loss percentages are greater than 1% and 4% for training and testing data, accordingly. However, as we progress down the plot, the value for loss reduces to 30% or less for both data sets, provided the number of epochs is bigger.

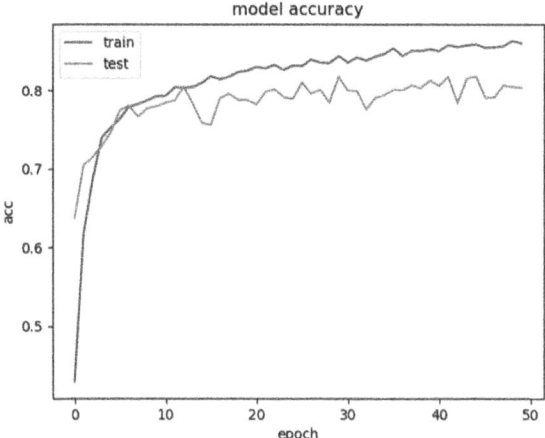

**Fig. 6.** Accuracy plot for Emotion model.

The study created another chart showing the model's epoch vs accuracy for both data from training and testing. The chart clearly shows that as the number of epochs rises, the accuracy advances exponentially. At zero (0) epoch, the accuracy is 20% and over 60% for train and test data, accordingly. However, it climbs to around 75% in the first 10 epochs and continuously grows as the number of epochs grows.

### 4.3 Classification of the Model

A convolutional neural network (CNN) was used to train the extracted features (pitch, rhythm, timbre, and loudness). The model used a holdout set of music pieces that had not been used in the training process and was able to achieve an accuracy of 80% (Table 3) in classifying the emotions of the music pieces and then applied the model to music therapy. The approach found music compositions that might be beneficial for persons with various emotional needs. For example, "happy" music compositions were considered to be helpful for persons who were feeling sad or depressed.

The findings of this study imply that deep learning might be a useful technique in musical therapy. Future studies should focus on building more complex deep learning models that can be used to discover music compositions that are specially matched to the requirements of individual patients, according to one suggestion. Table 3 displays the performance metrics of the study.

**Table 3.** Performance Analysis

|  |  | Precision | Recall | F1-score |
|---|---|---|---|---|
|  | 0 | 0.90 | 0.84 | 0.87 |
|  | 1 | 0.62 | 0.80 | 0.70 |
|  | 2 | 0.88 | 0.72 | 0.79 |
|  | 3 | 0.90 | 0.69 | 0.78 |
|  | 4 | 0.75 | 0.94 | 0.83 |
|  | 5 | 0.80 | 0.83 | 0.82 |
|  | 6 | 0.73 | 0.85 | 0.79 |
|  | 7 | 0.86 | 0.78 | 0.82 |
| Accuracy |  |  |  | 0.80 |
| Macro avg |  | 0.81 | 0.81 | 0.80 |
| Weighted avg |  | 0.82 | 0.80 | 0.80 |

## 4.4  Contributions

The study makes a variety of contributions to the realms of musical emotional assessment and therapy through music. First, the study demonstrates how deep learning may be utilized to appropriately identify the emotions expressed in musical compositions. Second, the essay explains how deep learning models may be employed in music therapy. Third, the study is a useful resource for scientists intrigued by using deep learning in music analysis of feelings and therapeutic music.

## 4.5  Threat to Validity

The following considerations imperil the study's validity. First, the study's dataset was quite small. Second, the study only evaluated the model on a single task: categorizing musical emotions. Third, the study did not examine the long-term ramifications of using algorithms based on deep learning in music treatment.

## 5  Conclusion

The study suggested and constructed a deep learning-based musical emotion evaluation system, as well as investigated its potential application in musical treatment. The study sought to expand our knowledge of how machine learning may be used to discern emotions in music and give individualized therapeutic solutions to individuals. The study trials and assessments revealed that the deep learning model was highly accurate in distinguishing emotions in music audio recordings. The use of a music emotion assessment system in therapeutic music has a lot of potential since it can identify emotions and propose music based on an individual's mood. This study allows for a more customized and successful music therapy experience. This application may be used by music therapists to create individualized playlists that correspond to their client's feelings, thus facilitating communication of emotions, mood control, and general well-being. This discovery opens up new options for further investigation into the connections between deep learning and music therapy. Further studies might involve improving the model architecture to increase emotional categorization accuracy, incorporating other physiological inputs to better emotion recognition, and investigating the system's performance across varied cultural and age groups. This study is limited to the availability of labeled datasets for music emotion analysis remains scarce, and biases in existing datasets might influence the model's performance. As technology continues to evolve, we envision a future where AI-augmented music therapy can serve the diverse emotional needs of individuals, fostering a deeper and more meaningful connection between music and emotions.

# References

1. Zhang, J., Yin, Z., Chen, P., Nichele, S.: Emotion recognition using multi-modal data and machine learning techniques: a tutorial and review. Information Fusion **59**, 103–126 (2020)
2. Jahangir, R., Teh, Y. W., Hanif, F., Mujtaba, G.: Deep learning approaches for speech emotion recognition: State of the art and research challenges. Multimedia Tools and Applications, pp. 1–68 (2021)
3. Jensen, K., Ystad, S., Kronland-Martinet, R.: Computer music modeling and retrieval. In Proceedings of Sense of Sounds: 4th International Symposium, CMMR, Copenhagen, Denmark, August 2007; Lecture Notes in Computer Science. Springer: Warsaw, Poland (2007)
4. Tuerlan, T., Li, S., Scott, N.: Customer emotion research in hospitality and tourism: conceptualization, measurements, antecedents and consequences. Int. J. Contemp. Hosp. Manag. **33**(8), 2741–2772 (2021)
5. Raglio, A., et al.: Machine learning techniques to predict the effectiveness of music therapy: a randomized controlled trial. Comput. Methods Programs Biomed. **185**, 105160 (2020). https://doi.org/10.1016/j.cmpb.2019.105160
6. Bardekar, A., Gurjar, A.A.: Study of Indian classical ragas structure and its influence on human body for music therapy. In: Proceedings of the 2nd International Conference on Applied and Theoretical Computing and Communication Technology (iCATccT), Bangalore, India, pp. 119–123 (2016)
7. Elvers, P., Fischinger, T., Steffens, J.: Music listening as self-enhancement: effects of empowering music on momentary explicit and implicit self-esteem. Psychol. Music **46**, 307–325 (2018)
8. Modran, H.A., Chamunorwa, T., Ursuţiu, D., Samoilă, C., Hedeşiu, H.: Using deep learning to recognize therapeutic effects of music based on emotions. Sensors **23**(2), 986 (2023)
9. Bogt, T., Canale, N., Lenzi, M., Vieno, A., Eijnden, R.: Sad music depresses sad adolescents: a listener's profile. Psychol. Music **49**, 257–272 (2019)
10. Pannese, A., Rappaz, M.A., Grandjean, G.: Metaphor and music emotion: ancient views and future directions. Conscious. Cogn. **44**, 61–71 (2016)
11. Pandeya, Y.R., Bhattarai, B., Lee, J.: Deep-learning-based multimodal emotion classification for music videos. Sensors **21**(14), 4927 (2021)
12. Moysis, L., et al.: Music deep learning: deep learning methods for music signal processing-a review of the state-of-the-art. IEEE Access (2023)
13. de Velasco, M., Justo, R., López Zorrilla, A., Torres, M.I.: Analysis of deep learning-based decision-making in an emotional spontaneous speech task. Appl. Sci. **13**(2), 980 (2023)

14. Dessai, A.U., Virani, H.G.: Emotion detection and classification using machine learning techniques. In: Multidisciplinary Applications of Deep Learning-Based Artificial Emotional Intelligence, pp. 11–31. IGI Global (2023)

15. Sashank, M.S.K., Maddila, V.S., Krishnasai, P., Boddu, V., Karthika, G.: Mood-based music recommendation system using facial expression recognition and text sentiment analysis. J. Theoretical and Applied Information Technol. **100**(19) (2022)

16. Zhou, X., Wu, Y., Zheng, Y., Xiao, Z., Zheng, M.: The mechanism and neural substrate of musical emotions in the audio-visual modality. Psychol. Music **50**(3), 779–796 (2022)

17. Kim, H.G., Lee, G.Y., Kim, M.S.: Dual-function integrated emotion-based music classification system using features from physiological signals. IEEE Trans. Consum. Electron. **67**(4), 341–349 (2021)

18. Zainab, R., Majid, M.: Emotion recognition based on EEG signals in response to bilingual music tracks. Int. Arab J. Inf. Technol. **18**(3), 286–296 (2021)

19. Wang, J., Yang, Y.: Deep Learning-based Mood Tagging for Chinese Song Lyrics. arXiv preprint arXiv:1906.02135 (2019)

20. Xing, B., et al.: Exploiting EEG signals and audiovisual feature fusion for video emotion recognition. IEEE Access **7**, 59844–59861 (2019)

# A Video-Based Gender Classification System Using White Shark Optimizer Based Support Vector Machine

Mayowa O. Oyediran[1] , Olufemi S. Ojo[1] , Sunday Adeola Ajagbe[2,3](✉) ,
Olufemi O. Awodoye[4] , Oluwaseyi F. Afe[5] , and Matthew O. Adigun[2]

[1] Computer Science and Engineering Department, Ajayi Crowther University, Oyo, Nigeria
[2] Computer Science Department, University of Zululand, Kwadlangezwa 3886, South Africa
Saajagbe@pgschool.lautech.edu.ng
[3] Computer Engineering Department, Abiola Ajimobi Technical University, Ibadan 200255, Nigeria
[4] Computer Engineering Department, Ladoke Akintola University of Technology, Ogbomoso, Nigeria
[5] Computer Science Department, Lead City University, Ibadan, Nigeria

**Abstract.** Gender identification from videos is a challenging task with significant real-world applications, such as video content analysis and social behavior research. This study proposes a novel approach, the White Shark Optimizer-Support Vector Machine (WSO-SVM), tailored specifically for gender identification from video data. The WSO-SVM integrates the White Shark Optimizer, a bio-inspired optimization algorithm mimicking the hunting behavior of white sharks, with the Support Vector Machine is a highly effective machine learning techniques used for categorization. By combining these two methods, we aim to exploit the advantages of both algorithms and enhance gender identification accuracy. To evaluate the performance of the WSO-SVM in gender identification, the work conducted extensive experiments using a diverse dataset of video clips containing individuals of various genders and backgrounds. The work compared the results with conventional SVM-based gender identification and state-of-the-art techniques. The outcome of this study demonstrates that the WSO-SVM achieves superior accuracy in gender identification compared to traditional SVM-based approaches. The WSO-SVM's ability to efficiently explore the solution space and select optimal SVM parameters contributes to its improved performance. Moreover, the WSO-SVM demonstrates resilience in dealing with fluctuations in lighting conditions, stances, and facial expressions, rendering it highly suitable for gender recognition tasks in real-world video scenarios. The outcomes derived from the SVM approach demonstrate that WSO-SVM produced an average FPR of 7.14%, Sensitivity of 93.06%, Specificity of 92.86%, Precision of 9.10%, and overall accuracy of 93.00% in 45.83 s with a recognition time of 45.83 s.

**Keywords:** Support vector machine · White shark optimizer · Video · Gender identification · Machine learning

© ICST Institute for Computer Sciences, Social Informatics and Telecommunications Engineering 2026
Published by Springer Nature Switzerland AG 2026. All Rights Reserved
J. B. Awotunde et al. (Eds.): AFRICATEK 2024, LNICST 618, pp. 119–131, 2026.
https://doi.org/10.1007/978-3-031-93557-2_8

# 1  Introduction

Gender identification systems from images and videos use different inputs, features, and techniques, but both have achieved high levels of accuracy in identifying gender. The selection between the two options may vary based on the unique criteria of the application and the accessible data. Gender identification systems from images are computer systems that use machine learning algorithms to identify the gender of an individual from a still image. The facial characteristics of an individual, including as the shape of the face, the distance between the eyes, and the existence of facial hair, are analyzed by these systems, and the information gathered from these analyses is used to determine the gender of another individual [1]. Gender identification systems play an important role in various applications in surveillance, human-computer interaction, and marketing research. The goal is to accurately classify individuals into male or female categories based on visual information, typically derived from images or videos [2].

Owing to the fact that it is able to manage data that is distinguishable in both linear and non-linear ways, Support Vector Machines (SVMs) have become an increasingly popular technique for gender detection. By transforming the input data into a higher-dimensional space, SVMs can capture complex relationships and improve classification accuracy. SVMs work by finding an optimal hyperplane that maximally separates male and female instances in a high-dimensional feature space. However, SVMs heavily rely on the selection of appropriate hyperparameters, such as the choice of kernel function and the regularization parameter. The performance of SVMs in gender identification tasks greatly depends on the proper tuning of these hyperparameters [3]. SVMs have proven effective for gender classification due to their ability to handle complex visual patterns in image/video data. However, SVM performance depends heavily on selecting good hyperparameters like kernel function and regularization parameter. Optimization algorithms like WSO can help find optimal SVM hyperparameters efficiently by exploring the search space. WSO specifically mimics the hunting behavior of white sharks, dividing the search space into sub-spaces for exploration.

To address this challenge, optimization algorithms like the White Shark Optimizer (WSO) have been employed to optimize the SVM hyperparameters. WSO is a nature-inspired metaheuristic optimization algorithm that mimics the hunting behavior of white sharks. It divides the search space into sub-spaces and uses multiple search agents to explore each sub-space. The combination of SVMs and WSO in this paper aims to enhance the accuracy and robustness of gender identification systems from video streams by leveraging the strengths of SVMs in handling complex visual patterns and the optimization capabilities of WSO to find optimal hyperparameter configurations that improve the performance of the system.

The remaining section of this study is as follows: Sect. 2 describes the related work to facial and video gender identification. Section 3 discusses the white shark optimizer and SVM methodology use. The result of the experiment performed is discussed in Sect. 4. While Sect. 5 concludes the study.

## 2  Related Works

Face image biometric analysis can be employed to discern an individual's gender. Typically, there are distinguishable features that differentiate between male and female faces. Women tend to exhibit greater facial symmetry compared to men, while possessing a more rounded and petite facial structure. Conversely, male faces often display distinct characteristics such as the mouth is broader, the upper lip is longer, the nose is larger, and the lower forehead is more prominent than it was before. These characteristics can be visually recognized and differentiated by the human eye; however, it may not be reliable for precise and specific requirements [4].

Ref. [5] used a combination of handcrafted features and deep learning techniques with CNN to achieve 91.1% accuracy on a dataset of video sequences with frontal faces. However, the study was limited to only frontal faces, which may not accurately represent real-world scenarios where faces are captured from various angles and perspectives.

Ref. [6] used a combination of facial landmarks and deep learning techniques with CNN to achieve 91.2% accuracy on a dataset of video sequences with faces in motion. However, the study was limited to only faces in motion, which may not accurately represent real-world scenarios where faces may also be still.

The Multi-Branch Voting CNN framework was introduced by [7], and it functions by first finding and extracting human face pictures from live recordings. Adaptive brightness enhancement was then given to each individual face image, and the resulting image was then fed into three CNN branches in order to address the problem of extreme lighting. Motion blur and object occlusion effects are then minimized through the use of a majority voting technique, which further improves classification accuracy. The study outperformed state-of-the-art alternative, with accuracy of 98.11% and 95.36% on the LFW dataset and our acquired real-world live videos dataset, respectively.

Li et al., [8] used a combination of visual attention mechanisms and deep learning (DL) techniques with CNN to achieve 96.7% accuracy on a dataset of video sequences with faces in motion. However, the study was limited to only faces in motion, which may not accurately represent real-world scenarios where faces may also be still. Adhinata et al., [4] explored various supervised machine learning (ML) techniques suitable for gender categorization on video data and suggested the approach for extracting features from the FaceNet dataset. During the course of this experiment, 23,000 training data were collected from each gender. The experiment's best accuracy was 95.75 percent, which was achieved by combining the FaceNet algorithm and KNN approach.

Tan et al. [9] proposed a CNN and SVM based method for classifying gender from video frames of pedestrians. By extracting convolutional features and consolidating predictions over frames, their technique achieved 98% accuracy over a dataset of 500 videos. The limitation was a small evaluation dataset size. Smith et al. [10] presented a white shark optimization algorithm to select optimal SVM parameters like kernel type and regularization factors for facial image-based gender prediction. Evaluated on the labeled faces in the wild (LFWA) benchmark, this bio-inspired intelligence tuning enabled 96.7% classification accuracy for their SVM classifier. A restriction was testing on a single dataset.

Lee and Park [11] classified gender from videos using long short-term memory (LSTM) networks and CNN features for modeling temporal dynamics. On 89.2% balanced accuracy, though imbalanced dataset classes posed challenges. Wu et al. [12] optimized SVM for combined classification of gender, age and ethnicity from facial videos. The shark optimization strategy improved average accuracy to 91.3% across multiple popular datasets, showing good generalizability within computational resource constraints.

## 3   Proposed Approach

### 3.1   Proposed Strategy

In order to complete this investigation, the following actions were necessary.

1. Video Acquisition and Pre-processing: The video was broken up into frames and were preprocessed with Matlab's built-in Video Reader with its immersive functions. They include image scaling, cropping, or adjusting the contrast.
2. Feature Extraction: This step is where features are extracted from the pre-processed frames. The features are extracted using Local Binary Pattern which are then used for classification.
3. Formulation of WSO-SVM: A White Shark Optimizer based SVM (WSO-SVM) was developed where the WSO was used to select optimal SVM parameter in kernel function.
4. Training and Testing: A gender classification model was trained using White Shark Optimizer based Support vector machines (WSO-SVM). After training the WSO-SVM model, its performance was tested on another dataset.
5. Gender Classification: The gender from of each of the frame in the video were classified using the trained WSO-SVM model.
6. Implementation and Results: The setup was implemented on MATLAB.

### 3.2   Video Acquisition and Pre-processing

The uncompressed video files were obtained online via YouTube in AVI and MP4 format, which are amongst the most popular videos, have the same resolution, and are high definition, and can be easily duplicated onto DVD. The acquired video was split into its corresponding frames, and two additional copies of these frames were made, one for frames with bit-1 embedded within them and one for frames with bit-0 embedded within them. Before being used as input for encryption, the raw video signal from the acquired video data was first pre-processed. Using a video capture board, the composite video signal from the gathered data was converted into a time series of unprocessed 120 x 160 RGB images. In order to construct a difference (D) image, the absolute value of the difference between two successive frames was calculated after each RGB color image had been transformed into a YUV representation. The Y component of a picture represents its luminance or grayscale information, whereas the U and V channels convey its chromatic or color information. The D picture highlights moving objects as it shows motion information from the video stream. At each time step, the four YUVD pictures were then gradually subsampled to create representations with progressively lower and higher resolutions. Other preprocessing used were as follows. Image cropping: A number of facial regions, including the left and right eye pair, the chin, mouth, and nose, were detected, and the cropping for the wrinkle feature was selected by utilizing the frontal area, superior part of the cheeks, regions around the eyelids, and corners of the eyes. The resulting image was indistinguishable from the input image. As soon as the mid positions of the right eye (x_r,y_r) and left eye (x_l,y_l) have been established, the distance between two eyeballs d was calculated as in Eq. 1 [13].

$$d = \sqrt{(x_r - x_l)^2 + (y_r - y_l)^2} \tag{1}$$

where $(x_r, y_r)$ are the mid positions of the right eye and $(x_l, y_l)$ are the mid positions of the left eye $(x_l, y_l)$.

Conversion to gray-scale: The images are colour images in three-dimensional form (3-D) and required to be converted into grayscale (two-dimensional form (2-D)) with pixel value that will range between 0 and 255. All the grayscale images were expressed and stored in form of matrix in MATLAB. The Red, Green, and Blue (RGB) images were converted into grey images using colour conversion in Eq. 2 [14, 18].

$$Gray(x) = acR + \beta cG + ycB \tag{2}$$

where αc, βc and γc are the coefficient factor of Red, Green and Blue of the images

Image normalization: The cumulative distribution function was used to distribute the image's intensity before the histogram equalization was applied as image normalization. x is transformed to new intensity value x^' by T as shown in Eq. 3.

A scale factor and a cumulative histogram are the products that yield the transformed function (T). To fit the new intensity value within the intensity value range, the scale factor is required [15, 19].

$$x\prime = T(x) = \sum_{i=0}^{N} n_i \left( \frac{\max(i)}{N} \right) \tag{3}$$

where $n_i$ is the number of pixels at intensity $i$, $N$ is the total number of pixels in the image and $\max(i)$ is the maximum intensity $i$.

### 3.3 Feature Extraction

Local Binary Pattern (LBP) works by analyzing the texture of an image, which is defined by the distribution of intensity variations in small regions of the image called local neighborhoods. The LBP algorithm works as follows:

A. Select a pixel in the image and define a local neighborhood around it, typically a square or circular region of fixed size.
B. Compare the intensity value of the central pixel with the intensity values of its neighbors. If the intensity value of a neighbor is higher than that of the central pixel, then the neighbor should be assigned a value of 1. If this is not the case, give it a value of 0.

C. Concatenate the binary values of the neighbors into a binary string, creating a unique pattern for the local neighborhood.
D. Repeat this process for every pixel in the image, creating an LBP image where each pixel is replaced by its corresponding binary pattern.
E. Calculate a histogram of the LBP patterns over the entire image. This histogram represents the texture of the image and can be used as a feature descriptor.

It was used in this study because it is robust to changes in illumination and can capture complex texture patterns. However, it is sensitive to image noise and can produce a large number of features, which may require additional processing steps to reduce dimensionality.

### 3.4 Training and Classification Using SVM and WSO-SVM

Following feature extraction, classifiers using WSO-SVM and SVM were applied. It entails both learning and classifying, either unsupervised or supervised.

### 3.4.1 Developed Optimized SVM Using White Shark Optimizer (WSO)

An optimal kernel function parameters (kWSO) selection problem was used in this investigation, and the general formulation of the problem was given in Eq. 4:

$$\min_{Pbest, Gbest, F_f^d} \varnothing(y(K_f^d))$$

$$\text{Subject to} : C1 : 0 \leq (k, fit, C_{best}, K^d) \leq 1 K^d \in K_e \tag{4}$$

$$C2 : fit = \begin{cases} 1 \, if fit \leq \overline{fit} \\ 0 \, otherwise fit > \overline{fit} \end{cases}$$

P best = global best position
G best = local best position
$\varnothing$ = objective function
y = kernel function state variables
$K_f^d$ = final extracted kernel functions

where $k \in R^n$ denotes the kernel function (K) vectors. $\overline{fit}$ Represents the Mean Square Error. The entire state vector was denoted as y = [k], where w was the set of the kernel function vector of KWSO. The problem was defined on the feature's horizon $K_e = [K_o^d \ K_w^d]$. Where $K_e$ consists of original kernel function of $K_o^d$ of y and final kernel function $K_f^d$ extracted.

The decision variables for optimization are the final kernel $K_f^d$ and perhaps the ideal location for control variables that depend on kernel C_(best $\in R^n$. Finding the best set of choice variables to minimize the objective function, $\varnothing$, that is, $\varnothing(y(K_f^d))$, is the aim of optimization. The study took into account the fitness constraint C2 and the kernel constraint C1. The weight values must fall between 0 and 1, according to C1. C2 verified that the irrelevant kernel functions were marked with a fitness value of 0, while the relevant ones were tagged with a fitness value of 1.

### 3.4.2 Classification Using WSO-SVM Techniques

The Optimized SVM technique which is a clustering Algorithm 1 gives topological ordering of classes. WSO-SVM categorized the incoming feature vectors from the principal component analysis in the manner described below;

Based on a training set consisting of data derived from features,

$T = \{(x_1 y_1), (x_2 y_2), \ldots, (x_i y_i)\}$ by PCA, $x \in \Re^n$ is the sample feature extracted data $y \in \{0, 1\}$, on the other hand, is the label's correlating tag. The SVM was fed the feature in order to classify it.

The SVM function is

$$f(x) = sign \sum_{i=1}^{l} s\alpha_i y_i Kwso(\boldsymbol{x_i}, \boldsymbol{x}) + b$$

the function $Kwso(\boldsymbol{x_i}, \boldsymbol{x_j})$ is a kernel function defined as follows:

$$Kwso(\boldsymbol{x_i}, \boldsymbol{x_j}) \equiv \Phi^T(\boldsymbol{x_i}) \Phi(\boldsymbol{x_j})$$

The Eq. 5 employed in this study, provides the kernel for the Radial Basis Function (RBF):

$$Kwso(\boldsymbol{x_i}, \boldsymbol{x_j}) = \exp\left(-\frac{\|\boldsymbol{x_i} - \boldsymbol{x_j}\|^2}{2\sigma^2}\right) \tag{5}$$

where the kernel width is indicated by the constant $\sigma$. The penalty or regularization parameter, $\sigma$, also affects the trade-off between the slack variable penalty and the size of the margin. In order to improve the "approximating function" known as selection technique, these parameters are set. SVM was used to analyze retrieved feature data sets after the collected parameters were supplied into the kernel. Figure 1 showed the block diagram for the system that was created.

### 3.5 Implementation of the Techniques and Evaluation Measure

MATLAB 2016a was used to create GUI. By analyzing the sensitivity, accuracy, average recognition time, specificity and FPR, the examined Gender classification applying WSO-SVM and SVM was evaluated for performance.

Algorithm 1: expressed the White Shark Optimizer Support Vector Machine Algorithm.

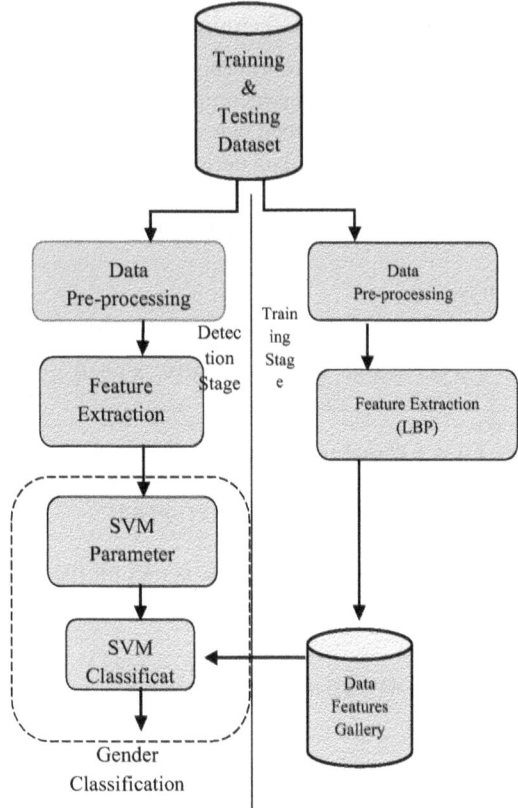

**Fig. 1.** Block diagram of WSO-SVM and SVM techniques

---

**Algorithm 1: White Shark Optimizer Support Vector Machine Algorithm**

INPUT: Input the SVM kernel functions

Step 2: Initialize the parameters of WSO

Step 3: Randomly generate the initial positions of WSO

Step 4: Initialize the velocity of the initial population

Step 5: Evaluate the position of the initial population

Step 6:  while (k<K) do

Update the parameters $v$, $p_1$, $p_2$, $\mu$, $a$, b, $w_o$, f, $m_v$ and $s_s$ using
$v = [n \times rand(1, n)] + 1$ where $rand(1, n)$ is a vector of random numbers generated with a uniform distribution in the range [0, 1].

$p_1 = p_{max} + (p_{max} - p_{min}) \times e^{-(4k/K)^2}$

$p_2 = p_{min} + (p_{max} - p_{min}) \times e^{-(4k/K)^2}$

Where $k$ and $K$ stand for the current and maximum number of iterations, respectively, $p_{min}$ and $p_{max}$ represent the initial and subordinate velocities.

$$\mu = \frac{2}{|2 - \tau - \sqrt{\tau^2 - 4\tau}|}$$

Where $\tau$ denotes the acceleration coefficient which is equal to 4.125.

$b = sgn(w_k^i - l) < 0$

$w_o = \oplus (a, b)$

Where $\oplus$ is a bit-wise XOR operation.

$$f = f_{min} + \frac{f_{max} - f_{min}}{f_{max} + f_{min}}$$

Where $f_{max}$ and $f_{max}$ denote the minimum and maximum frequencies

$$m_v = \frac{1}{(a_o + e^{(k/2)-k)/a_1})}$$

$s_s = |1 - e^{(-a_2 \times \frac{k}{K})}|$

Where $a_2$ is a positive constant utilized to control exploration and exploitation behaviors.

Step 7: For j=1 to n do

$v_{t+1}^j = \mu[v_k^i + p_1([w_{gbest_k} - w_k^i] \times c_1 + p_2([w_{best}^{v_k^i} - w_k^i] \times c_2]$

End for

Step 8:  For i=1 to n do

if $rand < m_v$ then

$$w_{k+1}^i = w_k^i \cdot \neg \oplus w_o + u.a + l.b$$

Else

$$w_{k+1}^i = w_k^i + v_k^i/f$$

End if

End for

Step 9:  For i=1 to n do

if $rand < s_v$ then

$$\overrightarrow{D_w} = |rand \times (w_{gbest_k} - w_k^i)|$$

If i=1 then

$$w_{k+1}^i = w_{gbest_k} + r_1\overrightarrow{D_w}sgn(r_2 - 0.5)$$

Else

$$w_{k+1}^i = w_{gbest_k} + r_1\overrightarrow{D_w}sgn(r_2 - 0.5)$$

$w_{k+1}^i = \frac{w_k^i - w_{k+1}^i}{2 \times rand}$

End if

End if

End for

Adjust the position of the SVM kernel functions that proceed beyond the boundary

Evaluate and update the new positions

$$k = k + 1$$

**End while**

Step 10: Output optimal SVM kernel function

---

## 4  Findings and Analysis

This section presents the results acquired by the SVM and WSO-SVM classifiers. The evaluation of the developed technique was conducted using performance measures such as False Positive Rate, Accuracy, Sensitivity, Precision, Specificity, and recognition time (which are denoted as FPR, ACC, SEN, PREC, SPEC and time respectively). All performance measures were analyzed using a square dimension pixel resolution, with thresholds of 0.13, 0.30, 0.40, and 0.75.

The results obtained using the SVM technique, as shown in Table 1 at the optimal threshold of 0.75, reveal that SVM achieved the following; accuracy 87.00%, Specificity 82.14%, FPR 17.86%, Sensitivity 88.89%, Precision 92.75%, and with a recognition time of 73.12 s. While The results obtained using the SVM technique, as shown in Table 2 and Fig. 3 at the optimal threshold of 0.75, reveal that WSO-SVM achieved the following; accuracy 93.00%, FPR 7.14%, Sensitivity 93.06%, Specificity 92.86%, Precision 9.10%, and a recognition time of 45.83 s (Fig. 2).

**Table 1.**  Result of the SVM for Gendal Classification

| TP | FN | FP | TN | FPR (%) | SEN (%) | SPEC (%) | PREC (%) | ACC (%) | Time (sec) | Threshold |
|----|----|----|----|---------|---------|----------|----------|---------|------------|-----------|
| 67 | 5  | 12 | 16 | 42.86 | 93.06 | 57.14 | 84.81 | 83.00 | 74.30 | 0.2 |
| 66 | 6  | 10 | 18 | 35.71 | 91.67 | 64.29 | 86.84 | 84.00 | 72.03 | 0.35 |
| 65 | 7  | 8  | 20 | 28.57 | 90.28 | 71.43 | 89.04 | 85.00 | 75.09 | 0.5 |
| 64 | 8  | 5  | 23 | 17.86 | 88.89 | 82.14 | 92.75 | 87.00 | 73.12 | 0.75 |

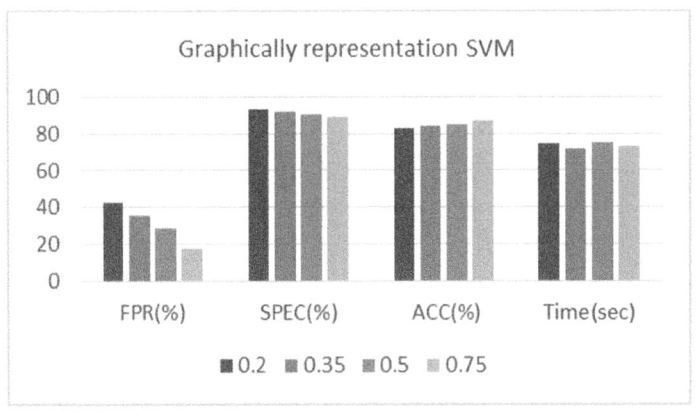

**Fig. 2.**  Graphically representation SVM Results

Considering the findings, it becomes evident that WSO-SVM outperforms the standard SVM in terms of accuracy, boasting a notable reduction in false positives without

**Table 2.** Result of the WSO-SVM for Gendal Classification

| TP | FN | FP | TN | FPR (%) | SEN (%) | SPEC (%) | PREC (%) | ACC (%) | Time (sec) | Threshold |
|----|----|----|----|---------|---------|----------|----------|---------|-----------|-----------|
| 70 | 2 | 10 | 18 | 35.71 | 97.22 | 64.29 | 87.50 | 88.00 | 47.49 | 0.2 |
| 69 | 3 | 7 | 21 | 25.00 | 95.83 | 75.00 | 90.79 | 90.00 | 48.41 | 0.4 |
| 68 | 4 | 4 | 24 | 14.29 | 94.44 | 85.71 | 94.44 | 92.00 | 46.69 | 0.5 |
| 67 | 5 | 2 | 26 | 7.14 | 93.06 | 92.86 | 97.10 | 93.00 | 45.83 | 0.75 |

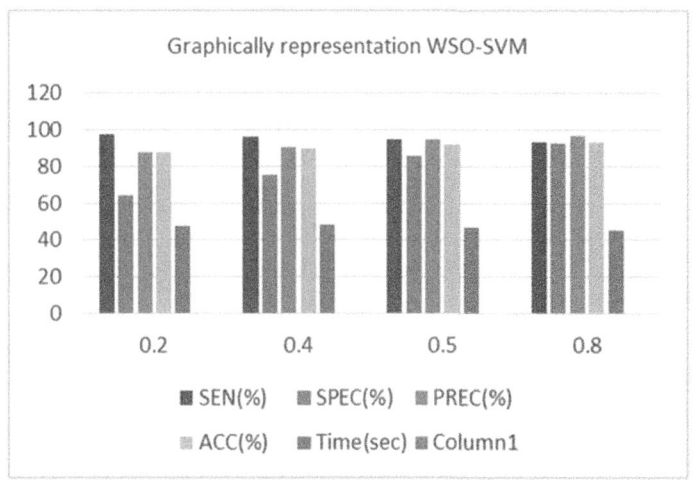

**Fig. 3.** Graphically representation WSO-SVM

compromising recognition speed. This achievement is attributed to the efficient selection of optimal parameters like the kernel function and penalty factor. Consequently, WSO-SVM demonstrates enhanced accuracy and a lower false positive rate. Moreover, the optimization of SVM parameters through WSO proves to be a substantial contributor to improving recognition rates and significantly reducing computational time. These results align with the findings of other researchers in the field such as [16, 17, 20].

## 5    Conclusion and Recommendations

In this paper, WSO has shown promising results in optimizing SVM hyperparameters for gender identification in videos. By efficiently exploring the search space, WSO can find optimal hyperparameter configurations that maximize the accuracy of gender classification. A popular ML approach named SVMs can be applied to classification and regression applications. In order to locate a hyperplane that divides two classes of data with SVMs explore all potential hyperplanes to find the largest margin, which is the distance between the hyperplane and the closest points in each class. SVMs are a strong method, however depending on the kernel function and regularization parameter that are used, they may be sensitive to the choice of hyperparameters. This is where optimization algorithms such as the WSO can be useful.

# References

1. Al_Dujaili, M.J., Salim ALRikabi, H.T., Niama ALRubeei, I.R.: Gender recognition of human from face images using multi-class support vector machine (SVM) classifiers. International Journal of Interactive Mobile Technologies, **17**(8) (2023)
2. Tareef, A., Al-Dmour, H., Al-Sarayreh, A.: An automated deep learning framework for human identity and gender detection. J. Advances in Information Technol. **14**(1) (2023)
3. Roy, A., Chakraborty, S.: Support vector machine in structural reliability analysis: a review. Reliability Engineering & System Safety 109126 (2023)
4. Adhinata F.D., Junaidi, A.: Gender classification on video using facenet algorithm and supervised machine learning. Int. J. Computing and Digital Systems **11**(1), 199–208 (2022)
5. Guo, H., Zhang, Z., Wang, L., Liu, Z.: Gender recognition from video sequences using fusion of handcrafted and deep features. Multimedia Tools and Appl. **77**(16), 21393–21409 (2018)
6. Jaiswal, A., Valiati, J.F., Silla, C.N.: Facial landmarks-based gender recognition from videos in motion. In: 2018 IEEE International Conference on Systems, Man, and Cybernetics (SMC), Miyazaki, Japan, pp. 4085–4090 (2018)
7. Chen, J., Liu, S., Chen, Z.: Gender classification in live videos. Proceedings - International Conference on Image Processing, ICIP, pp. 1602–1606 (2018)
8. Li, J., Wu, Y., Chen, Q., Wu, C.: Gender recognition from video sequences using visual attention mechanism. IEEE Trans. Circuits Syst. Video Technol. **29**(4), 1179–1191 (2019)
9. Tan, F., Ooi, B.C., Isa, D.: Automatic gender classification from video sequences. J. Vis. Commun. Image Represent. **60**, 273–286 (2019)
10. Smith, A., Lee, J., Kim, B.: Optimizing support vector machines for gender classification with white shark optimization. IEEE Trans. Evol. Comput. **24**(4), 666–679 (2020)
11. Lee, C., Park, K.: Video-based gender classification using convolutional neural network features and long short-term memory networks. Appl. Sci. **11**(3), 1220 (2021)
12. Wu, Z., Chen, W., Huang, J.: An Effective Gender Classification Framework for Facial Video Based on Optimized Support Vector Machine. Advance Online Publication, Applied Intelligence (2022)
13. Barnouti, N.H.: Improve face recognition rate using different image pre-processing techniques. American J. Eng. Research (AJER) **5**(4), 46–53 (2016)
14. Saravanan, C.: Color image to grayscale image conversion. In: 2010 Second International Conference on Computer Engineering and Applications, 2, pp. 196–199 (2010). IEEE
15. Tan, T., Zhang, X., Sun, Z., Zhang, H.: Noisy iris image matching by using multiple cues. Pattern Recogn. Lett. **33**(8), 970–977 (2012)
16. Houssein, E.H., Hosney, M.E., Oliva, D., Mohamed, W.M., Hassaballah, M.: A novel hybrid Harris hawks optimization and support vector machines for drug design and discovery. Comput. Chem. Eng. **133**, 106656 (2020)
17. Oyekunle, D.O., et al.: Artificial neural network algorithm in nutritional assessment: implication for machine learning prediction in nutritional assessments. In: Papadopoulou, P., Lytras, M., Konstantinopoulou, S. (eds.), Precision Health in the Digital Age: Harnessing AI for Personalized Care, pp. 253–276 (2025). IGI Global Scientific Publishing. https://doi.org/10.4018/979-8-3693-4422-4.ch013
18. Ajagbe, S.A., Adegun, A.A., Mudali, P., Adigun, M.O.: Performance of machine learning models for pandemic detection using COVID-19 dataset. 2023 IEEE AFRICON, pp. 1–6 (2023). Nairobi, Kenya: IEEE. https://doi.org/10.1109/AFRICON55910.2023.10293525

19. Ipeayeda, F.W., Oyediran, M.O., Ajagbe, S.A., Jooda, J.O., Adigun, M.O.: Optimized gravitational search algorithm for feature fusion in a multimodal biometric system. Results in Eng. **20**(3), 101573 (2023)
20. Sowmya, R., Kumar, T.A., Rajmohan, R., Kanimozhi, P., Ananth, C., Ajagbe, S.A.: A brief survey on recommendation system for a gradient classifier based inadequate approach system. Middle East Journal of Applied Science & Technology (MEJAST) **6**(2), 1–8 (2023)

# Optimization-Improved Genetic Algorithms and Advanced Classification Techniques for Efficient Big Data Analysis

Tolulope Olufemi[1]([✉]), Wilson Sakpere[1], and Chinonyelum Vivian Nwufoh[2]

[1] Department of Computer Science, Lead City University, Ibadan, Nigeria
Tolubiks67@gmail.com, Sakpere.wilson@lcu.edu.ng
[2] Computer Science Department, Federal College of Animal Health and Production Technology, Ibadan, Nigeria

**Abstract.** The exponential rise of digital data presents significant data acquisition and evaluation challenges. Efficient techniques are needed to handle the large and complex datasets in today's interconnected society. Traditional methods often struggle to derive meaningful insights from these vast data sets. We propose an Improved Genetic Algorithm (I-GA) integrated with a Support Vector Machine (SVM) and k-nearest Neighbors (kNN). This combination aims to efficiently extract features and accurately classify data from the CICIDS2017 dataset. The I-GA optimizes feature selection, while SVM and kNN handle the high-dimensional data classification. The I-GA-kNN model achieved superior performance with an accuracy of 97.71% and an F1 score of 97.53%. It outper- formed the I-GA-SVM model, which had an accuracy of 88.98% and an F1 score of 88.49%. The I-GA optimization process effectively reduces computational load, making it suitable for real-time applications. The hybrid I-GA approach significantly improves classification accuracy and efficiency. This makes it ideal for real-time applications by reducing computational overhead and enhancing an alytical dependability. The results underscore the I-GA algorithm's capacity to augment the efficacy of diverse classifiers in classification endeavours. Our study demonstrates that the I-GA, combined with SVM and kNN, enhances classifier performance. This method offers a robust solution for extensive data analysis, with potential for further development and application. Future research should explore integrating deep learning techniques to improve accuracy and applicability across different fields.

**Keywords:** Machine learning · Intrusion detection system · Optimization · Genetic algorithm · Classification

## 1 Introduction

The issue of cyber-security and safeguarding against various cyber-attacks has emerged as a pressing concern in recent times [1]. The primary factor contributing to this phenomenon is the significant expansion of computer networks and the extensive array of

© ICST Institute for Computer Sciences, Social Informatics and Telecommunications Engineering 2026
Published by Springer Nature Switzerland AG 2026. All Rights Reserved
J. B. Awotunde et al. (Eds.): AFRICATEK 2024, LNICST 618, pp. 132–148, 2026.
https://doi.org/10.1007/978-3-031-93557-2_9

pertinent applications used by people or collectives for personal or commercial purposes, particularly with the widespread adoption of the Internet of Things (IoT) [2]. Cyber-attacks have been shown to result in significant harm and substantial financial repercussions inside extensive network systems [2]. The current solutions, such as hardware and software firewalls, user authentication, and data encryption methods, are inadequate in addressing the impending demand and are regrettably incapable of adequately safeguarding computer networks from various cyber-attacks. The existing conventional security structures are insufficient in providing enough protection due to rapid and extensive advancements in infiltration methods [3–6]. A firewall only governs the regulation of network-to-network access, hence serving as a mechanism to impede inter-network connectivity. However, it fails to provide any indication of an internal breach. Implementing precise defensive tools, such as an ML-driven IDS, enhances the system's security.

An IDS monitors a network or computer system for any signs of intrusion or policy breaches. An IDS is a program that monitors a network or system during regular use to spot any malicious or suspicious behaviour. Its primary function is identifying security incidents, such as denial-of-service (DoS) attacks, that may occur on a network [7]. Unauthorized system activity, such as illegal access, modification, and destruction, may be detected determined, and managed using an intrusion detection system [8–10]. The user's perspective may be used to categorize intrusion detection systems into various groups. For instance, intrusion detection systems might be host-based or network-based [2]. Methods might vary from using a single computer to using a global network. A host-based intrusion detection system (HIDS) is set up on a specific machine, and it monitors the system files to see if anything out of the ordinary has happened.

In contrast, a network intrusion detection system (NIDS) analyzes network traffic to spot and stop potentially harmful intrusions. In contrast, the area of detection is home to two separate approaches: signature-based detection and anomaly-based detection [2, 11]. The signature-based IDS analyses the network route bytes. Analysis and remediation based on malware's malicious instruction sequences is possible. Antiviral software's emergence involves identifying and detecting specific groupings or patterns, often known as signatures. Signature-based IDS are limited in identifying assaults that lack a preexisting pattern. The anomaly-based IDS analyzes the network's activity and identifies patterns, subsequently generating a data-driven model to establish a profile of anticipated behaviour. Consequently, it can detect any deviations or abnormalities that may occur [11]. The primary advantage of using an anomaly-based IDS is its ability to detect and track contemporary, novel, and previously unobserved irregularities or cyber-attacks, such as denial-of-service incidents.

Examining distinct incident patterns and then using cybersecurity data to forecast potential risks is necessary to build computational methodologies for identifying diverse cyber-attacks. The technology is often called a data-driven intelligent IDS [2]. A comprehensive understanding of artificial intelligence, namely ML methodologies, is necessary to construct a data-centric intrusion detection model. However, the accurate prediction of cyber-attacks using ML techniques poses challenges owing to the varying outcomes of numerous classifiers in different situations, which are influenced by the properties of the data [12]. In light of this rationale, we examine two ML algorithms in the context of intrusion detection systems, focusing on their application in the use of cyber-security data. To fulfil this objective, two widely used machine learning classification methods, namely SVM and kNN, are used to provide intelligent functionalities within the field of cyber-security, explicitly focusing on intrusion detection. The efficacy of the proposed approach is assessed via a series of experiments conducted on cyber-security datasets, including two distinct classes of traffic. Effectiveness is evaluated by quantifying performance measures such as precision, recall, f1-score, and accuracy for the machine learning-based IDS models.

The remaining part of the article is structured as follows: section 2 provides an overview of the current literature on the subject matter. Section 3 provides a comprehensive examination of the dataset and proposed framework. The findings are further discussed in Sect. 4, while the primary conclusions are outlined in Sect. 5.

## 2   Related Works

A classifier called an Incremental Learning Algorithm using an SVM has been introduced by Myint and Meesad [13]. SVM enables the generation of predictions, streamlining the method's computational complexity and calculation requirements. This approach also minimizes the time required for recurrent training of the dataset and lowers the occurrence of errors within the dataset. The KDD Cup99 dataset is used to evaluate the system's performance. The suggested approach can predict 41 attributes from the incoming dataset. Farnaaz and Jabbar presented a model using the intrusion detection RF classifier [14]. Hence, Random Forest (RF) is used as an ensemble classifier, exhibiting superior discriminatory capabilities compared to conventional classifiers in identifying assaults. The dataset utilized for the implementation is NSL-KDD, and the suggested model has shown a successful performance with a high detection rate and a low false alarm rate, as indicated by reference [15].

Peddabachigari et al. (2004) have introduced STL-IDS, an efficient deep-learning technique to facilitate self-learning. Chowdhuri et al. proposed a framework [17] that can potentially be used for interactive learning and size reduction. It was necessary to provide sufficient time for preparation and testing to enhance the predictive accuracy of SVM. The existing solution effectively enhances the identification of network intrusion. Furthermore, the intrusion detection decision tree proposed by Chandre et al. [18] has undergone testing. The 1998 DARPA dataset evaluated intrusion detection, comparing the decision-based approach with traditional models. The findings indicate that the decision-based system exhibited superior accuracy in detecting intrusions. Once again, the results suggest that the test duraions and training times are more significant than the SVM. Muna and colleagues (2018) have presented a NIDS based on the Naïve Bayes paradigm.

The selected approach has exhibited superior efficacy regarding false-positive rates, computational efficiency, and cost-effectiveness for deploying the KDD Cup 99 dataset. In their study, Muna et al. (2019) introduced a navigation system that relies on the irregularity of the Internet Control System (ICS) and is specifically designed for Industrial Internet Control Systems (IICSs). This system can acquire and process data from Transmission Control Protocol/Internet Protocol (TCP/IP) packets. The proposed approach involves a sequential preparation phase using a feed-forward neural system and deep automated encoder. A comprehensive input system development is also nec essary to evaluate the approach's effectiveness. This evaluation will use two well-established data sets, NSL-KDD and UNSW-NB15, which are well-recognized and com- prehensible in the field. Based on the findings of the test results, it can be inferred that this particular strategy exhibits a superior detection rate and a lower incidence of false positives compared to the other eight ways. Consequently, it is plausible to consider revising the actual IICS requirements [19].

In their study, Shi et al. (2020) introduced an alternative method for simplification in- volving comprehensive training and selecting relevant elements. This technique aims to provide optimal solutions and emphasize essential aspects in the context of traffic arrangements. Moreover, the exploitation of symmetrical vulnerability is used in [21] to exclude extraneous highlights within the dataset of system traffic. One notable aspect that is unveiled by the process of feature age is its association with pertinent dimensional reduction features and the time of selection using deep learning techniques. Weighted Symmetric Complexity is employed to choose the most optimum characteristics by eliminating redundant ones. The proposed strategy has been shown to have a limited impact on the highlighted feature due to actual traffic patterns. Additionally, it has been observed that this approach may effectively address the adverse effects on both the machine learning approaches related to imbalanced multi-class classification and the dispersion of ideas [22].

In the realm of IDS research and development, the following ML approaches have been widely employed: The following ML algorithms were used in the study: Random Forest (RF) [23], kNN [24], SVM [25, 26], Decision Tree (DT) [27], Artificial Neural Networks (ANNs) [28], and Naive Bayes (NB) [13]. This article focuses on enhancing the genetic algorithm by integrating two machine learning (ML) techniques. This study assesses two widely used machine learning models: SVM and kNN. In this study, the CICIDS2017 Dataset is used to train our ML models. The performance of each model is then evaluated based on the findings obtained from the CICIDS2017 Dataset.

## 3   Materials and Methods

The methodologies and procedures that will be used to complete this study have been outlined in this section.

### 3.1   Description of Dataset

To efficiently identify anonymous intrusions, a network intrusion detection system must have regularly updated data to train the model. The publicly available datasets KDD-CUP99 and DARPA98/99 exhibit shortcomings in their ability to effectively incorporate and update information on new attack patterns. The CICIDS 2017 dataset includes both actual network traffic and a variety of widespread attacks that closely resemble real-world data. These data are stored in CSV format. In addition, the CIC Flow Meter facilitates the organization of network traffic analysis by categorizing flows according to various attributes such as time stamps, protocols, ports, source IPs, and destination IPs.

Additionally, this study encompasses the whole of network traffic, providing a compreensive data capture. It also considers a wide range of attack types, including webbased attacks, brute force attacks, DoS attacks, DDoS attacks, infiltration attacks, bot attacks, and scan attacks. Furthermore, this study acknowledges the heterogeneity of the collected data, which previous datasets have not addressed well. In addition, the dataset offers 84 attributes, including four categorical columns. 11 essential criteria play a significant role in developing a dependable dataset. These requirements include a fully configured network, a labelled dataset, interaction, and traffic. Data collection is now possible with the use of available protocols. Review and Criticism of Variability in Data, Features, and Metadata

## 3.2  Preprocessing of Dataset

The suggested architecture gathers information from the publicly available dataset, namely CICIDS 2017. Label encoders are then assigned values to the data's category characteristics. Since strings are not usable by any machine-learning-based technique, the label encoder transforms them into a numerical representation. Since using all of the data's features/parameters while creating the model is unnecessary, we employ the I-GA method to select the most useful ones. Next, we split this pool of information into training and test sets. SVM and kNN Models are then built based on the training data. Since it is unnecessary to include all data characteristics while constructing the model, I-GA is used to choose some of the best features. Data for training consists of 25192 rows and 42 columns, whereas data for testing consists of 22544 rows and 41 columns. Out of a possible 41 features, only 15. Next, we split this pool of information into training and test sets. Then, SVM and kNN models are constructed based on the training data. SVM and kNN fall under supervised learning methods, meaning they need training data to build a model, which is then used to evaluate test data. The training model is given test data to assess whether or not it is malicious, and if the data fits the profile of an attack, the training model will provide the classification of the attack. Normal 13449 and Anomaly 11743 are the two data types in the CICIDS2017 dataset.

## 3.3  Proposed Models

In this study, three models were used for the experimentation. The I-GA was used for feature selection, while SVM and KNN models were employed for the classification tasks. Each of the models is presented as follows:

**Improved Genetic Algorithm (I-GA)**
The key ideas and implementation strategies of an improved GA are carried out in this work, as shown in Fig. 1, to tackle the problem of GA having slow iteration with convergence speed and falling into the local optimum prematurely when handling complicated issues. Hence, a Lévy-GA is proposed in this study.

In this work, Algorithm 1 combines the principles of Levy Flight and Generic Algorithm to create a novel algorithm called I-GA. The method presented in this study integrates components from Genetic Algorithms and Levy flying to achieve optimization objectives. The algorithm employs genetic operators such as crossover, mutation, and

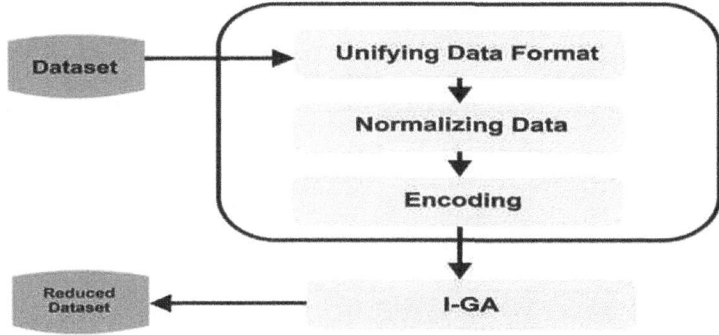

**Fig. 1.** Improved Generic Algorithm (I-GA) Model

Levy flight to systematically explore the search space and identify the optimal answer. It is necessary to obtain more clarity on the specifics of the parameters of the Genetic Algorithm and the fitness evaluation process to have a comprehensive understanding of the algorithm's functioning. Technique 1 is an optimization technique that utilizes a hybrid approach by combining Genetic Algorithms (GAs) with Levy flight. The algorithm starts by generating an initial population of people according to predetermined genetic algorithm parameters. The fitness of all individuals within the population is validated, and the most optimal solution discovered so far is documented. After that, the algorithm proceeds into a loop until it encounters a halting requirement. In each iteration of the loop, a Levy flight process is included. The Levy fly is a stochastic process that enhances the efficiency of search space exploration.

In the Levy flight process context, selecting parents from the population is followed by applying crossover and mutation procedures to create offspring. The fitness of the offspring is assessed and confirmed, after which they are included in the population. The population is partitioned into four groups following the Levy flight process. The updating of particle placements follows the determination of fitness values for individuals within the population. Each group's population and global optimum solution are updated following the ideal criteria. The method, after that, proceeds to go through another loop for each kth generation. Communication occurs among the various groups, and the most optimal Lévy flight solution from each group is selected. As mentioned earlier, the procedure is iterated until the task is fully accomplished. The method terminates the Levy flight procedure and outputs the optimal solution.

Figure 2 represents the iterative process of the Improved Genetic Algorithm. It starts with initializing the population, followed by selection, crossover, mutation, and fitness Evaluation. The process continues until a termination condition is met, at which point the best solution is returned. If the termination condition is unmet, the algorithm loops back to the initialization step and repeats the process.

The flowchart process is discussed more as follows:

- Initialize: This is the starting point of the algorithm. It involves setting up the initial population, which consists of a set of individuals representing potential solutions.

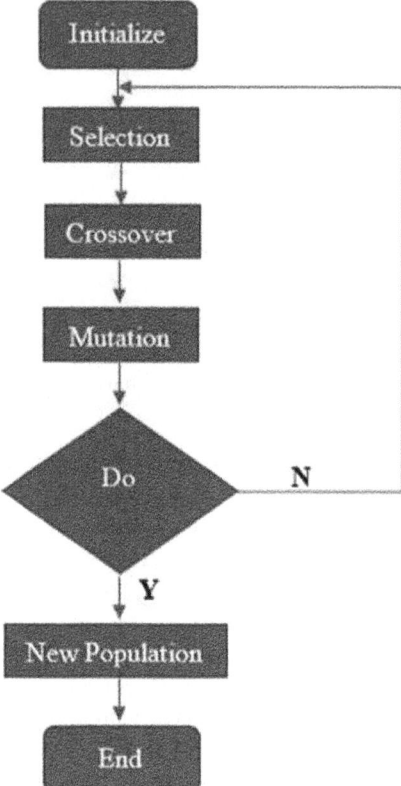

**Fig. 2.** Flowchart for I-GA

- Selection: The selection phase involves applying a method to the existing population to identify and pick individuals for reproduction, considering their fitness level. The likelihood of selection is higher for individuals with more excellent fitness since their increased probability of transmitting their genetic material enhances their reproductive success.
- The crossover process involves the chosen individuals undergoing genetic recombination, resulting in the creation of novel offspring. As mentioned earlier, the procedure emulates the phenomenon of mating and recombination seen in natural evolution.
- Mutation is crucial in the genetic algorithm process after the crossover operation. Its purpose is to create random alterations in the offspring's genetic material. Mutation helps maintain genetic diversity and allows for exploring new solution spaces.
- Do: This step represents the evaluation of the fitness of the newly generated offspring. Everyone's fitness is assessed based on a predefined fitness function or objective.
- If (yes): If the termination condition has been fulfilled, the algorithm proceeds to a decision point to assess the situation. Once the termination condition is met, such as reaching a desired fitness level or the maximum number of generations, the algorithm moves to the subsequent phase.

- New Population: The algorithm concludes and outputs the optimal answer if the termination condition is satisfied. Alternatively, a novel population is established by substituting the existing population with the progeny produced in the preceding iterations.
- Else: Alternatively, if the termination condition is not satisfied, the algorithm reverts to the first step, starting from the Initialize phase. The repetitive nature of the method permits the repetition of selection, crossover, mutation, and assessment steps until the termination condition is met.
- End: This point shows the conclusion of the algorithm. The termination condition is considered satisfied when the algorithm returns the best answer or reaches a certain maximum number of iterations.

**Support Vector Machine**

Prediction and classification are among the many SVM applications, and they are a kind of monitored learning. The SVM divides the two groups relatively by locating the hyperplane to improve prediction and classification. It's a binary classification; thus, it may separate groups in a dimensional space. Each category is further subdivided into normal and anomalous subtypes. Information is represented by a $+1$ and a $-1$. The primary goal of an assist vector machine is to locate the line that will maximize the difference in earnings between the two groups.

Vladimir Vapnik invented the SVM in 1995. To construct an algorithm that predicts many types of outcomes, such as classification, regression, and outlier identification, SVM is an ML algorithm. It's most used to analyze small and medium-sized datasets. SVMs have a generalization approach based on structural risk minimization that allows them to capture vast feature spaces (SRM). The Radial Basis Function (RBF) is proposed as the kernel of a Support Vector Machine (SVM) for classification. Two real-valued parameters, C and, must be optimized for the RBF kernel. This parameter trades the potential for training, for example, misclassification, for the ease with which the decision surface can be understood. The value determines how far an example can spread its impact. It was first scaled to values between zero and one for all feature vectors. In the second stage, a grid search process determines the best C and parameters for the classification. The parameters were scaled on an exponential scale in the first stage, and the results were fine-tuned around the parameter values that led to the best classification in the second step. The Leave-one-Out method is used to cross-validate each C and selection to generalize the classification findings and boost the system's dependability. It's also necessary to ensure that both training data sets are evenly sized by oversampling the smaller ones.

The SVM Algorithm applies a search process to find the best solution (lair) for the SVM classification problem. It utilizes either a Brownian walk or a levy walk to explore the search space and validate the fitness of each solution. The algorithm iterates until a stopping criterion is reached, and the best solution found is used to train an SVM classifier. By optimizing the selection of the best lair, the algorithm aims to improve the performance of the SVM classifier in classification tasks.

**k Nearest Neighbor**

Regarding statistical discrimination, the kNN algorithm is the most straightforward and user-friendly. When utilizing this strategy, a new observation is produced in the group of observations closest to the latest observation using variables. Distance measurements are used to determine similarity. A technique known as "kNN imputation" uses the kNN algorithm to find as many cases as possible that are statistically comparable to the missing data row. The kNNs were utilized to calculate an average of the missing data variables. Missing data were imputed using the five persons closest to the researcher in the current study (k = 5).

KNN Algorithm performs a classification task based on the nearest neighbours of a test data point. It calculates the distances between the test and known data points, sorts them in ascending order, and selects the k nearest neighbours. If there are equidistant samples, the algorithm handles them using specific equations. Finally, it assigns a predicted classification label to the test data point based on the majority class among the k nearest neighbours. The algorithm repeats this process until a termination condition is met. KNN is a simple yet effective algorithm for classification tasks, relying on the principle that similar data points tend to belong to the same class.

### 3.4  Data Processing

The data employed for experimentation contains several instances of The Jupyter Notebook platform used to implement this investigation. To run the code in Jupyter, you must first call the library involved, converting any dataset to '.csv' before calling it in the code using df = pd.read CSV('Kaggle.CSV).

Data is used to describe datasets in the application for calculating statistical statistics from a data frame's numerical values, such as mean, percentile, and standard deviation (std). The training data has 25192 rows & 42 columns, and the Testing data has 22544 rows & 41 columns.

Machine learning frequently divides data into train, test, and evaluation sets. The data were split into training and testing subsets for the standard scaler method to standardize the data and the label encoder for target data in the dataset. The training set was utilized as a basis for evaluation to fit the model and conduct testing. Table 1 shows the result obtained using the I-GA method for reduced features.

Testing data has 22544 rows & 41 columns.
Normal 13449
anomaly 11743
Name: class, dtype: inte4

**Table 1.** Reduced Data

| Rows | Columns |
|------|---------|
| 25192 | 15 |

This study's reduction of data, optimization, classification, and evaluation outcomes was made using Python, Google Collab, and Jupyter Notebook.

## 4    Results and Discussion

In this section, the results obtained from the experimentation performed are discussed. Two classification methods were implemented. I-GA with SVM and I-GA with kNN.

### 4.1   I-GA Subset (Reduced Dataset)

The optimization results obtained using the reduced data from the I-GA subset are of significant interest. By applying the I-GA in combination with dimensionality reduction techniques, an optimal subset of features that can effectively represent the original data while minimizing redundancy and noise is actualized. The I-GA algorithm works by iteratively evolving a population of candidate solutions, evaluating their fitness based on a predefined objective function, and applying genetic operators such as selection, crossover, and mutation to generate new candidate solutions. Through this iterative process, the algorithm searches for an optimal subset of features that maximizes the performance of a given task or model. The outcomes of the I-GA optimization model are depicted in Fig. 3, where the result generated comes in the form of a set of features selected for intrusion detection using the Improved GA.

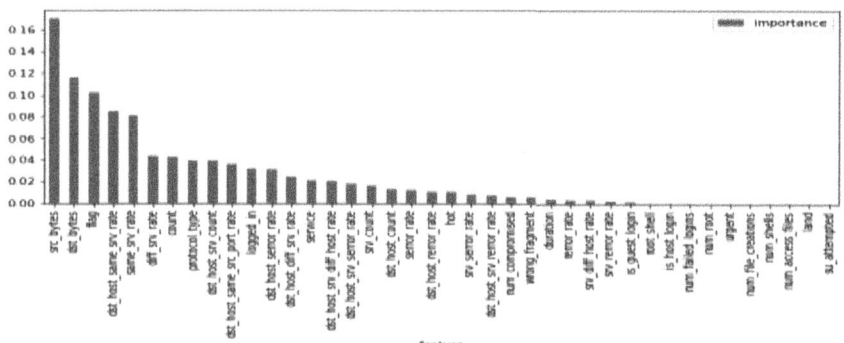

**Fig. 3.** I-GA Optimization Result (Reduced Data)

### 4.2   Classification Results

This section analyses the model's performance and accuracy in predicting the class labels of previously unknown data. The outcomes are often shown as evaluation metrics that appraise various facets of the model's performance. The current work utilizes the confusion matrix to depict the classification results of the models, using two machine learning techniques, namely SVM and kNN. This discussion focuses on the significance of TP (True Positive), TN (True Negative), FN (False Negative), and FP (False Positive) in the context being examined.

The confusion matrices for the I-GA with SVM and K-NN algorithms are shown in Figs. 4 and 5, respectively. The values inside these matrices are as follows: For I-GA-SVM, the TP value is 3202, the TN value is 3523, the FP value is 296, and the FN value is 537. For I-GA-kNN, the TP value is 3420, the TN value is 3965, the FP value is 78, and the FN value is 95. Using the I-GA in conjunction with classifiers, such as SVM and kNN, yields significant findings about the efficacy and efficiency of this hybrid methodology in the context of classification problems.

In the context of the I-GA-SVM, the findings indicate that the technique substantially enhances the classification accuracy by optimizing the SVM parameters. The distribution of TP, TN, FP, and FN is shown in the confusion matrix (Fig. 4). For example, based on the given values of TP = 3202, TN = 3523, FP = 296, and FN = 537, it can be shown that the I-GA-SVM model has effectively detected a substantial number of positive cases and minimized misclassifications. This finding suggests that the process of I-GA optimization has had a significant role in improving the performance of the SVM classifier.

Similarly, the I-GA with KNN classifier (as seen in Fig. 5) demonstrates a robust classification performance, characterized by elevated TP and TN values of 3420 and 3965, respectively, with comparably lower FP and FN values of 78 and 95. As mentioned earlier, the observation highlights the efficacy of the I-GA method in enhancing precision and mitigating the occurrence of FP and FN outcomes in the KNN classifier. Using the optimized parameter values acquired by the I-GA has led to developing a classification model with enhanced robustness and accuracy.

The observed uniform improvement in classification performance across several classifiers underscores the efficacy and broad applicability of the I-GA methodology. The effectiveness of using I-GA in conjunction with classifiers may be ascribed to the algorithm's capacity to systematically investigate and use the search space to identify each classifier's most advantageous parameter configurations. The I-GA technique leverages the complementary attributes of the genetic algorithm and classifiers to boost the classifier's performance. This is achieved by optimizing the classifier's parameters, resulting in improved accuracy and more excellent predictive capabilities.

The confusion matrix facilitates the assessment of classification performance beyond mere accuracy. This analysis offers valuable information into the model's efficacy in accurately discerning positive and negative occurrences and the prevalence of misclassifications. Comprehending the strengths and limitations of the I-GA with classifiers strategy is contingent upon acquiring this essential information, which may provide valuable insights for enhancing and refining the approach.

The outcomes obtained via the I-GA method's use with classifiers such as SVM and kNN demonstrate the I-GA method's efficacy in enhancing classifier performance and augmenting classification accuracy. The confusion matrices show that the obtained outcomes demonstrate the I-GA methodology's efficacy in correctly discerning and categorizing positive and adverse events. As mentioned earlier, the results underscore the I-GA algorithm's capacity as a robust instrument for augmenting the efficacy of diverse classifiers in classification endeavours.

We may compute diverse evaluation metrics to evaluate the I-GA-SVM classifier's performance using the given data. Standard metrics include accuracy, precision, recall, and F1 score. These metrics provide a more comprehensive understanding of the classifier's performance, considering both the true and false predictions.

Figure 6 presents the Receiver Operating Curve (ROC) AUC curve for the I-GA technique with the ML classifiers implemented in this study. The study obtained an AUC score close to 100%.

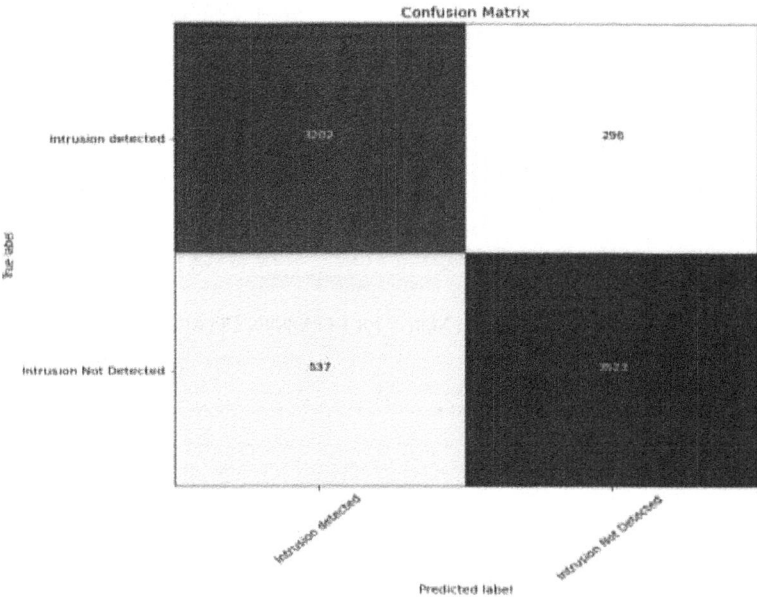

**Fig. 4.** Confusion Matrix for I-GA-SVM Classifier

Table 2 shows the performance evaluation between the two implemented classifiers with the I-GA. Figure 7 shows the bar chart of I-GA with the ML classifiers. It can be discovered from both the table and the figure that I-GA-kNN outperformed the I-GA-SVM in terms of accuracy, sensitivity, specificity, precision and f1-score. I-GA-kNN obtained an accuracy of 97.71%, over 88.98% obtained for I-GA-SVM; a sensitivity of 97.30% over 85.64% obtained for I-GA-SVM. The study also got a precision value of 97.77% for I-GA-kNN over 91.54% for I-GA-SVM. An f1-score value of 97.53% was obtained for I-GA-kNN over that of I-GA-SVM, with a value of 88.49%.

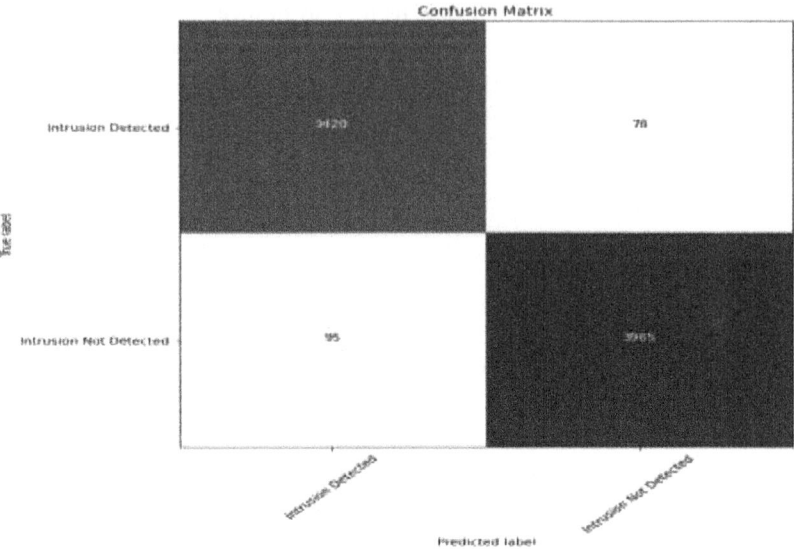

**Fig. 5.** Confusion Matrix for I-GA-kNN Classifier

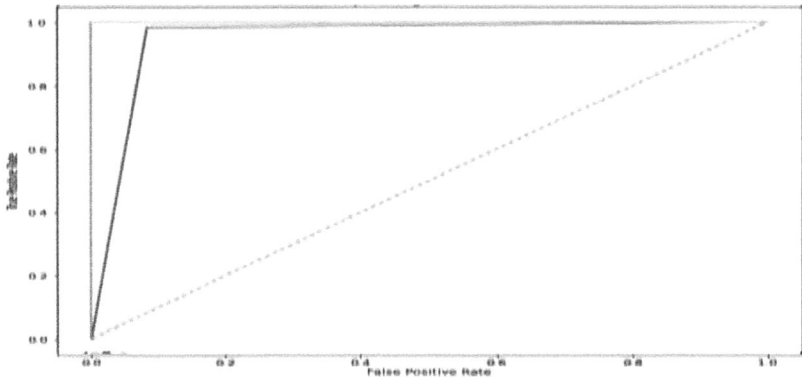

**Fig. 6.** Receiver Operating Curve for I-GA with classifiers

### 4.3  Discussion

The I-GA-SVM model achieved an accuracy of 88.98%, indicating that it correctly classified 88.98% of the instances. The sensitivity (TP) was 85.64%, which means the model successfully identified 85.64% of the positive instances. The specificity (TN) was 92.25%, indicating that the model accurately identified 92.25% of the negative instances. The precision (positive predictive value) was 91.54%, which shows the proportion of correctly predicted positive instances out of all instances predicted as positive. The F1 Score, which considers the balance between precision and sensitivity, was 88.49%.

The I-GA-kNN model showed excellent performance across all metrics. It achieved an accuracy of 97.71%, indicating a high level of correct classifications. The sensitivity

**Table 2.** Evaluation comparison of I-GA-SVM and I-GA-kNN with the classifiers

| | Accuracy ACC = (TP + TN)/(P + N) | Sensitivity TPR = TP/(TP + FN) | Specificity SPC = TP/(FP + TN) | Precision PPV = TP/(TP + FP | F1 Score F1 = 2TP/(2TP + FP + FN) |
|---|---|---|---|---|---|
| I-GA- SVMI- | 88.98 | 85.64 | 92.25 | 91.54 | 88.49 |
| GA-kNN | 97.71 | 97.30 | 98.07 | 97.77 | 97.53 |

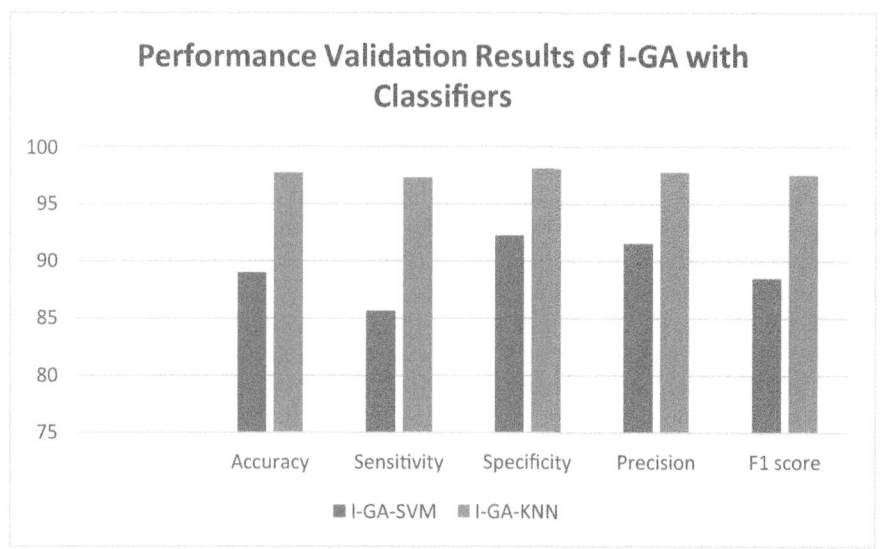

**Fig. 7.** Bar Chart of IGA with the classifiers

was 97.30%, indicating a strong ability to identify positive instances. The specificity was 98.07%, demonstrating a high accuracy in identifying negative instances. The precision was 97.77%, indicating a high proportion of correctly predicted positive instances. The F1 Score was 97.53%, reflecting a harmonious balance between precision and sensitivity.

These results suggest that the I-GA-kNN model outperformed the I-GA-SVM model in terms of classification accuracy, sensitivity, specificity, precision, and F1 Score. The higher accuracy and F1 Score of the I-GA-kNN model indicate its better overall performance in correctly classifying instances and maintaining a balance between precision and sensitivity. While the I-GA-kNN model showed superior performance in this study, the I-GA-SVM model still achieved reasonably good results and may be more suitable for specific scenarios. The I-GA approach combined with both SVM and kNN classifiers demonstrates promising performance in classification tasks, with the I-GA- kNN model showing robust results. These findings highlight the potential of using genetic algorithms to enhance the performance of classifiers in various domains.

## 5    Conclusion

The proposed study introduces an innovative approach to handling the challenges associated with the exponential rise of digital data in today's interconnected society. The researchers employ an improved Genetic Algorithm (I-GA) to efficiently navigate the massive and intricate CICIDS2017 dataset. Traditional methods struggle with extracting insights from large, complex datasets, but the I-GA method significantly enhances this process. The I-GA effectively identifies vital features within the dataset, ensuring crucial information retrieval while minimizing computational resources. The extracted data is classified using SVM and kNN. SVM and kNN, well-known for their ability to deal with high-dimensional data and intricate patterns, successfully classify the information. When the optimized GA is combined with support vector machines and kernel neural networks, a powerful data mining and classification framework is produced. The experimental results prove beyond a reasonable doubt the efficacy of the suggested method. The optimization-enhanced GA is a dramatic improvement over prior methods in terms of both precision and productivity. I-GA not only improves analytical trustworthiness via fine-grained classification, but it also decreases computing burden, making it appropriate for real-time applications. The results reveal that when comparing I-GA-kNN with I-GA-SVM, the former provides a more efficient and wellrounded method for classification tasks, as measured by accuracy, sensitivity, specificity, precision, and F1-score.

The suggested I-GA may be further developed, and hybrid models using deep learning approaches can be explored in future studies to improve accuracy. Responsible and successful deployment of sophisticated machine learning algorithms across domains will need more analysis of real-time applications, creating interactive platforms for expert cooperation, and considering ethical concerns.

## References

1. Ogundokun, R.O., Odusami, M., Sisodia, D.S., Awotunde, J.B., Tiwari, D.P.: A Novel PCA-Logistic regression for intrusion detection system. In: International Conference on Information Systems and Management Science, pp. 575–588. Springer International Publishing, Cham (2022)
2. Mohammad, H., Mohammad, S.R., Helge, J., Iqbal, H.S.: Detecting Anomalies in Blockchain Transactions using Machine Learning Classifiers and Explainability Analysis. Research and Applications, Blockchain ,100207, ISSN 2096-7209 (2024)
3. Mohammadi, S., Mirvaziri, H., Ghazizadeh-Ahsaee, M., Karimipour, H.: Cyber intrusion detection by combined feature selection algorithm. J. Information Security and Appl. **44**, 80–88 (2019)
4. Narayanan, S.L., Kasiselvanathan, M., Gurumoorthy, K.B., Kiruthika, V.:. Particle swarm optimization based artificial neural network (PSO-ANN) model for effective k-barrier count intrusion detection system in WSN. Measurement: Sensors, **29**, 100875 (2023)
5. Tapiador, J.E., Orfila, A., Ribagorda, A., Ramos, B.: Key-recovery attacks on KIDS, a keyed anomaly detection system. IEEE Trans. Dependable Secure Comput. **12**(3), 312–325 (2013)

6.  Tavallaee, M., Stakhanova, N., Ghorbani, A.A.: Toward credible evaluation of anomaly-based intrusion-detection methods. IEEE Transactions on Systems, Man, and Cy bernetics, Part C (Applications and Reviews) **40**(5), 516–524 (2010)
7.  Ogundokun, R.O., Misra, S., Babatunde, A.N., Chockalingam, S.: Cyber intrusion detection system based on machine learning classification approaches. In: 2022 International Conference on Applied Artificial Intelligence (ICAPAI), pp. 1–6 (2022). IEEE
8.  Milenkoski, A., Vieira, M., Kounev, S., Avritzer, A., Payne, B.D.: Evaluating computer intrusion detection systems: a survey of common practices. ACM Computing Surveys (CSUR) **48**(1), 1–41 (2015)
9.  Xin, Y., et al.: Machine learning and deep learning methods for cybersecurity. IEEE Access **6**, 35365–43538 (2018)
10. Aslan, Ö., Aktuğ, S.S., Ozkan-Okay, M., Yilmaz, A.A., Akin, E.: A comprehensive review of cyber security vulnerabilities, threats, attacks, and solutions. Electronics **12**(6), 1333 (2023)
11. Sarker, I.H., Abushark, Y.B., Alsolami, F., Khan, A.I.: Intrudtree: a machine learning-based cyber security intrusion detection model. Symmetry **12**(5), 754 (2020)
12. Sarker, I.H., Kayes, A.S.M., Watters, P.: Effectiveness analysis of machine learning classification models for predicting personalized context-aware smartphone usage. J. Big Data **6**(1), 1–28 (2019)
13. Myint, H.O., Meesad, P.: Incremental learning algorithm based on support vector machine with mahalanobis distance (ISVMM) for intrusion prevention. In: 2009 6th International Conference on Electrical Engineering/Electronics, Computer, Telecommunications and Information Technology, **2**, pp. 630–633 (2009). IEEE
14. Farnaaz, N., Jabbar, M.A.: Random forest modeling for network intrusion detection system. Procedia Computer Science **89**, 213–217 (2016)
15. Al-Qatf, M., Lasheng, Y., Al-Habib, M., Al-Sabahi, K.: Deep learning approach combining sparse autoencoder with SVM for network intrusion detection. IEEE Access **6**, 52843–52856 (2018)
16. Peddabachigari, S., Abraham, A., Thomas, J.: Intrusion detection systems using decision trees and support vector machines. Internat. J. Appl. Sci. Comput. **11**(3), 118–134 (2004)
17. Chowdhuri, S., Das, S.K., Roy, P., Chakraborty, S., Maji, M., Dey, N.: Implementation of a new packet broadcasting algorithm for MIMO equipped Mobile ad-hoc network. In: International Conference on Circuits, Communication, Control and Computing , pp. 372–376 (2014). IEEE
18. Chandre, P.R., Mahalle, P.N., Shinde, G.R.: Deep learning and machine learning techniques for intrusion detection and prevention in wireless sensor networks: comparative study and performance analysis. Design Frameworks for Wireless Networks, pp. 95–120 (2020)
19. Muna, A.H., Moustafa, N., Sitnikova, E.: Identification of malicious activities in industrial internet of things based on deep learning models. J. Information Security and Appl. **41**, 1–11 (2018)
20. Shi, H., Li, H., Zhang, D., Cheng, C., Cao, X.: An efficient feature generation approach based on deep learning and feature selection techniques for traffic classification. Comput. Netw. **132**, 81–98 (2018)
21. Fong, S., Li, J., Song, W., Tian, Y., Wong, R.K., Dey, N.: Predicting unusual energy consumption events from smart home sensor network by data stream mining with misclassified recall. J. Ambient. Intell. Humaniz. Comput. **9**, 1197–1221 (2018)
22. Mukherjee, A., Keshary, V., Pandya, K., Dey, N., Satapathy, S.C.: Flying ad hoc networks: a comprehensive survey. In: Information and Decision Sciences: Proceedings of the 6th International Conference on FICTA, pp. 569–580 (2018). Springer Singapore
23. Qi, Y.: Random forest for bioinformatics. Ensemble machine learning: Methods and applications, pp. 307–323 (2012)

24. Guo, G., Wang, H., Bell, D., Bi, Y., Greer, K.: KNN model-based approach in classification. In: On The Move to Meaningful Internet Systems 2003: CoopIS, DOA, and ODBASE: OTM Confederated International Conferences, CoopIS, DOA, and ODBASE 2003, Catania, Sicily, Italy, November 3-7, 2003. Proceedings, pp. 986–996 (2003). Springer Berlin Heidelberg.
25. Cheong, S., Oh, S.H., Lee, S.Y.: Support vector machines with binary tree architecture for multi-class classification. Neural Information Processing-Letters and Reviews **2**(3), 47–51 (2004)
26. Magán-Carrión, R., Urda, D., Díaz-Cano, I., Dorronsoro, B.: Towards a reliable comparison and evaluation of network intrusion detection systems based on machine learning approaches. Appl. Sci. **10**(5), 1775 (2020)
27. Diao, R., et al.: Decision tree-based online voltage security assessment using PMU measurements. IEEE Trans. Power Syst. **24**(2), 832–839 (2009)
28. Priddy, K.L., Keller, P.E.: Artificial Neural Networks: An Introduction, **68**. SPIE press (2005)

# Health Monitoring System for Underground Miners

Al Fezghari Omar$^{(\boxtimes)}$ and El Azhari Moulay El Hassan

Al Akhawayn University, P.O Box 104, Hassan II Avenue, 53000 Ifrane, Morocco
omar.el.fezghari@gmail.com, m.elazhari@aui.ma

**Abstract.** In spite of the evolution of Moroccan mining industry, underground mines still witness hazardous incidents happening to workers, aggravated by the non-availability of adequate health monitoring systems. This triggers the necessity of developing a solution ensuring workers' safety and allowing prompt intervention in cases of emergency. This paper presents a health monitoring system for underground miners in Morocco. The system provides continuous measurements of vital body signs, namely temperature and heartbeat rate, as well as gas concentration in the mine environment; it then communicates data wirelessly to be displayed on a command station. Particle Photon is used as the processing unit to allow suitable implementation of the system's logic. Pipedream (a platform enabling processing and piping data between apps using manual code development) and Node-RED (an integration for developing simple graphical user interfaces and wiring together hardware devices, online services, and application programming interfaces) are used to trigger events and generate dashboards to monitor miners' health as well as warn the user in case of dangers. The system exhibits instantaneous responses to changes in the measured parameters, proving the functionality of our novel health monitoring system design.

**Keywords:** Heartbeat rate · gas concentration · temperature sensor · alarm · IoT

## 1 Introduction

Morocco is known for its geological prosperity in natural resources, which makes it an adequate environment for investments in different national and international sectors.

The mining industry is not an exception as its activity has been increasing during last decades, benefiting from the minerals abundance as well as the enormous reserves of phosphate [1]. Therefore, the mining industry has become a part and parcel of the Moroccan economic power [1].

Nevertheless, social, and environmental challenges are increasingly emerging and hindering the mining activity in Morocco. The high demand on minerals and phosphate necessitates unfolding new mining sites, and the optimization of mining operations in existing sites. A study shows that additional efforts are still necessary to generalize safety measures in Moroccan mines although the number of occupational injuries decreased during the last years thanks to improvements in health and prevention systems [2].

© ICST Institute for Computer Sciences, Social Informatics and Telecommunications Engineering 2026
Published by Springer Nature Switzerland AG 2026. All Rights Reserved
J. B. Awotunde et al. (Eds.): AFRICATEK 2024, LNICST 618, pp. 149–154, 2026.
https://doi.org/10.1007/978-3-031-93557-2_10

Consequently, in an attempt to improve the safety regulations inside mines, the Moroccan government launched a new strategy targeting to increase production and exports while maintaining an improved working environment. A series of mines upgrades and reconstructions was held under patronage of international suppliers [3].

The development of health monitoring systems comes as a good solution to decrease the hazard in mines. Implementing these systems has increasingly become a necessity. In existing applications, S. Maheswari et al. suggest a wireless technology-based device that monitor workers' health continuously using nRF24L01 transceivers, which are wireless radio modules of receivers and transmitters [4]. The system is an optimization in material of the Cable Monitoring System (CMS) that was used previously, and an optimization of wireless ZigBee technology, a high-level communication protocol with limited working range [5]. T. Porselvi et al. focused on an IoT-based solution. This application makes use of wireless Long Range Wide Area Network (LoRaWAN) module operating on exceedingly long operating distances with low cost. IoT is used to store communicated data of miners in a webpage [6]. J. Colaco and R. Lohani propose the use of Zigbee technology rather than using Radio transceivers or IoT solutions. However, Zigbee only operates reliably over short distances making it quite difficult to cover wide areas [7].

This paper builds upon existing literature to attempt a design of a health monitoring system for underground miners in the Moroccan context. This system monitors vital signs of underground miners, namely heartbeat rate and temperature, as well as an external factor: harmful gas concentration (smoke, Methane, and Carbone Monoxide.). In case of emergencies, the system reacts by generating alarms of adequate degree (either by medium or high degree depending on the severity of the situation). The results of monitoring are to be displayed wirelessly in a central command station outside the mine.

## 2   Proposed Components for the System

### 2.1   Particle Photon

STM32 ARM Cortex M3 is a Wi-Fi IoT device with a Reduced Instruction Set Computer (RISC) architecture. It has 18 general purpose Input and Output pins (GPIOs) and advanced peripherals divided into 2 ports (a port is a group of 8 pins) for analog-to-Digital conversion (ADC) and digital-to-analog conversion (DAC) [8].

### 2.2   Pulse Sensor

SEN-11574 is an electronic device constituted of an infrared light emitting diode (IR LED) and a photo diode. It has 3 pins: a power pin, a ground pin, and an output pin. Some pulse sensors also have a clip that can be connected to the human finger [9].

### 2.3   Temperature Sensor

CJMCU-906 MLX90614ESF IR is a non-contact electronic device that measures the temperature using infrared radiations. It features 4 pins: a power pin, a ground pin, an SDA pin for Inter Integrated Circuit (I2C) data line, and an SCL pin for I2C clock line. It operates on a wide range (-70 C to 382 C) and has an accuracy of ± 0.5 C and a very low power consumption [10].

## 2.4 MQ Gas Sensor

MQ is a measuring device that senses based on changes of resistances when exposed to harmful gas. It is powered by a DC voltage and detects a multitude of gases such as smoke, Methane, and Carbone Monoxide. It has 4 pins, two are ground and power pins, and the other two give a digital output determining the presence or the absence of a gas, and an analog input of gas concentration [11].

# 3 Proposed Health Monitoring System Design

The system consists of a portable module that has a processing unit and a sensing unit meant for continuous monitoring of the miners' vital signs and environmental conditions, as well as a fixed module that consists of a remote monitoring unit in the command station outside the mine. Figure 1 depicts the functional architecture of the system.

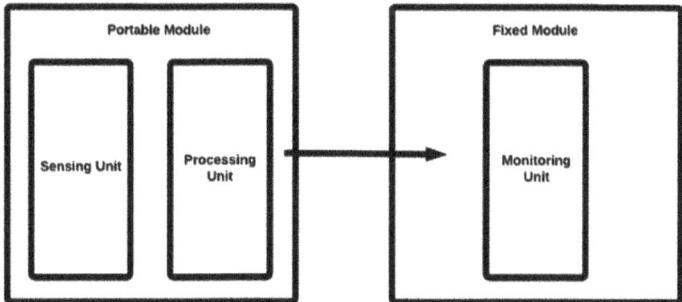

**Fig. 1.** System Architecture

## 3.1 Portable Module

The portable module, that is attached to the miners for monitoring purposes, is wired as illustrated in Fig. 2. The sensing unit consists of temperature, pulse, and MQ gas sensors that provide analog data for the processing unit which is a Particle Photon. The ADC port of the Particle Photon takes care of converting the analog signal into a digital signal to be processed. The portable health system consists of one item of each component mentioned in the figure. After interfacing this module, a buzzer is added to the portable device to warn miners in emergency cases.

## 3.2 System Algorithm

The algorithm is programmed in the Particle Photon and sets the working environment and IoT cloud to activate the sensors that continuously read data. If the measured parameters are within the specified thresholds by the program, data is displayed in a dashboard. Otherwise, there is also an activation of the alarms.

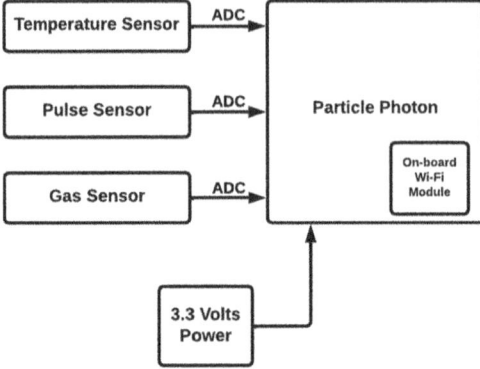

**Fig. 2.** Portable Module Design.

### 3.3 Fixed Module

The fixed module is represented by a monitoring screen outside the mines, placed to have visibility over the changes and miners' measured data. It consists of a dashboard developed using Node-RED that varies lively with miners' health conditions.

## 4 Implementation, Logic, and Results

### 4.1 Implementation and Wiring

The proposed system is built using a breadboard. For the pulse sensor, the ground pin is wired to the ground rail, the Vcc pin is connected to the power rail, and the third pin (Vout pin) is wired to the analog pin A1. For the temperature sensor, the Vin pin is wired to the power rail, the ground pin is connected the ground rail, the SCL pin is connected to the digital Particle Photon pin D1, and the SDA pin is connected to the digital Particle Photon pin D0. When it comes to the MQ135 gas sensor, the Vcc pin is connected to the power rail, the ground pin is connected to the ground rail, and the A0 pin is connected to the analog pin A0 of the Particle Photon. For the alarm system, a buzzer and an LED are attached to the breadboard. The buzzer is wired in such a way that it is connected to the digital pin D2 and to the ground rail. The LED is wired to the digital pin D7 that contains an on-board LED as well. This wiring allows the blinking of the two LEDs simultaneously. The LED is also wired to the ground rail. A current limiting resistor is used before the LED.

### 4.2 Logic

If the value of the temperature is out of the normal range (which was set to 35–40 °C as a proof of concept), or the concentration of $CO_2$ gas is out of the normal range (which was set to 0–350 ppm as a proof of concept), or the heartbeat rate is out of the proposed human range (set to 50–80 bpm as a proof of concept), the alarm is sent depending on the degree of danger: (1) Medium degree of danger, defined with the temperature being above 40 but below 42, or the temperature being below 35 °C but above 30 °C, or the gas concentration is above 350 ppm but below 420 ppm. The buzzer tones with a frequency of 1000 Hz and the LEDs toggle each 200 ms. (2) Extreme degree of danger, if the temperature goes beyond 42 °C or below 30 °C, or the gas concentration goes beyond 420 ppm. The buzzer tones with a higher frequency of 3000 Hz a nd the LEDs flash each 100 ms. It is worth noting that the ranges of values are chosen for limiting danger cases as a proof of concept, but it is possible to change them upon need. Improving the precision of the response may need hardware upgrade.

### 4.3 Proteus 8 Testing Phase

Before real implementation, the system was tested using a simulation software called Proteus 8 that offers a wide range of electronic and electric components that can be interfaced with microcontrollers. Since Proteus 8 does not feature Particle Photon in the default libraries, the system was tested using AVR ATmega 32 microcontroller. The gas sensor library was imported to the simulation to use the MQ Gas Sensor.

### 4.4 Results

Particle Photon allows for a console that displays the values of measured data. The data is imported to the cloud. Particle Photon also offers the possibility of adding online integrations such as Pipedream. Pipedream is a platform offering multiple Application Programming Interfaces (APIs), triggers, and workflows. It permits the connection between different applications and the development of event-driven automations [12]. Pipedream is used in this system to generate HTTP webhooks. These are a type of triggers that listen to data. The HTTP webhook listens to the published event of temperature value, MQ gas value, or the heartbeat rate value. The integration used in this case is "sending an email" to the monitor in case of danger. The system is tested by monitoring the vital signs of a student as well as the toxic gases' concentration surrounding the student. The system exhibits instantaneous responses to any changes in the measured signs, which means that it is working properly. For temperature and heartbeat rates, measured data is displayed in the published variables of Particle Photon IoT cloud as well as in a dashboard. This is done using another integration called Node-RED. Node-RED is a programming tool and editor permitting the integration of APIs, hardware, and services as well as the creation of flows [13]. Node-RED is used in the system to develop a simple graphical user interface (dashboard) to visualize measured values of temperature, heartbeat rate, and gas concentration.

## 5    Conclusion and Future Work

This paper presented a health monitoring system for underground miners in Morocco to improve the safety systems in such environment. The solution uses the pulse sensor, the MQ Gas sensor, and the MLX temperature sensor, as well as the Particle Photon as a processing unit. This latter allows for online integrations platforms such as Pipedream and Node-RED. The actual system exhibits satisfactory results revealed as exhibited by the instantaneous responses to changes in the vital and environmental parameters. Future work may be summarized as follows: (1) developing local command stations prototypes to monitor the miners' health. (3) A localization feature can be developed as well in the system to specify the position of a certain miner, or at least to specify which Wi-Fi access point the miner is present in its vicinity. The offered design allows to improve the safety of Moroccan miners according to the specified needs by taking advantage of the IOT technologies as well as mechanical and electronics novel designs.

## References

1. Atalayar Economy and Business page, https://atalayar.com/en/content/morocco-wants-emphasise-its-leading-position-miningsector. Accessed 12 Mar 2023
2. https://www.mem.gov.ma/en/Pages/secteur.aspx?e=7. Accessed 12 Mar 2023
3. https://europepmc.org/article/med/10596544. Accessed 5 Feb 2023
4. https://howtomechatronics.com/tutorials/arduino/arduino-wireless-communicationnrf24l01-tutorial/. Accessed 11 Mar 2023
5. Maheswari, S., Ashwini, S., Gayathri, S., Geetha, K.: Wireless health monitoring system in mine areas. International Research Journal of Engineering and Technology (IRJET) **6**(3), 2800–2806 (2016)
6. Porselvi, T., Sai Ganesh, C., Janaki, B., Priyadarshini, K., Shajitha Begam, S.: IoT based coal mine safety and health monitoringsystem using LoRaWAN. International Conference on Signal Processing and Communication (ICPSC), Coimbatore (2021)
7. Colaco, J., Lohani, R.: Health monitoring system for underground miners. Department of Electronics & Telecommunications Engineering, GEC, Ponda (2016)
8. Particle Photon: Wi-Fi. https://docs.particle.io/photon/. Accessed 1 Apr 2023
9. Heart Beat Sensor Library for Proteus. https://www.theengineeringprojects.com/2017/09/heart-beat-sensor-library-proteus.html. Accessed 24 Feb 2023
10. https://lastminuteengineers.com/mlx90614-ir-temperature-sensor-arduino-tutorial/. Accessed 2 Apr 2023
11. https://lastminuteengineers.com/mq2-gas-senser-arduino-tutorial/. Accessed 1 Mar 2023
12. Pipedream Homepage. https://pipedream.com/explore. Accessed 13 Apr 2023
13. NodeRED Homepage. https://nodered.org/. Accessed 19 Apr 2023

# Environmental Monitoring, Smart Agriculture and Smart Education

# EduSim: A Multi-agent Model for Simulating the Impacts of Urban and Demographic Growth on School Infrastructures Demand and Offer in the City of Ouagadougou

Yacouba Ouedraogo[1]([⊠]), Mahamadou Belem[1], Dramane Coulibaly[1], Mehdi Saqalli[2], Mesmin Dandjinou[1], and Marie Yves Théodore Tapsoba[1]

[1] Laboratoire d'Analyse, de Mathématiques Discrètes et d'Informatique, Université Nazi BONI, 01, BP 1091 Bobo-Dioulasso, Burkina Faso
ouedyac@gmail.com

[2] CNRS Université Toulouse 2 Jean Jaurès, Toulouse, France

**Abstract.** The education system in African cities and particularly in Ouagadougou, Burkina Faso is characterized by unequal distribution. This results in long distances for students to travel to their schools. This is observed as a mismatch between educational supply and demand. This phenomenon is even more pronounced with the continued increase in population and other uses of urban space in African cities. The paper examines the impact of urbanization and demographics on school infrastructure demand and supply, predicting future developments. It compares complex systems and proposes a generic model called the Education Simulation Model (EduSim) to simulate urban and demographic trends. Modeling by allowing the abstraction and integration of different types of data collected from different sources and its ability to predict the behavior of the actors in the complex system is relevant to analyze the impact of demography on the development of school infrastructure. For this study, we first showed to what extent the education system is a complex system. To do this, we compared the characteristics of complex systems and the education system. Then, we presented the different approaches to modeling the education system. Of these approaches, the most relevant and suitable for our study is agent-based modeling. It allows the study of the behavior of actors in order to analyze the results of their actions on the educational, urban and demographic systems as well as their interactions. The model assesses student enrollment and tracks school inequalities. Results show that urban growth, population growth, and distance constraints affect school infrastructure demand and enrollment. The model proposes new schools based on population needs and criteria. The resulting model from the analysis is a decision-making tool in predicting urban and demographic growth and also in planning school provision in African cities. In perspective, the model expects to couple information models as well as migration models and propose more research criteria for decision-makers.

**Keywords:** Simulation · agent-based modeling · multi-formalism simulation · school choice · enrollment · Burkina Faso

© ICST Institute for Computer Sciences, Social Informatics and Telecommunications Engineering 2026
Published by Springer Nature Switzerland AG 2026. All Rights Reserved
J. B. Awotunde et al. (Eds.): AFRICATEK 2024, LNICST 618, pp. 157–176, 2026.
https://doi.org/10.1007/978-3-031-93557-2_11

# 1 Introduction

The population and the urban area are constantly increasing in the agglomerations of developing countries. Several studies have highlighted these attributes common to these cities [1–4]. In Africa, the provision of services and education have not followed this increase [1, 5, 6].

For policy makers, the provision of social services like education and health to the population is mandatory. In developing countries, the lack of sufficient schools and the poor urban planning create inequalities and inadequacies in the accessibility of schools. For that, decision makers need to analyze the trends of this population increase and its effects on schools offer in order to provide better schools access to the population. Many studies have shown the impacts of the population growth on the demand of school infrastructures in the city of Ouagadougou [1–3].

While these studies demonstrate that there is an unequal distribution of schools in Ouagadougou, they are based on past and current data. This therefore does not allow for an analysis of the future impacts of population growth on school provision in the city. Furthermore, these studies do not present an equitable distribution of schools in Ouagadougou. It is therefore necessary to propose an innovative study that takes into account these limitations of past studies.

The school system is a complex system. Several actors (students, parents, school managers, policy makers, planners, etc.) interacting with each other intervene at different levels. These actors differ both in their attributes and their decision-making processes. Also, the school system is a place of interaction between different processes (economy, demography, land use and urban mobility). Therefore, the design of the system requires a multi-disciplinarily approach deploying a multiplicity of point of views [7]. In addition, it is important that the validation of the system considers the diversity of actors in the education system and also the different objectives and their interactions. This requires on the one hand to integrate the points of view of different actors to be efficient and on the other hand to evaluate the system under different scenarios in the short and long term. Modeling is best suited for this type of study because of its ability to integrate multiple data sources and predict different future states of a system, thus making it possible to analyze the impact of population growth on the development of school infrastructure.

Different approaches are used to model the educational system. From these approaches emerge the statistical, spatial and agent-based modeling approaches, considering that they are not to be opposed to one another. The statistical approach based on mathematical models uses "linear" methods while the education system has a non-linear character [8]. Interactions between actors are unpredictable, actions arise from reactions and behaviors do not follow a linear pattern, which makes it difficult to schematize them in a mathematical formula. An advantage of using the spatial approach is that it allows to analyze on a map the different actors of the education system and their attributes. However, this approach remains limited to study the behaviors of the actors. The agent-based approach allows to analyze the interactions and behaviors of the actors of the system, which allows to better study the complexity of the education system [9, 10].

This study aims to propose an agent-based model to analyze the interactions of actors in the education system as well as the consequences of demographic and urban growth on the educational offer in Ouagadougou. The objectives of the study are to (1) implement different scenarios to find an answer to the inequality of access to schools in Ouagadougou, (2) represent the education system through a conceptual framework using agent-based modeling, and (3) analyze under various scenarios the links between the future increase in the population and the demands for school infrastructure.

Based on agent-based modeling approach, we develop a generic model that accepts different parameters. This model is the dynamic decision tool capable of adapting to different hypotheses.

The simulation results show an increase in population following an increase in urban space.

At the scenario level, enrollment rates differ depending on the choices of households and the location of schools in urban space. The enrollment rate is higher when households choose a school far from their living place.

In the remainder of the paper, the different approaches to modeling interaction between the educational, urban and demographic systems are presented. Then, we present the methodology used as well as the tools and the conceptual model. Finally, the simulations carried out are presented and the results.

## 2   Education System Modeling Approaches

Within the framework of the education system, the modeling focussed on understanding and simulating different aspects of the education system, among others, the choices of learners, the construction of new schools, the layout of school infrastructure in the urban space, the impact of educational policies, school admission choices etc. Our review has enabled us to identify three main approaches of modeling the education system. Depending on the choice of analytical methods, statistical, spatial and agent-based modeling approaches can be considered in modeling the education system.

### 2.1   Statistical Approach

Several variables come into play within the framework of the education system. Whether one is interested in the layout of schools, the choice of studies, or the socio-economic composition of learners, there are as many subjects for research. The objectif of a statistical model is to represent the characteristics of the real model with the best approximation. The differential and confirmatory approach makes it possible to validate or invalidate the hypotheses formulated a priori or after the exploratory phase, and to extrapolate certain properties of the sample to a larger population. The hypotheses are validated by the use of statistical tests or probabilistic models. [11]. Thus, research on the study choice process that uses statistical modeling aims to be able to estimate the effect that can be attributed specifically to a certain variable, after controlling for the effect of other variables, which constitutes its main interest and ultimately its usefulness. [12]. Statistical modeling of the education system has mainly been the work of researchers in educational sciences, anthropologists, economists, sociologists, demographers and geographers. This modeling concerned subjects of study such as the choice of learners, the geographical location of schools, inequalities of access to the education system, school performance. This approach makes it possible to use several variables.

## 2.2 Spatial Approach

The use of spatial models in the education system seems natural given the variables and contexts related to the education system. This is, among other things, the location of schools in space that can lead to access problems and thus create inequalities, not yet even considering students' transportation issues, between paths and means of transportation. Still connected to these provisions, students' parents must select which schools their children should attend, according to location, prices and reputation, among other things. Researchers try to analyse if these choices are the sole criteria for schools' location and their importance [13, 14]. These different school choices by households can be studied to analyze the weight of the location of schools, the reputation of schools as well as their impact on the academic career of students and the quality of education in these schools. So many questions and research topics related to the location of schools. The different themes of the education system are therefore excellent subjects for study with the spatial approach. The conviction of geographers is made on the importance of discipline in the educational question. "What unites geographers is a belief that geography matters. This is nowhere more clearly seen than in the provision of educational services. The fact that geography matters in relation to educational provision applies in a number of different ways. For example, it is unequally distributed across space". [15]. Geographic Information Systems (GIS) as a database of spatial information remains a key component in the spatial modeling approach. This use of GIS makes it possible to better develop school cartography. It turns out to be an effective tool in decision-making.

## 2.3 Agent-Based Approach

The agent-based approach in the modeling of the education system is based on the consideration that the education system is a complex system, meaning several factors acting in an intricate and not on a determinate way on the system outputs. Having clues on these dynamics is supported on the numerous works on which the model is based. Studies on modeling complex systems underline the limit of "traditional" straightforward representations: the essential criticism concerns the fact that such "traditional" models use "linear" methods while the educational system has a non-linear character. For instance, the actions and reactions of actors constantly modify the processes. Households' choice of schools can change depending on the location of schools, which can also change depending on the size of the population in the area. When there are large uncertainties, ABM (Agent-Based Modeling) is much more flexible than equation-based modeling to perform scenario analyses and provide critical information needed for policy decision-making. [8]. Because of its "emergent" characteristic, the properties of the educational system cannot be the summation of the properties of the agents of the system [16]. This characteristic of the education system shows the limit of mathematical methods in the modeling of complex systems. Unlike these approaches, the agent-based approach is a simulation approach characterized by modeling the behavior and interaction of individual agents, from which emerge complex and dynamic macro-models [8]. ABM is adequate to represent the social dimension and to better represent the heterogeneity of households and their interactions [17]. Several researchers use this approach as the most reliable for modeling complex systems, such as here, the behavior and interaction between the educational and school construction policies, students' transportation practices, household demographic trends and other actors' characteristics in the education system.

ABMs make it possible to present the agents of the system with their attributes and their behaviors and to analyze the interactions. The actions and reactions of the agents show the dynamics of the system and its functioning. Although it has many advantages in the description of complex systems, it should be remembered that the multi-agent approach is far from being a panacea [8]. George E. P. Box's famous quote illustrates this: "Essentially all models are wrong, but some are useful".

## 3   Materials and Methods

### 3.1   Study Site

Ouagadougou, the capital city of Burkina Faso, formerly Upper Volta, is located in the center of the country in the province of Kadiogo (Fig. 1).

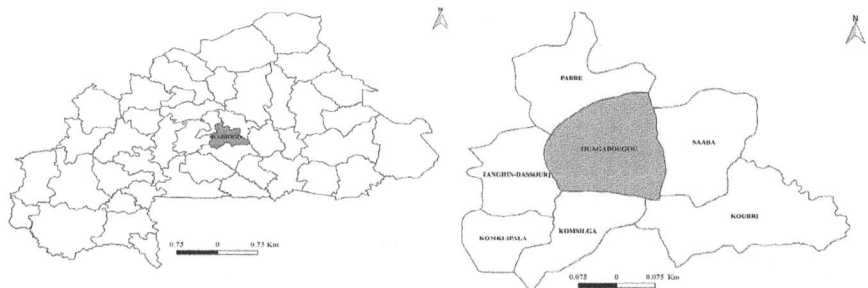

**Fig. 1.** Geographical location of Kadiogo and Ouagadougou (Source IGB/BNDT 2002, [2])

When Upper Volta gained independence in 1960, the city of Ouagadougou had a total of 10 secondary schools, 3 of which were public. The number of secondary schools has increased considerably since then, so that in 2013–2014 the city has more than 390 secondary schools [1]. At the same time, Ouagadougou is experiencing strong demographic growth (its intercensal growth rate between 1996 and 2006 is 7.6%) [4], with the corollary of a significant need for basic social infrastructure (education and health), and a spreading fast city area. In terms of population, it seems unimaginable to note that at the dawn of independence, Ouagadougou had "only" 59,000 inhabitants (estimate from the first demographic survey) [2]. Since then, the population has continued to grow until reaching more than 2.5 million inhabitants according to the 2019 General Population and Housing Census (RGPH). The city area having been multiplied by 200 in fifty-six years, from 1,400 ha in 1960 to 280,500 ha in 2016 [2]. However, this decrease seems to slow down the annual growth of the municipal population: between 2006 and 2012 it reaches 4.44% while the corresponding value between 1996 and 2006 was 7.59%. [4].

This rapidly growing population is obviously composed of very young people. Indeed, 47.3% of the population is under 20 and the average age is 23.1. Examination of the school-age population (3–29 years) shows that 69.8% were schooled in 2006/2007. [4], raising questions about the various reasons explaining why nearly half of the children do leave school. Among important reasons, such as the need for income within the family, the simple fact that accommodation capacity of post-primary schools may not be enough is of crucial importance, as it is here a task on which governing powers could more rapidly act. The other aspect of this school offer is its distribution in the city of Ouagadougou. Indeed, this school offer is characterized by its unequal distribution. While the outlying districts bring together more than 48% (941,193 for a total of 1,933,306) of the population, they only have 28% of the schools of the city according to data from [1]. This also gives rise to situations for a student to travel more than 20 km on a motorcycle to get to his/her school in the city center. [1, 2], reinforcing the school leaving dynamic as a result.

## 3.2  Methodological Approach and Tools

### 3.2.1  Conceptual Framework

The urban system is a complex system in which many agents intervene. These agents act among themselves and also act within the framework of subsystems contained in the urban system. This vision of the urban system coupled with the education system highlights several subsystems acting and interacting in relationships [18], distinguishes eight (8) subsystems which evolve at different scales of space and time, namely: population, employment, buildings, urban space planning, transport, environment, public finances and public services.

The grouping of these subsystems into models highlights the different models that are of interest to us: the demographic model (subsystem: population), the economic model (subsystems: employment, public services, public finances), the model of urban mobility (subsystems: transport, environment) and the land use model (subsystems: buildings, environment, land use). In addition, we considered the school selection process, the dynamics of social networks between parents and the choice of schools by households.

### 3.2.2  Methodology

In order to understand the apprehension and also determine the different actors of the education system in Ouagadougou, a workshop held in 2018 in Ouagadougou brought together urban planners, researchers (geography, demography and IT), school founders and teachers. During the seminar, the exchanges made it possible to determine the many actors of the educational system from school buildings to students' enrollment as well as the educational path of the students. It was also the place to analyze the interaction between these actors and the problems of the school offer in the city with regard to the growth of the population and the urban area. From these analyses, scenarios have been developed to analyze the different scenarios and determine the optimistic scenario for the school offer. After, the data sources to be used were determined.

Based on results of the workshop, a conceptual model has been proposed using the protocol ODD (Overview, Design concepts, and Details). Our approach was based on multi-formalism approach, i.e. the integration of different types of models to come out with complex and realistic model. Then, existing models have been identified. After, using the Gama platform, EduSim has been developed based on the integration of identified models. Data have been collected, harmonized and integrated for the simulations.

### 3.2.3 Tools

A range of tools have been used to develop the model among them, we have UML [19], QGIS [20], GAMA [21], Raster model [22] and Gen*[23].

**UML** for Unified Modeling Language (UML) is used to describe models. It is a relevant tool for the visualization of models in the description of the system.

Thus, UML is used to present the actors of the model and their interactions, the entities that make up the system and their properties, the conceptual framework of the system's functionalities [19].

**QGIS** to develop the map of Ouagadougou with schools, homes and urban population, Quantum Geographic Information System (QGIS) allowed us to process geographical data on the city of Ouagadougou. It is an effective platform which was used for the preparation of the map and the representation of the data but also to analyze spatially the various geographical data of Ouagadougou. [20].

**GAMA:** GAMA is an easy-to-use open source modeling and simulation environment (https://gama-platform.org/) for creating spatially explicit agent-based simulations. It has been developed to be used in any field of application: urban mobility, adaptation to climate change, epidemiology, design of disaster evacuation strategies, urban planning, are some -one of the application areas in which GAMA users are involved and for which they create models [21]. It is a generic platform that provides several possibilities for modeling complex systems.

**Raster Model:** The Raster Model, consisting of dividing space into homogeneous spatial units (in terms of internal state), has the advantage of requiring less data (or at least less precise data) and of being simpler to implement, especially with the many platforms that exist [22].

It is an urban growth model used to predict the future expansion of urban areas. The model has been implemented and integrated into the models available in GAMA Platform. In the case of Ouagadougou, it is appropriate to plan the expansion of the city based on spatial and non-spatial factors. The model also requires little data to implement.

**Gen*:** Gen* is a generic tool, that makes it possible to generate, locate and structure a synthetic population through a social network, directly usable in GAMA [23]. With the map of Ouagadougou and demographic data, an urban and demographic representation could be produced. Given the size of the population, it is not relevant to present the entire population of the city on a map of Ouagadougou for the simulation. Thus, Gen* is the appropriate tool that generates synthetic populations for simulation. Developed and integrated into GAMA, Gen* allows several parameters to be taken into the generation of a population of agents. Thus, socio-demographic and economic parameters of households resulting from city statistics can be taken into account as well as social ties in generating the population for the simulation.

### 3.3   ODD Conceptual Model Protocol

The conceptual model is represented with the ODD protocol. The aim of ODD is to standardize the descriptions of the models mainly individual and agent-based (ABMs). The primary objectives of ODD are to make model descriptions more understandable and complete, thereby making ABMs less subject to criticism for being irreproducible [24].

#### 3.3.1   Objective of the Model

The aim of this study is to analyze the impact of urban and demography growth on the demand of school infrastructure in Ouagadougou. This involves studying the effects of school offer and demand in Ouagadougou at the post-primary and secondary levels according to urban dynamics and demographic dynamics. The model is intended for decision-makers as a decision-making tool in planning urban development and the construction of new schools. It is used to analyze different scenarios in order to optimize the construction of school infrastructure in demographic and urban forecasts.

#### 3.3.2   Entities and Agents of the System

Four main agents determine the functioning of the education system as described in Fig. 2 which interactions determine how the system operates.

**Household**  is the main actor in the model. The household has attributes such as status, its financial income, the level of schooling of the head of household, the number of children in the household and their school preferences. The household evolves in a social environment and therefore has social ties with other households. To inform itself, the household takes into consideration the information coming from its social network. And the importance of this information depends on the weight of this social relationship.

**Student**  is a household member. Their main attributes are age, sex, educational level. The students represented in the system belong to households.

**School**  describes the different classes of a school. The main characteristics of the school are the capacity, the area of the school, the success rates in exams, the reputation, and the location.

**Authority:**  The authority is at the center of interactions in the system. It also determines the school institutional orientation and environment as well as the policies related to the city and its links with the development of schools. It is the authority that is also in charge of defining the conditions of access to public schools, the area of schools and the conditions required to build schools in urban areas.

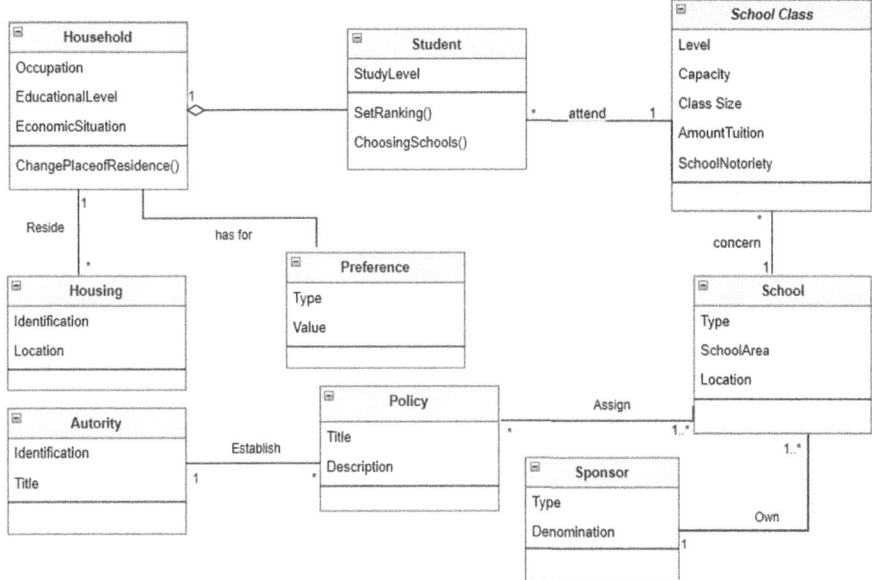

**Fig. 2.** Model class diagram

### 3.3.3 Sub-models

Three sub-models are represented in the model. These are urban model, demographic model and school choice. These three sub-models share the same urban space. The interaction dynamics of these sub-models determine the behavior of the system to be modeled.

**Urban Growth Model:** This sub-model makes it possible to observe and analyze the increase in urban space over the course of the simulations. It is represented by a cellular automaton using the raster model, implemented in the GAMA platform. In the model, space is divided into cells. A cell is characterized by:

- its construction state: this state has three (3) possible values (1. Is Built, 2. Is not built, 3. Forbidden to build). It is not possible to build on water reservoirs and roads
- Its constructability: this is the level of constructability of the cell which has a boolean value (0 and 1): 0 for means the low probability for the cell to transform into a residential area and 1 for the high probability that the cell becomes a residential area.

An unbuilt cell is transformed into a residential area depending on its constructability. The constructability of a cell is a function of the distance to the nearest road, the distance to the city center and urban density. Density is determined by the number of surrounding constructed cells. It must be a number between 0 and 6. Cells closest to roads and the urban center are likely to be urbanized (Fig. 3).

**Demographic Growth Model:** this sub-model describes the occupation of urban space by households and also their interactions with urban model. This demographic dynamic

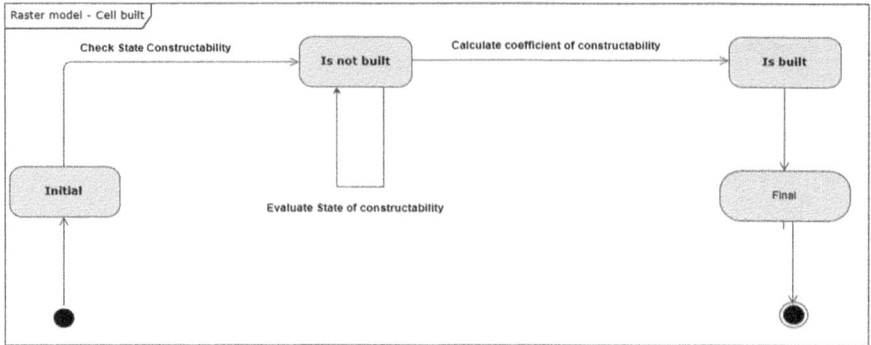

**Fig. 3.** State transition diagram of raster model

is based on the population generation model implemented in the GAMA platform [23]. Generating a population consists of random generation of individual characteristics.

**Schools' Choice Model:** One of the behavior of students is their choice of schools. This choice is based on the Boston mechanism [25]. The ordering of the process in this sub-model concerning the choice of schools highlights the different sub-models involved in this process. Different variables from the other sub-models are considered in this process. This shows the interaction between the different agents, and the actions of some influencing the reactions of others. Based on their choice, students look for schools and schools enrol students considering their capacity. The process for all the choices of the students when they are not enrolled and up to the maximal capacity of the schools. The algorithm is presented in Fig. 4.

## 4  Simulations

### 4.1  Input Data

We used different data from studies, projects and statistics. Also, certain data were collected in the field, such as the geographical coordinates of certain schools. With the update of the school database, the location of some schools needed to be updated. Field trips made it possible to record the new GPS coordinates of these schools to integrate them into the geographic database. The various data were also updated with recent available and validated data. The table below lists the different data sources.

The geographical data of the schools come from the ASPENO Project (Permanent and Digital School Atlas of the city) [1, 2, 4].

The population data comes from the General Population and Housing Census of 2006 and 2019 carried out by the Burkina Institute in charge of Statistics and Demography (INSD) [28, 29]. These data made it possible to extract the socio-economic and demographic components of the city of Ouagadougou. And also, to have data on the school population of the city. The work carried out by [1, 2] and [4] also used census data and allows a good presentation of data on school population and household characteristics. The criteria for the construction of schools and distance for students are taken from a

1. E = the student
2. N = student's level of study
3. S = school
4. CapEcole (N) = Capacity of the school for level N
5. Number of Schools: Total of schools in the city
6. Enroller: Boolean which gives the student's enrollment status
7. Function: Search function which searches for a free place for a student taking as parameters the student, their choices, their level of study and the school
8. Start
9. i=0
10. Enroll = false
11. As long as (i < NbrSchools and Enroller = false)
12. T = Search (E, S, N)
13. If (T == true)
    Enroll =true
    CapSchool(N) = CapSchool(N)-1
14. Otherwise
    i=i+1
    End If
16. End While
17. End

**Fig. 4.** Algorithm of school choice

decree of the Ministry of Urbanization, data from UNESCO and studies on the school map. The area of Ouagadougou as well as its delimitation are taken from data from the Ministry of Urban Planning and data from the City of Ouagadougou [29].

**Table 1.** Sources of Ouagadougou data of the model.

| Data Source | Issue | Reference |
|---|---|---|
| School | Schools 'size and students' composition | [1–3, 27] |
| School Choice | Parents'school choice process | [1, 2] |
| School typology | schools classification | [1–3, 27] |
| Household | Households | [1–3, 28, 29] |
| Demographic | Demography | [28, 29] |
| positionings | Spatial positioning of schools and households | [26, 29] |

### 4.1.1 The Map of Ouagadougou City

To represent Ouagadougou, a 200x200m map, with the geographical data of the main roads and water reservoirs, was used with a 2018 shapefile map from the National Topographic Data Base (BNDT) source. We generated the raster file in ASCII form from this shapefile (Table 1).

### 4.1.2  Demographic Data

The following data is used (Table 2).

- the map of the districts of the city of Ouagadougou designed from BNDT 2012 data. It is a geographical representation of the 12 municipalities of the city of Ouagadougou. It contains the population numbers. This data comes from RGPH 2019 data [29], and we reduced the size for representation in the model.

**Table 2.** Model population with RGPH 2019 data as source, INSD, Monograph of the commune of Ouagadougou.

| District | Population | Population in the model |
| --- | --- | --- |
| District 1 | 102 528 | 102 |
| District 2 | 83 436 | 83 |
| District 3 | 311 406 | 311 |
| District 4 | 207 647 | 207 |
| District 5 | 129 984 | 129 |
| District 6 | 222 854 | 222 |
| District 7 | 282 837 | 282 |
| District 8 | 152 880 | 152 |
| District 9 | 336 483 | 336 |
| District 10 | 263 969 | 263 |
| District 11 | 254 928 | 254 |
| District 12 | 66 314 | 66 |
| TOTAL | 2 415 266 | 2407 |

2407 agents are generated and the annual growth rate of the city's population is 4%. These data come from RGPH 2019 data and we adapted to the model.

- the composition of the population by age, gender and economic activity: the data was designed using data from the RGPH 2019 and school statistics from the Ministry of Education from 2019. It was necessary to adapt because in the RGPH, the branch of activity was codified according to the nomenclature of activities of the AFRISTAT member states, NAEMA rev.1 and this nomenclature is different from the professions taken from school statistics. The economic activities are: Artisan, Other, Farmer, Breeder, Commercial employee, Private sector employee, Public sector employee, Liberal profession, Retired. For the age groups, we used: 15 to 19 years, 20 to 24 years, 25 to 29 years, 30 to 34 years, 35 to 39 years, 40 to 44 years, 45 to 49 years, 50 to 54 years, 55 to 59 years old, 60 to 64 years old.
- the population structure by age and sex: the data comes from RGPH 2019 data on the city of Ouagadougou.

Table 3. Population size by age group by sex (Source: RGPH, 2019)

| Age group | Sex | | |
|---|---|---|---|
| | Masculine | Feminine | Total |
| Less than 4 years old | 156 611 | 155 533 | 312 144 |
| 5–9 | 135 165 | 142 921 | 278 086 |
| 10–14 | 118 096 | 138 183 | 256 279 |
| 15–19 | 108 919 | 152 382 | 261 301 |
| 20–24 | 115 539 | 142 336 | 257 875 |
| 25–29 | 115 615 | 126 166 | 241 781 |
| 30–34 | 111 725 | 104 013 | 215 738 |
| 35–39 | 90 824 | 76 845 | 167 669 |
| 40–44 | 69 816 | 53 021 | 122 837 |
| 45–49 | 49 005 | 37 238 | 86 243 |
| 50–54 | 36 163 | 29 763 | 65 926 |
| 55–59 | 25 965 | 23 434 | 49 399 |
| 60–64 | 20 369 | 17 760 | 38 129 |
| 65–69 | 12 654 | 11 309 | 23 963 |
| 70–74 | 8 394 | 8 839 | 17 233 |
| 75–79 | 4 102 | 4 874 | 8 976 |
| 80–84 | 2 094 | 3 449 | 5 543 |
| 85–89 | 818 | 1 508 | 2 326 |
| 90–94 | 347 | 858 | 1 205 |
| Plus de 95 ans | 1 336 | 1 277 | 2 613 |
| Total | 1 183 557 | 1 231 709 | 2 415 266 |

### 4.1.3  School Data

The school location data comes from geo-referenced school data from 2015 provided by the ASPENO project [1, 2, 4]. ASPENO is a project implemented by three (3) research institutes, namely the Research Institute for Development (IRD), the Institute of Social Sciences (INSS) and the Higher Institute of Population Sciences (ISSP) [26]. The aim of the ASPENO Project was to set up a digital school atlas of the city (Table 3).

Two main sources of data were used for the geo-referencing of schools in the city. The first is a directory of around a hundred schools with their geographical coordinates collected as part of the Ouagadougou Geographic Information Platform project later transformed into the Burkina Faso Geographic Information Platform (PIGEO). The second source of data is the database of the Ministry of National Education for the 2013–2014 school year [1].

This data has been updated with data from the Ministry of Education2016 and 2021 school statistics. [27].

## 4.2  Configuration of Simulations

To observe the operation of the model, simulations were configured. To do this, we described the simulated scenarios as well as the objectives of these simulations and also presented the simulation environment.

### 4.2.1  Simulation Scenarios

The scenarios simulated as explained concern the distance. Depending on the distance considered as a parameter of the model, students and households are enrolled by a school located within a radius of the distance. To do this, households make their choices and schools agree to enroll based on their choices and also availability. This availability depends on the school's capacity to accommodate the level of study requested by the student. The choice taken into account in the model is proximity to the household's home. The objectives of the model are above all to study the impact that distance has on enrollment and also to carry out a qualitative analysis of enrollment as a function of distance. And with urban model and demographic model, the model is simulated to generate schools in new residential areas taking into account the distance to be traveled by the students.

Two scenarios have been simulated. In the first scenario, we assume that students must travel at maximum 2 km to reach its school. We call this scenario, scenario2km. In the second scenario, we assume that students must travel at maximum 5 km to reach its school. We call this scenario, scenario5km.

### 4.2.2  Context of Simulations

To simulate these scenarios, it was necessary to configure the model with the initial data. Given the nature of the data from the different sub-models, the model uses the spatial, demographic and statistical data described above.

For urban model, the initial data are those described in the data description to develop the raster model. These are $W_1 = 0.5$, $W_2 = 1.0$, $W_3 = 1.0$; and also 250 for the construction area of a house and 4 as a density radius. $W_1$ is the weight of the distance to the nearest road, $W_2$ the weight of the distance to the city center and $W_3$ the weight of urban density.

For demographic model, the population size is 2407 individuals. These individuals are distributed in 1207 households. The annual growth rate of the city's population is 4%.

In terms of school and student data, 393 schools and 500 students are the initial data.

The model takes as input the map of Ouagadougou as well as the various system data based on the parameters. These parameters concern the agents of the system, namely households, schools and students. These parameters are defined in Table 4.

**Table 4.** List of parameters and their descriptions

| Parameters | Description |
|---|---|
| Number of schools | These are secondary schools in Ouagadougou |
| Number of students | All students from households |
| Number of households | The number of households distributed according to the 3 zones of the city of Ouagadougou on the map (Centre, First Peripheral Ring, Second Peripheral Ring) |
| School capacity | Capacity of the school and the different classes |
| Amount of tuition | Amount of registration fees in the school |
| Household income | Average household income |
| Distance from school | The distance between households and schools |

### 4.2.3  Simulation Environment

As a simulation environment, the model is simulated on the GAMA platform, version 1.8.2 RC2. We use a laptop, Core(TM) i7-7500U CPU @ 2.70 GHz 2.90 GHz, with 8 GB of RAM and installed Windows 10 Enterprise, x64-based processor. In terms of performance, we had to reduce the number of agents to simulate because the larger the population to generate, the longer the execution time was excessively long with "Out of memory" messages very often.

The model runs on average in 3 min and consumes more than 2 GB of RAM. This execution time is indicative because it very often depends on the processes running on the computer. This execution time observed in the execution console also varies from model to model. Generating the population takes more time given the complexity of the mathematical and statistical calculations that make up its algorithm. The other two models have less complex calculations and the algorithm has been optimized with run condition and output loops to optimize model performance.

## 5  Results

### 5.1  City and Population Growth

The simulation of the model produces as output, the map of the city and the layout of the unenrolled students. In terms of urban model, the expansion of the city with the construction of new homes (in yellow) follows the main roads and the approaches to water reservoirs. This expansion is taking place around the city Center which the expansion of the city revolves (see Fig. 5).

The growth of the city occurs from the center of the city. This center shows all its importance with demographic model. The populations who occupy the new buildable areas with the expansion of the city try to be close to this center. This leads to significant density in the city. The results show a certain consistency between the growth of the city and the demographic growth. The city grows with the increase in population and these populations occupy the growing area of the city.

In addition, we observed that new constructions are developing along the main roads and populations are settling in these built-up areas as observed in Fig. 5

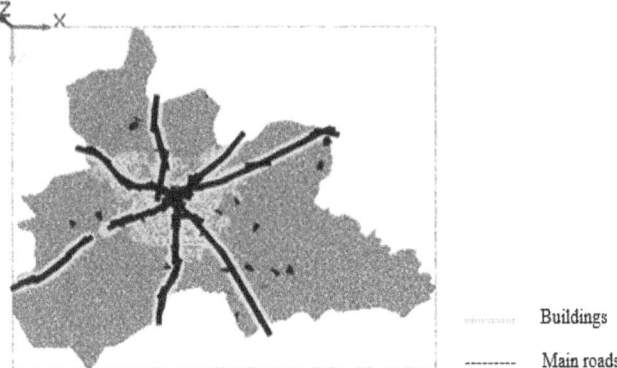

**Fig. 5.** Simulation of urban model

On the graph in Fig. 6 for a simulation of 25 steps, we observe a continuous increase in the number of new constructions in blue.

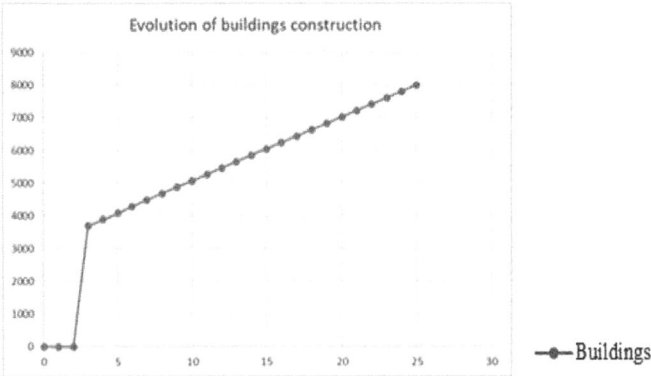

**Fig. 6.** Graph of urban model simulations

In terms of the demographic model, the simulation over 25 steps shows the settlment of new populations (in red) at the level of new constructions (in yellow) which materialize the increase of the city along the main roads (see Fig. 7).

### 5.2 Impact of Distance on Student Enrollment

The enrollment rate is higher in scenario5km than in scenario2km (Table 5). A qualitative analysis of this rate shows that students in peripheral areas are the lowest. The majority of schools are located in the center of the city, which has fewer households than the

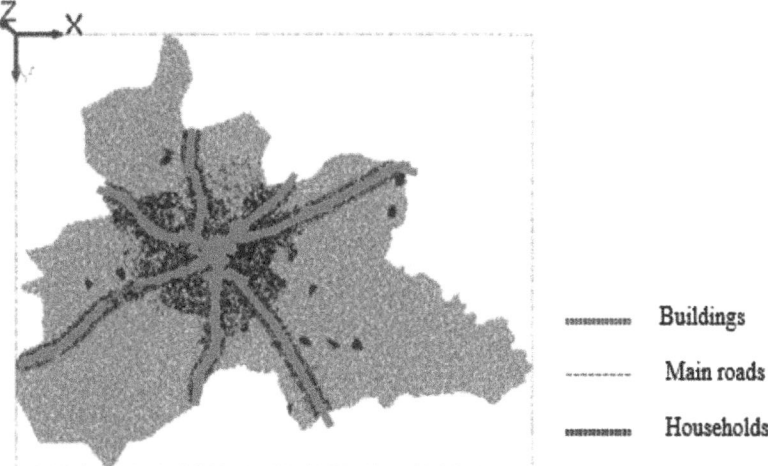

**Fig. 7.** Simulation of demographic model

outlying districts (Figs. 8 and 9). While students in the outskirts lack schools, schools in the city center lack students if we apply the distance criterion of 2 km. This is at the origin of the unequal distribution of schools. This phenomenon is exacerbated with the increase in the city growth and the settlement of new populations in new areas. We observ low enrollment rates in these new areas. The unequal distribution is thus reinforced with a much greater insufficiency in school provision. This insufficient offer is the result of the impact of urban growth and demographic growth. The creation of new schools based on schools brings schools closer to households, reducing this unequal distribution and the effects of insufficient school provision. The generation of new schools in these areas is therefore essential.

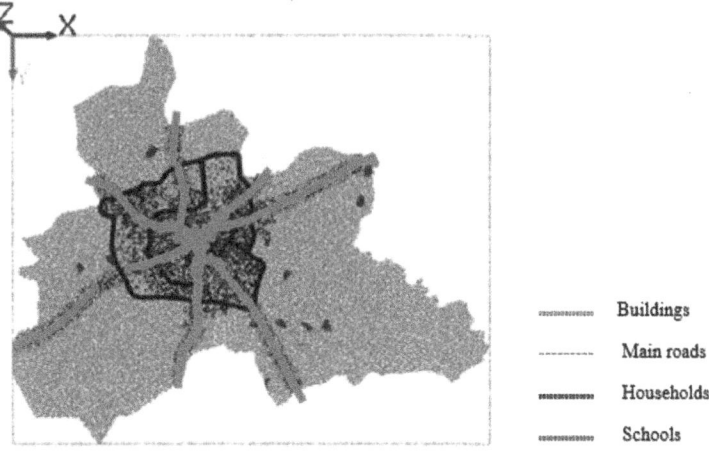

**Fig. 8.** Simulation of school choice by students - Scenario5km

The simulation for a radius of 2 km shows that fewer students are enrolled. ( Fig. 9).

**Fig. 9.** Simulation of school choice by students – Scenario2km

**Table 5.** Enrolment rate by distance

|  | Distance at 5kms | Distance to 2kms |
|---|---|---|
| Total number | 500 | 500 |
| Not enroled | 112 | 178 |
| Enolment Rate | 78 | 64 |

# 6  Conclusion

The objective of this study was to assess the impacts of urban growth and population dynamics on school infrastructure demands in the city of Ouagadougou. Our approach was based on multi-formalism approach as we coupled an agent-based model with a range of models. Then the raster model has been used to simulate the urban dynamics from spatial point of view and Gen* model has been used for population generation.

The resulting model is generic. The genericity of the model allows the definition of different parameters depending on the study themes and the choice of study parameters. The observation made is consistent with the observations of previous studies on the unequal distribution of school provision in the city of Ouagadougou. Results show that urban growth, population growth, and distance constraints affect school infrastructure demand and enrollment.

In the future, the model will propose the generation of new schools based on the criteria and the needs of populations. Simulation will consider different enrollment criteria such as the school fees, the reputation of the school, the social status of the school and also the coupling of the model will integrate information models and migratory models. The creation of a massive database for simulations is part of the work planned for the remainder of our study.

# References

1. Ouedraogo, I.: Inégalités spatiales d'éducation post-primaire et secondaire à Ouagadougou : enjeux de gouvernance et d'aménagement du territoire, PhD Thesis Université de Caen Normandie, pp. 122–136 (2018)
2. Boly, D.: Inégalités scolaires en milieu urbain. Le cas d'une capitale, Ouagadougou, dans les années 2000. PhD Thesis, université Paris Descartes 1, pp. 104–132 (2017)
3. Soma, A.: Vulnérabilité et résilience urbaines: perception et gestion territoriale des risques d'inondation dans la ville de Ouagadougou. PhD Thesis in Geography, Université de Ouagadougou, pp. 10–75 (2015)
4. Ouedraogo, H.: Les inégalités d'accès et de parcours scolaire au post-primaire à Ouagadougou, PhD Thesis, Université de Paris, 80 p. (2019)
5. Cadot, E., Harang, M.: Offre de soins et expansion urbaine, conséquences pour l'accès aux soins. L'exemple d'Ouagadougou (Burkina Faso). Espace populations sociétés **2–3**, 329–339 (2006)
6. El Hedi Arouri, M., Ben Youssef, A., Nguyen-Viet, C., Soucat, S.: Effects of urbanization on economic growth and human capital formation in Africa. halshs-01068271, HAL, pp. 1–6 (2014)
7. Belem, M., Müller, J.-P.: Toward a conceptual framework for multi-points of view analysis in complex system modeling: orea model. In: Proceedings of the 7th International Conference on Practical Applications of Agents & Multi-Agent Systems (PAAMS 2009), 55 of Advances in Intelligent and Soft Computing, pp. 548–556 (2009)
8. Ning Wang, C.H.: Agent-based overlapping generations modelling for educational policy analysis. Walden Dissertations and Doctoral Studies, pp. 33–85 (2017)
9. Lakon, C.M., et al.: Simulating dynamic network models and adolescent smoking: the impact of varying peer influence and peer selection. Am. J. Public Health, 2438–2448 (2015)
10. d'Aquino, P., Bah, A., Turner, B.L.: Multi-level participatory design of land use policies in African drylands: a method to embed adaptability skills of drylands societies in a policy framework. J. Environ. Manage., 207–219 (2014)
11. Rambaud, F.: Caractérisation, Analyse et Modélisation statistiques de fragments osseux crâniens pour la prédiction de paramètres mécaniques lésionnels. Autre. Université de Valenciennes et du Hainaut-Cambresis, p. 40 (2007)
12. Alvaro Gonzalez Sanzana, A.:. La modélisation du processus de choix d'études supérieures : apports et limites. Les Cahiers de recherche du Girsef 97. hal-00980190, pp. 7–8 (2014)
13. Carlos, K.M.R., Julius, N.M., Corneille, K.V.: Multi-agent decision-making model for the construction of schools. Int. J. Comput. Appl. **178**(40), 4–13 (2019)
14. Maroulis, S., Bakshy, E., Gomez, L., Wilensky, U.: Modeling the transition to public school choice. J. Artif. Soc. Soc. Simul. **17**(2), 3 (2014)
15. Nasser Marshad Al-Zeer, N.: Analysis of the spatial distribution of public secondary girls' and boys' schools in Riyadh, Saudi Arabia, Thesis (2005)
16. Jacobson, M.J., Levin, J.A., Kapur, M.: Education as a complex system: conceptual and methodological implications. Educ. Res. **48**(2), 112–119 (2019). https://doi.org/10.3102/001 3189X19826958

17. Belem, M., Saqalli, M.: Development of an integrated generic model for multi-scale assessment of the impacts of agro-ecosystems on major ecosystem services in West Africa. J. Environ. Manage. **202**, 117–125 (2017). https://doi.org/10.1016/j.jenvman.2017.07.018.hal-01683535

18. Laurini, R.: les systèmes d'information pour la gestion des villes. données urbaines, 25 (1994)

19. OMG: Unified modeling language specification (2017). https://www.omg.org/spec/UML/2.5.1/PDF

20. QGIS.org: QGIS Geographic Information System. QGIS Association (2023). http://www.qgis.org

21. Taillandier, P., Gaudou, B., Grignard, A., et al.: Building, composing and experimenting complex spatial models with the GAMA platform. Geoinformatica **23**, 299–322 (2019). https://doi.org/10.1007/s10707-018-00339-6

22. Taillandier, P., Banos, A., Drogoul, A., Gaudou, B. Marilleau, N.T., Quang, C.: Simulating urban growth with raster and vector models: a case study for the city of Can Tho, Vietnam. In: International Conference Autonomous Agents and Multiagent Systems (AAMAS 2016), Singapore, Singapore, p. 17 (2016)

23. Chapuis, K., Taillandier, P., Gaudou, B., Amblard, F., Thiriot, S.: Gen*: an integrated tool for realistic agent population synthesis. hal-03097016 (2019)

24. Grimm, V., Berger, U., De Angelis, D.L., Polhill, J.G., Giske, J., Railsback, S.F.. The ODD protocol: a review and first update. Ecol. Model., 2760–2768 (2010)

25. Abdulkadiroglu, A., Sonmez, T.: School choice: a mechanism design approach. Am. Econ. Rev. **93**(3), 729–747 (2003)

26. Projet ASPENO, Atlas Scolaire PErmanent Numérique de Ouagadougou et ses environs. IRD, INSS, CNRST, ISSP, Burkina Faso (2014)

27. Conseil National de la Statistique : Statistiques scolaires de l'Education, Burkina Faso (2023). http://cns.bf/

28. Institut national de la statistique et de la démographie (INSD) : Recensement Général de la Population et de l'Habitation de 2006, RGPH 2006, Monographie de la commune urbaine de Ouagadougou, Décembre 2009. https://www.insd.bf/

29. Institut national de la statistique et de la démographie (INSD): Cinquième Recensement Général de la Population et de l'Habitation, RGPH 2019, Monographie de la commune de Ouagadougou, Décembre 2022. https://www.insd.bf/

# Designing an e-Voting System Based on Blockchain and Smart Contracts in Developing Countries

Giovani M. Babagbeto[1]([✉]) [iD] and Eugene C. Ezin[1,2]

[1] Institut de Formation et de Recherche en Informatique, University of Abomey-Calavi, Abomey-Calavi, Benin
babagbetgeovani@gmail.com, eugene.ezin@uac.bj
[2] Institut de Mathématiques et de Sciences Physiques, University of Abomey-Calavi, Dangbo, Benin

**Abstract.** Voting practices in developing countries are often the subject of controversy and suspicion of corruption. To address these issues, electronic voting systems have been touted as a potential remedy. However, modern democracies face the challenge of instilling trust, security, and transparency in current electronic voting systems, which often struggle with scalability issues, security vulnerabilities, and doubts about trustworthiness. This paper presents an innovative solution that uses smart contracts and blockchain technology to revolutionize e-voting. The network is structured with a hierarchy of nodes that perform different functions: *Mining nodes* validate transactions for blockchain integrity, *Storage nodes* securely store and control access to the election database, *Compiling nodes* publish final election results while overseeing local vote counting, *Administrative nodes* act as election management bodies managing parameters and permissions, and *Voting nodes* enable voters and candidates to directly participate in the election process. Contracts implemented on this network facilitate the systematic and straightforward implementation of various electoral laws. Beyond its technical prowess, this architecture is adaptable across different legal frameworks and geographical boundaries, fostering wider adoption and inclusivity, even in remote areas. It is a beacon of hope for a future where every vote is trusted, every voice is heard and democracy thrives through scalability, security and transparency.

**Keywords:** e-Voting · Smart contracts · Blockchain · Security · Transparency · Trust · Scalability · Architecture · Remote voting

## 1 Introduction

Traditional approaches to democratic elections, which rely on complex logistics and human oversight, are vulnerable to error, manipulation and lack of transparency. This vulnerability is particularly acute in developing countries, where resources are scarce and trust in institutions is often fragile. As a result, elections can become sources of controversy and even violence, as illustrated by the infamous Angolan Halloween massacre

© ICST Institute for Computer Sciences, Social Informatics and Telecommunications Engineering 2026
Published by Springer Nature Switzerland AG 2026. All Rights Reserved
J. B. Awotunde et al. (Eds.): AFRICATEK 2024, LNICST 618, pp. 177–188, 2026.
https://doi.org/10.1007/978-3-031-93557-2_12

of 1992 and the recent unrest in Equatorial Guinea [12, 18, 21]. Such episodes underline the urgent need for alternative voting mechanisms that promote trust, transparency and security.

Electronic voting (e-voting) systems have emerged as a potential solution, promising to reduce logistical burdens and increase confidence in electoral processes. However, while a variety of e-voting systems exist, their global adoption has been slow. Concerns about security, transparency and technological complexity have been major obstacles.

- This paper reviews current e-voting systems, identifies their inherent flaws, and proposes an alternative blockchain architecture designed to mitigate many of these inherent limitations. This innovative design serves as a potential foundation for a secure, flexible and accessible e-voting system specifically tailored to the needs of developing countries.
- It then analyses the limitations of this proposed architecture and explores possibilities for improvement.

## 2   Survey on Electronic Voting Systems

### 2.1   Concept of Electronic Voting

Electronic voting, or e-voting, encompasses a range of technologies designed to digitize and modernize traditional voting processes. These technologies have the potential to streamline the casting and counting of votes, reduce costs and improve voter convenience. [9, 10]. However, designing effective e-voting systems requires careful consideration of fundamental characteristics [1]. Figure 1 illustrates these characteristics.

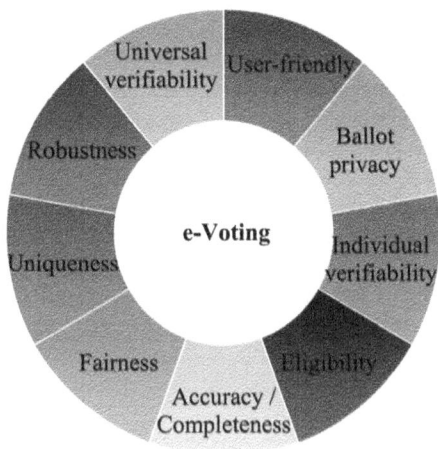

**Fig. 1.** Characteristics of an e-Voting System

Balancing these features is often challenging, as certain features may inherently conflict with each other. For example, ensuring individual verifiability can potentially compromise voter confidentiality. The design of a robust e-voting system must effectively manage these trade-offs in order to maintain both integrity and voter privacy.

## 2.2 e-Voting in the World

By 2023, a growing number of countries- 34 in total- will be using e-voting technologies in controlled or uncontrolled environments, either for all voters or for specific groups such as expatriates. [13]. These deployments include a variety of technologies, including:

- Direct Recording Electronic (DRE) voting machines: These machines record and store votes with or without a voter-verified paper audit trail (VVPAT) [11, 17].
- Electronic ballot printers (EBPs): These printers generate paper ballots or tokens reflecting voters' choices [17].
- Internet voting systems: These systems enable online vote casting, though security concerns limit their widespread adoption.
- Optical Mark Recognition (OMR): These systems recognize votes made on specially marked paper ballots.
- SMS voting systems: These systems allow voters to cast their votes via text message, but raise concerns about accessibility and potential manipulation.

Table 1 provides a detailed overview of the global distribution of these technologies in political elections.

**Table 1.** e-Voting Apparition across the World.

| e-Voting technologies | DRE with VVPAT | DRE without VVPAT | EBPs | Internet voting systems | OMR or OCR | SMS voting systems |
|---|---|---|---|---|---|---|
| Countries | Albania Bulgaria Fiji India Mexico Oman Panama Paraguay Russian Federation United States Venezuela | Bangladesh Bhutan Brazil France Namibia United States | Argentina Belgium Democratic Republic of Congo Ecuador Fiji | Armenia Australia Canada Ecuador Estonia France Mexico New Zealand Oman Pakistan Panama Republique of Korea Russian Federation United Arab Emirates | Canada Dominican Republic Iraq Kirgizstan Mongolia Philippines Russian Federation United States | Mongolia |

Although not yet widespread, several countries are actively exploring the feasibility of e-voting technologies through trials and pilot projects.

## 2.3 Flaws of e-Voting Technologies

While e-voting offers potential benefits such as convenience and efficiency, it also has inherent flaws that raise concerns about its integrity and reliability [5]. These challenges include:

- *Verification and Transparency*: Ensuring that voters can independently verify their vote and have confidence in the voting process remains a critical issue. Traditional paper-based systems provide tangible evidence such as ballot papers, while some e-voting systems lack comparable mechanisms for individual verifiability [4, 11].
- *Security and Vulnerability*: e-Voting systems introduce new attack vectors compared to traditional methods. Potential risks include hacking, manipulation of electronic records, and vulnerabilities in software or hardware. Robust security measures and comprehensive audit trails are crucial to mitigate these risks.
- *Confidentiality and Privacy*: Maintaining voter anonymity is essential to prevent coercion and influence. However, some e-voting systems struggle to completely hide voters' choices, especially in online voting scenarios. Strong cryptographic algorithms and privacy protocols are essential to ensure privacy.
- *Accessibility and Inclusivity*: Not all voters have equal access to, or comfort with, e-voting technologies. Ensuring equal participation for people with disabilities or limited technological skills requires careful design and consideration of alternative access methods.
- *System Complexity and Reliability*: E-voting systems often involve complex software and hardware infrastructure, which increases the potential for technical glitches and malfunctions. Reliable systems require rigorous testing, redundancy measures and contingency plans to deal with potential problems.

These challenges highlight the need for continued research and development of e-voting technologies. Finding solutions that address these limitations while maintaining the fundamental principles of secure, transparent and fair elections is a critical objective.

## 2.4 Use Cases of Blockchain and Smart Contracts for e-Voting

The inherent challenges of existing e-voting technologies have spurred the exploration of alternative solutions, particularly those based on blockchain and smart contracts. [20]. These emerging technologies hold potential to address the key limitations discussed earlier.

A blockchain is a distributed system without a controlling authority, used to store and transmit information transparently and securely [16]. It ensures a high level of security since the transactions that occur are completely anonymous.

Electronic voting using Blockchain technology offers immutability, irreversibility, redundancy, autonomy and resilience.

Smart contracts extend and leverage Blockchain technology. A smart contract is a computerized transaction protocol that executes a contract terms [14]. Smart contracts allow total transparency in the inner workings of e-voting systems using them and also increase efficiency and precision in the voting processes.

Blockchain technology and smart contracts are therefore a good lead for better e-voting systems. Therefore, since the popularization of blockchain technologies, a lot of scientific work has been done. In 2022, Ali Benabdallah and his colleague in *Analysis of Blockchain Solutions for E-Voting: A Systematic Literature Review* identified specific criteria for the design of electronic voting systems using Blockchain technologies [3]. Their study was based on a comparative analysis of existing e-voting solutions using Blockchain technologies. Table 2 summarizes the applications studied in the research based on the determined comparison criteria. In their 2019 paper on *Distributed E-voting and E-bidding systems based on smart contract*, Raylin Tso and his colleagues proposed a dynamic contract that enables voters to verify their ballots and count votes during the result calculation [22].

In 2023, Wenjie Tang et al. in their publication *Distributed Anonymous e-Voting Method Based on Smart Contract Authentication*, described a voting system whose authentication module would be based on smart contracts [19].

### 2.5 Inadequacies of Existing Blockchain and Smart Contract Based e-Voting Solutions

Existing e-voting solutions based on blockchain and/or smart contracts lack comprehensiveness. They tend to focus on specific mechanisms of the voting system, such as voting and counting.

The 2022 review published by Ali Bendallah and his colleagues shows that most related research focuses on verifiability, integrity, personal data protection, confidentiality and such voting properties [3]. Encryption mechanisms and resistance to attacks are also of great interest in this research, as shown in Table 2. While all these criteria should be considered when designing an e-voting system, it's also necessary to consider the remaining electoral processes, such as voter registration and the selection of the persons or organizations accredited to publish the official election results [15].

Smart contracts are extremely suitable for coding an electoral process while ensuring complete transparency. Raylin Tso and his colleagues have proven this fact with their publication of 2019 with a dynamic contract managing vote counting and ensuring individual verifiability [22]. Wenjie Tang and his peers on the other hand have shown how smart contracts can build an authentication module [19]. But these researches are targeting specific electoral processes once more.

Setting up the election according to various law regulations, identifying the voters and hierarchizing the electoral system actors are seldom targeted in existing researches and applications. A complete and flexible e-voting system based on Blockchain and smart contract has yet to be built and adopted. This paper endeavors to propose an architecture for such a system.

**Table 2.** Overview of Blockchain based e-Voting Systems Features

| Criteria | Methods | Number of concerned works |
|---|---|---|
| Authentication | Phone number | 01 |
| | ID document | 02 |
| | Reference validation (public/private keys) | 07 |
| | Biometric identification | 06 |
| Encryption/hashing algorithms | SHA-256 function | 05 |
| | Homomorphic encryption | 15 |
| | Zero Knowledge Proof | 12 |
| | Blind Signature and Ring Signature | 15 |
| | Ethereum hashing function (keccak 256) | 07 |
| Attack resistance | DDOS | 09 tested resistant applications 09 non-resistant applications |
| | Sybil attack | 04 tested resistant applications 01 non-resistant applications |
| | Man-in the-Middle attack | 02 tested resistant applications |
| | Byzantine fault | 08 tested resistant applications 01 non-resistant applications |
| | Coercion | 07 tested resistant applications 14 non-resistant applications |
| | Brute force attack | 02 tested resistant applications |
| Voting security properties | Audit | 26 |
| | Individual verifiability | 49 |
| | Possibility for voters to modify their vote | 12 |
| | Integrity | 36 |
| | Personal data protection | 46 |
| | Confidentiality | 24 |
| | Fairness | 21 |
| | Eligibility | 39 |
| | Transparency | 10 |
| | Unprovable ballot | 13 |

# 3 Constructing a Secure and Collaborative e-Voting System with Smart Contracts

## 3.1 Viability of Smart Contracts Technologies for e-voting

The potential of smart contracts to revolutionize e-voting is undeniable, but ensuring their practical implementation requires careful consideration. Figure 2 outlines key questions that must be addressed to assess their feasibility.

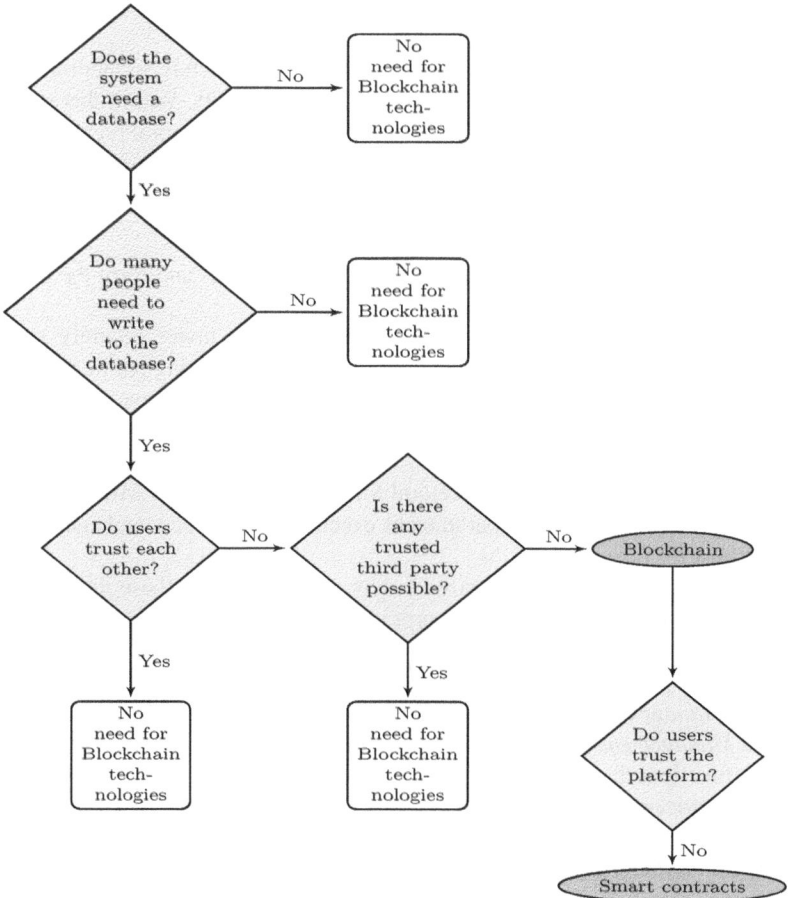

**Fig. 2.** Block Diagram of Smart Contracts for e-Voting System

Beyond verifying their technical suitability, gaining widespread acceptance presents a major hurdle. Research by Mohamed Kamel Alomari highlights how government approval and voter trust are critical factors in developing countries [2]. This approval hinges on demonstrating the system's security, fairness, and compliance with electoral regulations.

Studies by Carter, Schaupp, and Belanger further emphasize the importance of trust, both in the internet and the government, as key drivers of e-voting adoption [7, 8]. Similarly, Alomari et al.'s model for Jordan identifies four key factors influencing citizen adoption: government trust, internet attitudes, system simplicity, and perceived usefulness [2].

While a secure, location-independent, and training-free smart contract-based e-voting system addresses several adoption criteria, governments have a crucial role to play in fulfilling the remaining requirements and building trust amongst the electorate.

## 3.2    Architecture of a Smart Contracts Based e-Voting System

The proposed system leverages a distributed network architecture to facilitate collaborative efforts in maintaining and enhancing electoral integrity. Within this structured network, smart contracts act as impartial digital enforcers of electoral regulations.

The proposed e-voting system employs a semi-public blockchain architecture, fostering transparency and security while safeguarding sensitive data. This network is structured around a hierarchy of nodes, each fulfilling distinct roles:

- *Mining Nodes*: These nodes diligently validate transactions and form the backbone of the blockchain's integrity.
- *Saving Nodes*: Chosen for their trustworthiness, these nodes securely store the electoral database, ensuring controlled access while maintaining public availability.
- *Compiling Nodes*: Empowered to publish final election results, these nodes represent authorized entities, upholding the integrity of the results while allowing other nodes to participate in vote counting locally.
- *Administering Nodes*: Acting as Electoral Management Bodies (EMBs), these nodes meticulously establish election parameters, execute new contracts, and manage access permissions for other nodes.
- *Voting Nodes*: Comprising authorized voters and candidates, these nodes form the heart of the system, enabling direct participation in the electoral process.

The key smart contracts' responsibilities include[1]:

- *Election Management Contract*: Defining election parameters and details.
- *Scrutin Management Contract*: Implementing diverse electoral systems. It includes tallying functions that determine the final seat distribution for the respective elections.
- *Voters Management Contract*: Identifying voters, assigning them to respective districts, managing their voting process, and keeping track of eligible voters.
- *Candidates Management Contract*: Managing vote delegation processes.

These contracts serve as general guidelines and provide a broad framework for further implementation. Specific contracts tailored to each type of electoral law are essential for detailed implementation.

This two-pronged approach leverages the power of blockchain for verifiable security and transparency, while smart contracts automate electoral processes for efficiency and accuracy, as depicted in Fig. 3.

---

[1] For the smart contracts' prototype in Solidity, refer to this GitHub repository: SyVoElSe Contracts.

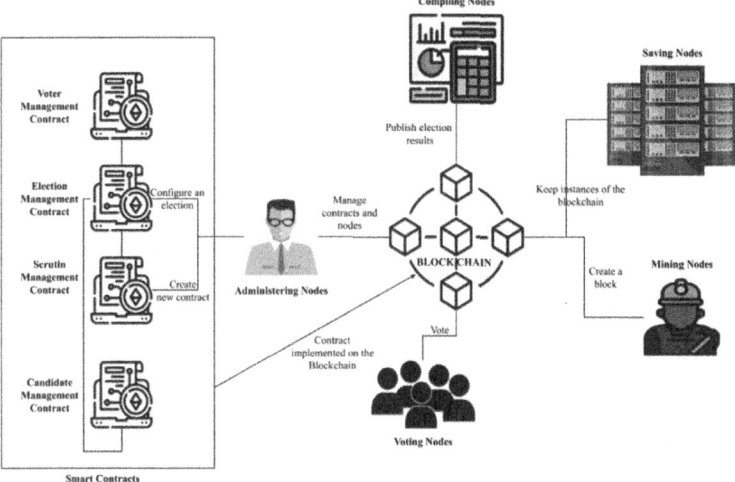

**Fig. 3.** Architecture of the Proposed System

# 4  Discussion

## 4.1  SWOT Analysis of the Proposed Architecture

Table 3 presents a rigorous SWOT analysis of the proposed architecture, comparing it to traditional e-voting and paper-based voting approaches. This analysis employs the evaluation criteria established by Cabuk et al. (2020) for comprehensive examination [6].

## 4.2  Limitations of This Solution

The proposed e-voting system suffers from two substantial limitations: robust voter authentication and internet connectivity dependence, potentially disenfranchising citizens in resource-constrained regions. While hybrid approaches combining e-voting and paper voting seem attractive, they risk inheriting vulnerabilities from both systems and diluting their individual strengths.

A more promising solution lies in the deployment of blockchain-powered voting machines as independent nodes within local government infrastructure. These offline machines circumvent internet dependence and facilitate participation for geographically-isolated populations. Biometric identification protocols integrated within these machines, coupled with optional voice recognition modules, can guarantee secure voter authentication and address accessibility concerns for illiterate voters. Furthermore, the issuance of official electronic voting cards can significantly enhance remote voter authentication protocols, mitigating potential security risks.

**Table 3.** SWOT Analysis of Smart Contracts Integration in e-Voting

|               | Smart Contracts based e-Voting | Simple e-Voting | Traditional Voting |
|---------------|--------------------------------|-----------------|--------------------|
| Strengths     | Immutable records. Record deletion is nearly impossible Provides transparency with privacy Cheaper in the long term Enables elastic elections: variable duration, conditions, and target groups Provides instant results Trust assured by the smart contracts Security ensured by cryptographic measures Redundant Can support frequent elections | Cheaper in the long term Enables elastic elections Many existing samples | People trust paper-based voting and counting, as long as the process is transparent Does not rely on the internet and computers, good for regions with low internet existence/usage |
| Weaknesses    | Initial deployment costs are salient if the concept wants to remain independent, but lower than a naive solution | Initial deployment costs are high Perception of trust is low Internal processes and casted votes are less transparent Uses non-scalable classical databases. Existing unsuccessful attempts may disrupt the motivations | Costs are very high in the long term In-person attendance may be hard and annoying Physical security is tough and expensive Not cost-effective to set vote centers in small and far-away settlements Crowded vote centers become open targets for terrorism |
| Opportunities | New solutions to improve voting transparency Secure remote participation and voting Secure storage and records Once learned, easier for elderly and disabled people Might bring more democracy to government units Less bureaucracy | Secure remote participation and voting Once learned, easier for elderly and disabled people Might bring more democracy to government units Less bureaucracy | Less prone to conspiracy theories Easier and cheaper for smaller and not spread out groups |
| Threats       | Subpar or malicious implementation may lead to heavy security failures | People's perception of trust is significantly lower The centralized processing and storage architecture creates a single point of failure The centralized structure creates an easier target for attackers, too | Human-factor may cause errors during counting Physical attacks may block or distort the voting process Re-holding elections are extremely costly, in case of appeals Difficulties regarding holding elections may result in having fewer elections Humans can be corrupted |

# 5 Conclusion

The transformative potential of smart contracts and blockchain technology resonates deeply within the realm of democratic processes. Our proposed architecture, meticulously crafted to address the Achilles' heels of traditional e-voting methods, stands as a testament to the relentless pursuit of innovation. Through a tapestry woven from specialized node roles, robust security measures, and transparent smart contracts, we have constructed a fortress of integrity, impervious to the shadows of doubt and manipulation. Scalability no longer poses a formidable foe, as our design gracefully scales to accommodate even the most populous nations. Security, once a precarious hope, takes root in the fertile ground of blockchain technology, its roots fortified by cryptographic shields and distributed network architecture. And transparency, the lifeblood of a thriving democracy, courses through the veins of our smart contracts, empowering voters to witness the inviolable audit trail of their entrusted ballot.

But the true strength of our architecture lies not merely in its technical prowess, but in its potential to bridge the chasm between citizens and their governance. Our adaptable design transcends legal and administrative frameworks, welcoming a kaleidoscope of nations into the embrace of secure and inclusive e-voting.

Following the future implementation and live testing of the proposed e-voting system, the ultimate validation lies in its application within a genuine government election. Such a large-scale deployment presents not only an exciting opportunity to assess its real-world efficacy but also valuable insights for further refinement and optimization. Analyzing post-election data, voter feedback, and potential challenges encountered will unveil invaluable information on scalability, security, and user experience in a high-stakes environment. This real-world testbed will pave the way for further enhancements and pave the path for potential global adoption, ultimately proving the proposed architecture's ability to revolutionize the future of secure and transparent democratic processes.

# References

1. Al-Ameen, A., Talab, S.A.: The technical feasibility and security of e-voting. Int. Arab J. Inf. Technol. **10**(4), 397–404 (2013)
2. Alomari, M.K.: E-voting adoption in a developing country. Transforming Gov. People, Process Policy **10**(4), 526–547 (2016)
3. Benabdallah, A., Audras, A., Coudert, L., El Madhoun, N., Badra, M.: Analysis of blockchain solutions for e-voting: a systematic literature review. IEEE Access (2022)
4. Bishop, M., Wagner, D.: Risks of e-voting. Commun. ACM **50**(11), 120 (2007)
5. Bokslag, W., de Vries, M.: Evaluating e-voting: theory and practice. arXiv preprint arXiv: 1602.02509 (2016)
6. Çabuk, U.C., Adiguzel, E., Karaarslan, E.: A survey on feasibility and suitability of blockchain techniques for the e-voting systems. arXiv preprint arXiv:2002.07175 (2020)
7. Carter, L.C.S.L., Schaupp, C.: E-voting: from apathy to adoption. J. Enterp. Inf. Manag. **18**(5), 586–601 (2005)
8. Carter, L., Bélanger, F.: The utilization of e-government services: citizen trust, innovation and acceptance factors. Inf. Syst. J. **15**(1), 5–25 (2005)
9. Collins Dictionaries: E-voting definition and meaning. https://www.collinsdictionary.com/dictionary/english/e-voting. Accessed Jun 2023

10. Driza Maurer, A.: Update of the council of Europe recommendation on legal, operational and technical standards for e-voting–a legal perspective. Jusletter IT (2016)
11. Election Cybersecurity Glossary: Direct Recording Electronic (DRE) voting machine. https://www.electionsecurityglossary.com/glossary/direct-recording-electronic-dre-voting-machine. Accessed Jun 2023
12. Hoekstra, Q.: Conflict diamonds and the Angolan Civil War (1992–2002). Third World Q. **40**(7), 1322–1339 (2019)
13. International IDEA: Advanced search. https://www.idea.int/advanced-search?th=ICTs+in+Elections+Database&amp;region=&amp;question=. Accessed Apr 2023
14. Jake, F., Erika, R., Suzanne, K.: What are smart contracts on the blockchain and how they work. https://www.investopedia.com/terms/s/smart-contracts.asp. Accessed Jun 2023
15. LOI: Code électoral– Charte des partis politiques– Constitution de la République du Bénin. Office Nationale d'Imprimerie et de Presse (ONIP), Bénin (2019)
16. Money: What is Blockchain. https://money.com/what-is-blockchain/. Accessed Jun 2023
17. National Democratic Institute: Common electronic voting and counting technologies. https://www.ndi.org/e-voting-guide/common-electronic-voting-and-counting-technologies. Accessed Jun 2023
18. Stille, A., Chitunda, J.K.: Famous Assassinations in World History: An Encyclopedia [2 Volumes], p. 96 (2014)
19. Tang, W., Yang, W., Tian, X., Yuan, S.: Distributed anonymous e-voting method based on smart contract authentication. Electronics **12**(9), 1968 (2023)
20. Tanwar, S., Gupta, N., Kumar, P., Hu, Y.C.: Implementation of blockchain-based e-voting system. Multimedia Tools Appl. **83**(1), 1449–1480 (2024)
21. Today News Africa: Biden administration condemns sham elections in Equatorial Guinea that gave longest serving president in the world Teodoro Obiang Nguema Mbasogo 94.9
22. Tso, R., Liu, Z.Y., Hsiao, J.H.: Distributed E-voting and E-bidding systems based on smart contract. Electronics **8**(4), 422 (2019)

# Artificial Intelligence Impact on Learner Outcomes in Distance Education: A Process-Based Framework and Research Model

M. D. Adewale[1]([✉]), A. Azeta[2], A. Abayomi-Alli[3], and A. Sambo-Magaji[4]

[1] Africa Centre of Excellence on Technology Enhanced Learning, National Open University of Nigeria, Abuja, Nigeria
mdadewale@gmail.com, ace22140007@noun.edu.ng

[2] Department of Software Engineering, Namibia University of Science and Technology, Windhoek, Namibia

[3] Department of Computer Science, Federal University of Agriculture, Abeokuta, Nigeria
abayomiallia@funaab.edu.ng

[4] Digital Literacy and Capacity Development Department, National Information Technology Development Agency, Abuja, Nigeria
asambo@nitda.gov.ng

**Abstract.** Several prior studies emphasised artificial intelligence's (AI) massive potential in making education more accessible. However, the open and distance learning (ODL) environment has not fully realised the expectations of AI. The heart of the challenge lies not in recognising AI's potential but in harnessing its capabilities effectively within dynamic educational environments. This current study investigates the transformative impact of AI in ODL. The critical need to understand how AI influences learner outcomes in ODL environments was addressed. A process-based framework and research model tailored for AI applications in ODL were developed in this research paper. The study utilised diverse elements comprising AI adoption drivers, its ensuing consequences on academic achievements, the predictive capabilities of machine learning, and inherent gender and regional disparities. Our findings demonstrate the framework's adaptability across various AI algorithms, offering significant implications for enhancing learner's experiences in ODL. The research community would benefit significantly from the developed framework and research model by integrating machine learning algorithms such as support vector machines (SVM). This integration, slated for future endeavours, promises to enhance the predictive efficacy and adaptability of the framework in real-world ODL scenarios.

**Keywords:** Academic performance · AI adoption · Machine Learning · ODL · Prediction

© ICST Institute for Computer Sciences, Social Informatics and Telecommunications Engineering 2026
Published by Springer Nature Switzerland AG 2026. All Rights Reserved
J. B. Awotunde et al. (Eds.): AFRICATEK 2024, LNICST 618, pp. 189–205, 2026.
https://doi.org/10.1007/978-3-031-93557-2_13

# 1 Introduction

Artificial intelligence (AI) is pivotal in revolutionising educational terrains, heralding transformative shifts in pedagogical practices to enhance learners' experiences (Wang et al., 2021). AI champions personalised learning through intricate data-driven strategies, optimising educational outcomes and significantly enhancing students' academic trajectories (Haenlein & Kaplan, 2019). With AI's proliferation in education, especially within open and distance learning (ODL) domains, it is paramount for educators, policymakers, software developers and AI stakeholders to discern its comprehensive implications (Hwang et al., 2020; Picciano, 2017).

While studies by Chen et al. (2020) and Hwang et al. (2020) delve into AI's transformative pedagogical role, a nuanced understanding of its direct impact on academic performance within ODL settings remains unresolved. Findings from Seo et al. (2021), Zhou et al. (2021), Tiwari (2023), and Hashim et al. (2022) highlighted implementation challenges and successes but scarcely touched upon AI's direct impact on ODL students' performance. Moreover, the research landscape fails to address AI's disparate effects across genders and regions, as Daraz et al.'s (2022) study in the Canadian context amplifies the need for inclusivity-centric AI efforts.

This study bridges these gaps by developing a procedural framework and a research model that is not tied to particular machine-learning algorithms. This all-encompassing methodology is essential given that the educational environment continuously evolves, risking framework obsolescence if tethered to a particular algorithm (Hwang et al., 2020; Adewale et al., 2024). Establishing an algorithm-independent framework guarantees flexibility, adaptability, and longevity. An exhaustive 2014–2024 literature review fortified efforts, providing an empirical foundation spotlighting key determinants of AI integration in ODL (Haenlein & Kaplan, 2019), unveiling gender disparities in AI application (Daraz et al., 2022), and shedding light on AI's predictive capabilities for academic outcomes (Picciano, 2017). The goal encourages tailoring AI tools to resonate with diverse distance education student cohorts, pioneering enhanced educational experiences, advocating for gender equality, and ensuring needs-based AI roles (Hwang et al., 2020; Adewale et al., 2024).

This study's unique contribution lies in developing a comprehensive integration of various theoretical model frameworks seamlessly, tailored explicitly for successfully integrating AI in ODL contexts. Contributions address existing knowledge gaps by introducing a model unifying technological, psychological, and contextual factors - pivotal for grasping AI adoption's complexities in ODL environments (Chen et al., 2020). The model's integration of these diverse factors advances academic discourse while offering practical guidance for educators and policymakers to effectively incorporate AI tools in ODL settings, enhancing user engagement and system efficacy (Haenlein & Kaplan, 2019). This dual theory-practice bridge marks a stride in applying AI to distance education.

The subsequent segments are structured as follows: Section Two engages with the review of the literature. Section Three delineates the materials and methodologies, encompassing the procedural framework and the design of the research model. Section Four investigates the implications and constraints, whereas Section Five provides a conclusive summary of the paper.

## 2 Literature Review

AI has swiftly revolutionised the educational landscape, particularly in the realm of distance learning, by augmenting educational outcomes, individualising the learning experience, and enhancing the efficiency of delivery mechanisms. Despite considerable progress, existing gaps persist, prompting the necessity for a process-oriented framework and research model specifically designed to address the intricacies of AI integration within distance education. This literature review examines the multifaceted contributions of AI to education, emphasising its advantages, challenges, and prospective developments, particularly in the context of ODL paradigms.

The incorporation of AI into ODL has fundamentally transformed pedagogical methodologies, mentorship, and content dissemination. Researchers such as Liu and Huang (2022) have underscored AI's potential to refine ODL approaches, while Gao (2022) and Tanjga (2023) accentuate the improvements AI introduces to e-learning platforms via adaptive and intelligent features. However, the incomplete incorporation of AI within ODL, as highlighted by Dua (2021) and Huang et al. (2021), represents a notable gap. This deficiency emphasises the necessity for a comprehensive, process-driven framework to facilitate the seamless implementation of AI in these platforms, ensuring the full realisation of its capabilities in ODL settings (Adewale et al., 2024).

Personalised learning, propelled by AI, is vital for fostering student engagement and enhancing outcomes in distance education. Although research conducted by Hwang et al. (2020) and Almaiah et al. (2022) acknowledges the significance of adaptive learning methodologies, there remains an absence of systematic strategies for effectively incorporating AI into personalised learning within broader educational structures. Recent scholarly discourse underscores the pivotal role of personalised learning in ODL, with elements such as productivity, economic efficiency, and increased involvement propelling AI adoption (Haenlein & Kaplan, 2019; Almaiah et al., 2022). Moreover, emotional responses, real-time feedback, and learning-related anxiety have been shown to affect AI adoption, illustrating the beneficial influence of AI-powered platforms on learner success through customised education and prompt feedback (Dua, 2021 ). Previous studies on ODL include (Ayo et al., 2014; Nicholas-Omoregbe, 2017; Azeta & Van Der Merwe, 2022).

The integration of AI into ODL is influenced by factors delineated in prominent technology acceptance theories, including the Technology Acceptance Model (TAM) (Charness & Boot, 2016), the Information Systems Success Model (Sabeh et al., 2021), and the Unified Theory of Acceptance and Use of Technology (UTAUT) (Yakubu & Dasuki, 2018). These theoretical frameworks elucidate essential determinants such as ease of use, perceived usefulness, user satisfaction, system quality, and social influence. Furthermore, investigations by Ouyang et al. (2023) illustrate AI's predictive capabilities in evaluating student performance trajectories. Chen et al. (2020) highlight AI's contribution to enhancing interactions between educators and students in digital contexts. Nguyen et al. (2022) advocate for an in-depth examination of variables such as gender and regional differences to ensure a comprehensive understanding of AI's impact on education.

Nonetheless, the incorporation of AI within the educational sector encounters various impediments, notably apprehensions regarding its omnipresence, the potential for inherent biases, and its influence on autonomous learning (Seo et al., 2021; Wang et al., 2021). These impediments necessitate the establishment of a comprehensive predictive, process-oriented framework that capitalises on the advantages offered by AI while simultaneously alleviating its associated risks. It is of paramount importance to take into account moderating variables such as gender and geographic disparities, particularly when assessing AI's ramifications on ODL across both developed and developing territories. Research conducted by Gardner et al. (2019) and Kumar and Choudhury (2022) accentuates the prospective ramifications of gender biases in AI interactions, while Toplic (2021) cautions against the possibility of AI intensifying the digital divide, mainly affecting women in both developed and developing environments. The prevailing academic discourse frequently neglects demographic and geographical differences in AI adoption, which are instrumental in shaping learner engagement with AI-enhanced educational instruments. A thorough, process-oriented framework is indispensable for the effective integration of these moderating factors into the design and implementation of AI, ensuring that AI tools are inclusive, equitable, and advantageous for all learners (Adewale et al., 2024).

The Support Vector Machine (SVM) has emerged as a prominent AI algorithm for forecasting the performance of students in ODL, with alternative methodologies such as evolutionary computation and random forests exhibiting potential for the early identification of students at risk and the enhancement of educational outcomes (Mduma et al., 2019; Tomasevic et al., 2020; Ayouni et al., 2021; Ouyang et al., 2023; Jiao et al., 2022; Holicza & Kiss, 2023; Adewale et al., 2024). Nevertheless, the concentration on particular algorithms often overlooks the broader educational framework, resulting in a disjointed comprehension of AI's function within education. The formulation of a process-oriented framework and research model that transcends dependence on specific algorithms is imperative for establishing a more versatile and adaptable methodology for the integration of AI in distance education.

This literature review serves as a foundational basis for our investigation, which seeks to create an all-encompassing, process-oriented framework and research model. Our methodology consciously refrains from depending on specific predictive algorithms, thereby devising a universally adaptable model. By incorporating variables such as the drivers of AI adoption, gender considerations, and regional disparities, we aspire to align our framework with UNESCO's 2030 educational objectives, thereby ensuring flexibility and inclusivity across diverse communities and regions. The deficiencies identified within the current literature, including inadequate AI integration in ODL, the urgent need for personalised and adaptive learning strategies, and the importance of addressing demographic and geographic disparities, underscore the necessity for such a framework. By tackling these challenges, our proposed framework and model endeavour to enhance the efficacy and inclusiveness of AI in distance education, ultimately advancing learner outcomes across varied educational contexts (Table 1).

## 3  Materials and Methods

In the previous section, a comprehensive review of related work was undertaken to formulate a process-driven framework and research model aimed at predicting the impact of AI integration on students' academic performance, utilising insights from prior studies

**Table 1.** Summary of the main features of the references discussed

| S/N | Reference | Main Features |
|---|---|---|
| 1 | Haenlein & Kaplan (2019) | Focus on bespoke learning through data-driven strategies |
| 2 | Hwang et al. (2020) | Discuss the democratising potential of AI in education |
| 3 | Chen et al. (2020) | Highlight AI's role in enhancing educator-student rapport in online settings |
| 4 | Seo, Tang, Roll, Fels, & Yoon (2021) | Examine AI's impact on learner-instructor interaction in online learning |
| 5 | Zhou et al. (2021) | Spotlight on implementation challenges and successes of AI in education |
| 6 | Huang et al. (2021); Sabeh et al., 2021 | Review of AI in Education and technology acceptance theories like TAM, D&M and UTAUT |
| 7 | Almaiah et al. (2022) | Asserts that efficacy, economic viability, and enhanced student involvement are fundamental to the integration of AI in ODL |
| 8 | Horowitz and Kahn (2021) | Discusses the emotion, immediate feedback and anxiety pertaining to learning in relation to AI integration |
| 9 | Dua (2021) | Focus on AI-driven platforms improving student performance through personalised learning experiences |
| 10 | Ouyang et al. (2023); ; Adewale et al. (2024) | Demonstrate AI's forecasting abilities in evaluating the trajectories of student performance |
| 11 | Nguyen et al. (2022); ; Adewale et al. (2024) | Advocate for investigation of factors such as gender and geographical variations in AI's educational dynamics |
| 12 | Seo et al. (2021); Wang et al. (2021) | Raise apprehensions regarding the pervasive nature of AI in education and the potential for inherent biases |
| 13 | Gardner et al. (2019); Kumar & Choudhury (2022) | Highlight gender biases in AI and its implications |
| 14 | Mduma et al. (2019); Tomasevic et al. (2020); Ayouni et al. (2021); Ouyang et al. (2023); ; Adewale et al. (2024) | Discuss AI algorithms like SVM for predicting student performance |

to enhance the conceptual framework and model. The methodology employed is elaborated systematically in the following sections. We divided our method into a design process and a systematic literature review, emphasising a design-centric approach.

### 3.1 Design of Process Framework and Research Model

This phase also necessitated meticulous examination of the framework and model to demonstrate significant theoretical coherence and logical consistency. It necessitated an in-depth review of the constructs and their systematic organisation to accurately depict the interactions and dynamics of AI adoption and its effects on students' academic performance.

I. **Identification of Fundamental Elements**

    From the consolidated literature, essential elements driving AI adoption and its impact on student outcomes were discerned and underpinned the foundation of innovative design.

II. **Framework Formulation**

    A preliminary version of the process-oriented framework was crafted, drawing on insights from the review of related work to outline the sequence and connections between key elements, ranging from the factors influencing AI adoption to their ultimate effect on educational outcomes.

III. **Model Development**

    Next, we developed the research model, detailing the variables, their interconnections, and their underlying theoretical bases. This was designed to offer a thorough understanding of how the integration of AI could potentially forecast academic outcomes.

IV. **Assessment and Enhancement**

    The proposed framework and model underwent multiple rounds of refinement. This iterative process involved revisiting relevant literature to ensure alignment with identified factors and making necessary adjustments for clarity and coherence. After the initial designs were developed, they were subjected to a series of evaluations and revisions to ensure their robustness, relevance, and applicability. The frameworks were thoroughly scrutinised for any inconsistencies, redundancies, or gaps, and necessary modifications were made to enhance their comprehensiveness and coherence.

V. **Tool Selection**

    Considering the emphasis on design, tools were selected to convey and represent the procedural framework and research model visually. Applications like Lucidchart and Microsoft Visio offered the essential resources to craft clear, visually appealing, and comprehensive diagrams, ensuring that the final designs were academically sound, robust, and accessible to users.

### 3.2 The Process-Based Framework

The research proposes a systematic process-based framework to guide the analysis of predicting AI integration's impact on students' outcomes. This structured approach aims to provide a coherent and effective methodology, ensuring consistent outcomes. The framework comprises several key steps executed sequentially to enable a comprehensive investigation. While the framework is indifferent to particular machine learning methodologies, SVM is well grounded in the literature as the most effective algorithm for predicting student outcomes. We use SVM as a representative example to enhance clarity throughout the framework description. The following steps were engaged in designing the process framework:

I. **Identification of Key Factors:** This step involves identifying and selecting the key factors that influence AI integration on the academic achievements of students within ODL environments. We review relevant literature and empirical studies to identify the critical factors significantly influencing learning outcomes in AI-integrated ODL environments.

II. **Research Model Formulation:** This phase merges key factors with constructs from TAM, D&M, and UTAUT, shaping independent variables that affect student performance. It also defines moderating factors like gender and regional differences to assess their influence on this relationship.

III. **Data Collection and Preprocessing:** The process framework collects relevant data related to the identified key factors in this step. Data sources, such as student performance records, demographic information, AI usage data, and other relevant indicators, will be considered. Preprocessing techniques will be applied to ensure data quality and prepare the dataset for analysis.

IV. **Feature Engineering and Selection:** This step involves transforming the collected data into meaningful features that can be utilised in the prediction process. Feature engineering techniques, such as data normalisation, dimensionality reduction, and feature extraction, will create a representative set of features for SVM modelling.

V. **Machine Learning Modeling and Prediction:** Machine Learning Models should be employed as the predictive modelling algorithm using the processed and engineered features. The machine learning model should be trained on historical data, leveraging its ability to analyse patterns and make predictions based on the identified key factors. The model's performance should be assessed using appropriate evaluation metrics.

VI. **Interpretation and Validation:** The final step of the process framework involves interpreting the results of the SVM model and validating the predictions against the actual students' academic performance in ODL. This step aims to assess the accuracy and reliability of the predictive model and gain insights into the influence of integrating AI on educational outcomes.

This methodological framework (Refer to Fig. 1) offers a structured, methodical and organised strategy for predicting the influence of AI integration on students' academic achievements in distance learning through the application of machine learning techniques such as SVM. By amalgamating the foundational principles of AI, distance learning, and machine learning techniques like SVM, this framework aids in elucidating the intricate interconnections between AI integration, significant determinants, and educational outcomes. The framework operates independently of specific machine learning methods. It serves as a guide for forthcoming empirical investigations and practical applications, thus empowering academic institutions to effectively leverage AI in distance learning to improve learners' academic outcomes and overall educational experiences.

In conclusion, the methodological framework employed for this research endeavour embodies a holistic approach that encompasses a comprehensive literature review, formulation of research inquiries, data acquisition, meticulous evaluation, predictive modelling, and insights generation from the results. By following this structured approach, the investigation aspires to uphold methodological integrity and yield substantive insights regarding the correlation between AI integration and learners' educational outcomes in distance learning contexts. Figure 1 shows a comprehensive process framework design that weaves in the factors discerned from the requirements elicitation phase, aiming to amplify insights into AI adoption within ODL settings.

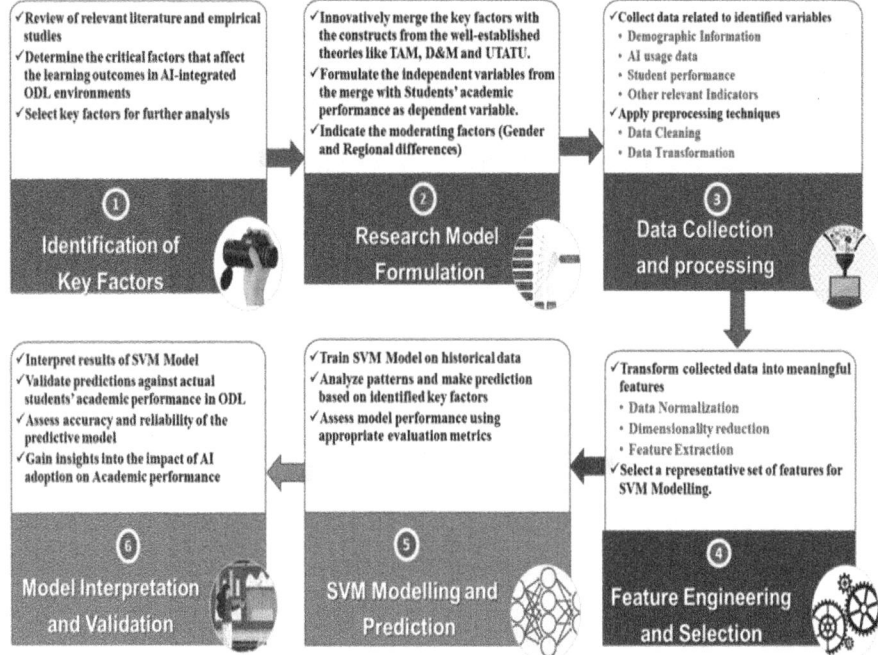

**Fig. 1.** The Process-Driven Framework for Analysing the Influence of Artificial Intelligence Implementation on the Academic Outcomes of Students in ODL

### 3.3 The Research Model

The study combined the core constructs of renowned theories–TAM, D&M, and UTAUT–with specific factors inherent to the ODL context, refining them into eight primary independent variables. These variables, depicted in Fig. 2, directly influence the implementation and utilisation of modern AI technologies in ODL settings, with students' academic performance as the dependent variable. The influence of these primary factors is further moderated by gender(G) and geographical location/region(R) as described below:

I. **AI Alignment and Relevance:** Evaluates the congruence of artificial intelligence with the requirements of students and institutions, incorporating Institutional Alignment, elements of Attitude toward Technology, and dimensions of Perceived Usefulness.

II. **Comparative Advantage of AI:** Analyses the advantages presented by artificial intelligence in comparison to conventional methodologies, merging Comparative Advantage with elements of Perceived Usefulness.

III. **Ease and Enjoyment of Use:** Assesses the straightforwardness and enjoyment associated with the utilisation of AI, synthesising elements of Perceived Ease of Use and dimensions of Perceived Enjoyment.

IV. **AI-induced Learning Anxiety:** Identifies the anxiety associated with learning facilitated by artificial intelligence.

V. **AI Readiness and Facilitating Conditions:** Appraises the preparedness for the integration of artificial intelligence and the prevailing supportive conditions.

VI. **Interactive Capability (IC):** Evaluates the readiness for and improvements in online interactions enabled by artificial intelligence.

VII. **Knowledge Absorption and User Satisfaction (KAUS):** Investigates the influence of artificial intelligence on knowledge acquisition and overall user satisfaction.

VIII. **Systems Quality and Social Influence (SQSI):** Assesses the calibre of the AI system and the impact of social factors on its adoption.

These refined constructs provide a comprehensive, generalisable research model for AI adoption in ODL, marrying proven theories such as TAM, D&M, and UTAUT with ODL-specific factors. We chose these models because of their proven effectiveness in evaluating technology adoption, particularly in the educational sector, ensuring a comprehensive approach to AI adoption in ODL. This work introduces a distinct research model that synergistically integrates key components from renowned models with particular attributes germane to ODL environments, fortifying the study's comprehensiveness and adaptability.

This model advances beyond these established theories by addressing unique ODL challenges, such as stress linked to AI-based learning, which existing models do not fully encapsulate. Our model fills gaps in current theories like TAM, D&M, and UTAUT, which, while effective in general technology adoption contexts, do not entirely cater to the unique dynamics of AI adoption in ODL. For instance, it considers institutional alignment and comparative advantage, which are less emphasised in traditional models. Given their proven significance in technology adoption, we adapted factors from TAM, UTAUT, and other models to the ODL context. This includes incorporating technological ease of use and acceptance in remote learning environments, where learner engagement and interaction with AI differ from traditional settings. For our research model, variables were included based on their relevance and impact in the context of AI adoption in ODL settings, ensuring a comprehensive analysis of how AI impacts student learning and engagement in these environments. Factors that did not directly contribute to this understanding or overlapped without adding significant value were excluded to maintain a focused and relevant model.

Our integrated model offers specific advances over existing theories by providing a more holistic view of AI adoption in diverse ODL environments. It acknowledges the

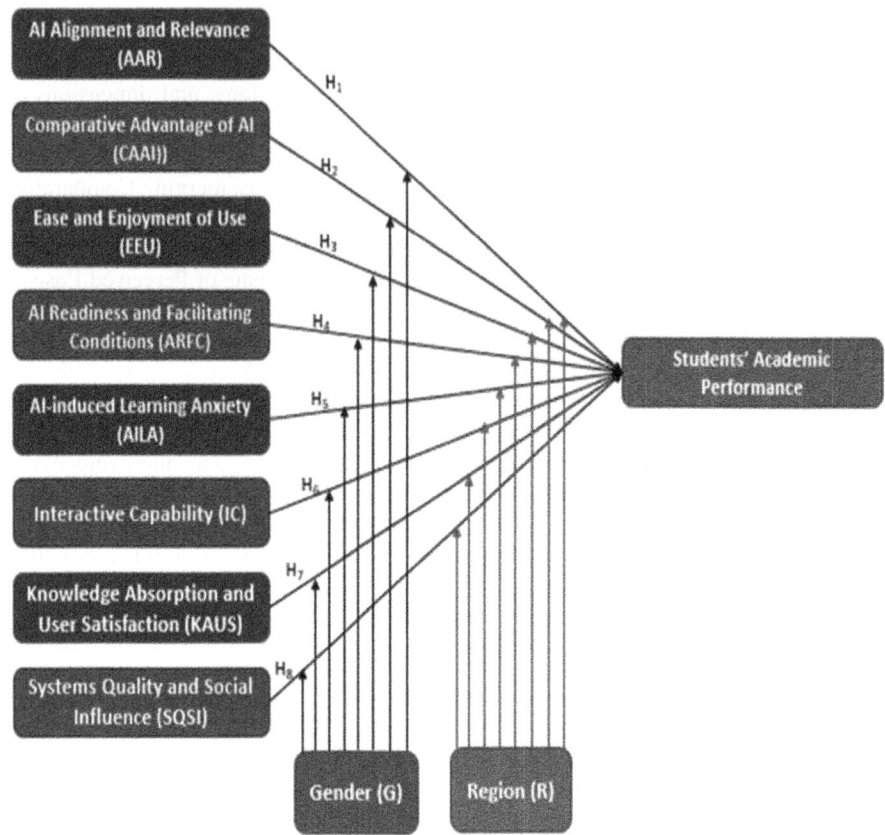

**Fig. 2.** Research Model

multifaceted nature of AI implementation, considering the technological aspects and socio-psychological elements, such as user satisfaction and system quality. This comprehensive approach enables a deeper understanding of the nuances and complexities involved in AI adoption in ODL, which individual models like TAM, D&M, or UTAUT may not fully capture. This strategic approach ensures a detailed, context-specific analysis and enhances the model's practical relevance. It addresses diverse ODL needs, making it a globally applicable framework. The research model contributes significantly to academic discussions and is poised to redefine our understanding of AI integration within ODL systems.

The following hypotheses (H1, H2 to H8) should be tested in the proposed research model shown in Fig. 2:

 I. H1: AI Alignment and Relevance (AAR) significantly impacts Students' academic performance prediction.
 II. H2: Comparative Advantage of AI (CAAI) significantly impacts Students' academic performance prediction.

III. H3: Ease and Enjoyment of Use (EEU) significantly impacts Students' academic performance prediction.
IV. H4: AI Readiness and Facilitating Conditions (ARFC) significantly impact Students' academic performance prediction.
V. H5: AI-induced Learning Anxiety (AILA) significantly impacts Students' academic performance prediction.
VI. H6: Interactive Capability (IC) significantly impacts Students' academic performance prediction.
VII. H7: Knowledge Absorption and User Satisfaction (KAUS) significantly impact Students' academic performance prediction.
VIII. H8: Systems Quality and Social Influence (SQSI) significantly impacts Students' academic performance prediction.

### 3.3.1 Moderating Factors

In our research model, gender and regional disparities are posited as moderators between AI adoption and students' academic performance. These variables are crucial for capturing the diverse impacts of AI in education, acknowledging the varying degrees of technology acceptance and access across different genders and regions. We propose that gender differences may influence the use and impact of AI in learning, possibly due to varying degrees of engagement and access to technology-related resources. Similarly, the model considers the influence of regional factors, acknowledging that students in developed regions may experience AI tools differently from those in developing areas due to infrastructure and internet access disparities. We will conduct subgroup analyses to discern the differential effects across genders and between developed and developing regions, ensuring our AI adoption strategies are responsive to these critical variables.

### 3.4 Research Design

In achieving the study's objective of investigating the intricate association between the integration of AI and the academic achievements of students within ODL settings, a process framework that can be implemented by employing the SVM or any other suitable algorithms and integrating key constructs from established theories has been developed. As part of the study to understand requirement elicitation and state-of-the-art technologies, a systematic literature review should be conducted using the following research design:

I. **Search Strategy.**
   Multiple academic databases were explored to ensure the collection of An extensive array of pertinent literature was examined. A meticulous search was conducted across distinguished academic databases:

   - Scopus
   - Web of Science
   - Google Scholar

   The inquiry utilised an amalgamation of terminology including: ("Artificial Intelligence" OR "AI") AND ("student performance" OR "academic outcomes") AND ("adoption factors" OR "integration").

II. **Criteria for Inclusion and Exclusion.**
   **Inclusion Criteria:**

- Articles subjected to peer review and conference papers focused on AI in ODL settings were included.
- The literature discusses models, frameworks, or theories about AI adoption in education.
- Publications in English from the last eight years were included to maintain relevance and timeliness.

   **Exclusion Criteria:**

- Non-academic and non-peer-reviewed articles or conference proceedings were excluded.
- Studies do not specifically address the incorporation of AI within ODL frameworks.

III. **Extraction of Data.**
   From every pertinent scholarly article:

- Contributors and the year of publication
- Objectives or research questions
- Findings, especially about AI adoption factors
- Relevant frameworks, models, or theories discussed

### 3.5   Ethical Considerations in AI Applications for Education

The establishment of a novel process-based framework and research model for predicting academic success in ODL environments emphasises ethical considerations to guarantee that AI-driven solutions uphold the highest standards of privacy protection, data security, and fairness. The framework includes robust privacy safeguards and secure data handling protocols to protect student confidentiality and rights. In order to cultivate equitable learning opportunities, the framework integrates comprehensive techniques for mitigating bias, considering factors such as gender and geographic location to prevent disparities. These critical elements underscore our commitment to responsible and ethical AI deployment in educational settings. We align our practices with societal expectations and regulatory requirements, which include data anonymisation, stringent data security measures, and systematic checks for algorithmic bias. This approach enhances the predictive accuracy of student performance in ODL contexts while ensuring that technological advancements contribute positively to the educational landscape, promoting fairness and inclusivity.

### 3.6   Practical Guidelines for Implementing the Process Framework

To effectively implement the process framework for predicting student academic performance in ODL environments, institutions should define the objectives and scope to ensure alignment with their educational goals. The next step is identifying and selecting critical factors influencing AI adoption based on a thorough review of relevant literature and empirical data. Data collection should involve gathering information from various sources, including student records, surveys, and academic performance metrics, followed by meticulous data preprocessing to ensure accuracy and consistency. Developing relevant features from the raw data enhances the model's predictive power, which is then trained using machine learning techniques such as SVM. Model validation is crucial to ensuring accuracy and reliability, utilising appropriate metrics. Once validated, the model should be deployed within the institution's existing data infrastructure, with continuous monitoring and evaluation to make necessary adjustments based on feedback and new data. Ethical considerations, including compliance with data privacy regulations, must be maintained throughout the implementation process. By following these practical guidelines, educational institutions can effectively leverage AI to enhance student academic performance and learning experiences in ODL settings.

## 4   Practical Implications, Future Research Endeavour and Limitations of the Study

The proposed model offers practical insights for educational institutions, guiding them in strategically adopting AI to enhance learner outcomes in ODL. It provides a framework for understanding the impact of AI on learning processes and outcomes, aiding in decision-making and policy formulation. While the current study is conceptual, future research will focus on implementing the model in real-world ODL settings. We plan to collaborate with educational institutions to apply our framework and assess its effectiveness in improving learner outcomes through controlled studies and qualitative feedback from educators and learners.

In our forthcoming research, building on the conceptual foundation of this study, we aim to empirically validate our model with quantitative data from ODL students, focusing on AI usage and performance metrics. We will analyse this data using machine learning algorithms, particularly SVM, and supplement it with performance metrics such as mean absolute error, mean squared error, and root mean squared error. Additionally, we will employ traditional statistical methods, including regression analysis and structural equation modelling, to reinforce the findings from machine learning, ensuring a multifaceted and thorough validation of our model. This future research is a critical extension of our current conceptual work, blending advanced computational analytics with established statistical approaches for a comprehensive evaluation.

This study acts as a clarion call, emphasising the imminent real-world applications of AI in ODL. By seamlessly intertwining theoretical underpinnings with tangible applications, this research stands out as an emblem of the harmonious union between AI's vast capabilities and the intricate challenges and prospects intrinsic to ODL environments. Our presented research model incorporates essential elements from acclaimed theories like TAM, D&M, and UTAUT. Beyond that, it is further enriched with distinct features tailored to the unique attributes and nuances of the ODL environment, ensuring its precision in capturing the multifaceted experiences typical of such contexts.

The process framework and the research model, rooted deeply in established educational theories, provide a holistic lens, offering an expansive view of AI's profound potential impacts on the academic realm. While amplifying the essence of AI, their design underscores the transformative shifts and nuanced challenges that arise with the infusion of technology in education, particularly in digital and remote learning contexts. Their construction showcases a masterful blend of varied theories and methods, symbolising the harmonious marriage of different paradigms to form a unified, cohesive structure. This structure is adept at exploring the intricate tapestry of experiences that define ODL. Beyond its theoretical richness, the work shines a light on the path ahead, guiding future research endeavours with fresh insights and pioneering approaches, paving the way for a crucial phase of empirical investigation. The subsequent step will involve a comprehensive examination and corroboration of the process framework using real-world evidence, establishing its reliability and applicability in predicting student academic outcomes in ODL environments.

## 5   Conclusion

This study meticulously unveils a process framework and research model based on the comprehensive insights presented in our preceding literature review. At its core, the process-based framework seeks to predict the repercussions of AI adoption on student academic achievements in ODL contexts, understanding AI's immense transformative potential and its inherent challenges. This paper delineates the workflow of this process framework, which is notably independent of any machine learning algorithm. This research magnifies the potential of melding cutting-edge technological solutions with deep-rooted theoretical knowledge, paving the way for an adaptive tool that's well-equipped to traverse the dynamic landscapes of modern education.

The developed framework and research model would benefit significantly from integrating machine learning algorithms such as SVM. This integration, slated for future endeavours, promises to enhance the predictive efficacy and adaptability of the framework in real-world ODL scenarios. Rigorous empirical validation of the framework and model in diverse ODL environments will further cement their reliability and applicability. By endorsing these proposals, we foresee a substantial enhancement in the domain of AI within ODL, propelling significant transformation and promoting scholarly excellence.

**Disclosure of Potential Conflict of Interest.**   All the authors have said that no financial or personal ties between them could be seen as having influenced the work reported in this paper.

**Authors Contributions.**   The contributions of the authors in this study are as follows. M.D. Adewale provided the conceptualisation, methodology, software, data curation, and writing for the original draft preparation. Others participated in the validation, project administration, and writing for review and editing. All authors have given their approval to submit the manuscript to this journal. This work is derived from M.D. Adewale's PhD thesis.

**Data Availability Statement.**   All data for this systematic review are sourced from public academic databases, including Scopus, Google Scholar, and Web of Science. Please direct any additional inquiries to the corresponding author.

**ORCID Information.** The document contains ORCID information regarding the corresponding author, with an ORCID Number of https://orcid.org/0009-0007-9267-5601.

# References

Adewale, M. D., Azeta, A., Abayomi-Alli, A., & Sambo-Magaji, A.: Impact of artificial intelligence adoption on students' academic performance in open and distance learning: A systematic literature review. Heliyon, **10**(22), e40025 (2024). https://doi.org/10.1016/j.heliyon.2024.e40025

Almaiah, M.A., et al.: Examining the impact of artificial intelligence and social and computer anxiety in E-learning settings: students' perceptions at the university level. Electronics **11**(22), 3662 (2022). https://doi.org/10.3390/electronics11223662

Ayo, C.K., Odukoya, J.A., Azeta, A.A.: A review of open and distance education and human development in Nigeria. Int. J. Emerg. Technol. Learn. **9**(6), 63–67 (2014). Index in Scopus. ISSN: 1863-0383

Ayouni, S., Hajjej, F., Maddeh, M., Al-Otaibi, S.: A new ML-based approach to enhance student engagement in online environment. PLoS ONE **16**(11), e0258788 (2021). https://doi.org/10.1371/journal.pone.0258788

Azeta, A.A., Van Der Merwe, T.M.: The effects of blended learning approaches on class attendance scores in two final-year undergraduate financial accounting courses. In: Proceedings of International Conference on Information Systems and Emerging Technologies (ICISET) and International Conference on Data Science, Machine Learning and Artificial Intelligence (DSM-LAI) held at Namibia University of Science and Technology (NUST) from 23 to 25 November 2022. Elsevier SSRN: https://ssrn.com/abstract=4331723 or https://doi.org/10.2139/ssrn.4331723

Charness, N., Boot, W.R.: Technology, gaming, and social networking. In: Handbook of the Psychology of Aging, pp. 389–407 (2016). https://doi.org/10.1016/b978-0-12-411469-2.00020-0

Chen, X., Xie, H., Zou, D., Hwang, G.J.: Application and theory gaps during the rise of Artificial Intelligence in Education. Comput. Educ. Artif. Intell. **1**, 100002 (2020). https://doi.org/10.1016/j.caeai.2020.100002

Daraz, L., Bouseh, S., Chang, B.S.: Subpar: the challenges of gender parity in Canada's Artificial Intelligence Ecosystem. Comput. Inf. Sci. **15**(2), 1 (2022). https://doi.org/10.3389/frai.2022.931182

Dua, A.: Applications of artificial intelligence in open and distance learning. TechnoLearn Int. J. Educ. Technol. **11**(2) (2021). https://doi.org/10.30954/2231-4105.02.2021.1

Gao, H.: Online AI-guided video extraction for distance education with applications. Math. Probl. Eng. **2022**, 1–7 (2022). https://doi.org/10.1155/2022/5028726

Gardner, J., Brooks, C., Baker, R.S.: Evaluating the fairness of predictive student models through slicing analysis (2019). https://doi.org/10.1145/3303772.3303791

Haenlein, M., Kaplan, A.: A brief history of artificial intelligence: on the past, present, and future of artificial intelligence. Calif. Manage. Rev. **61**(4), 5–14 (2019). https://doi.org/10.1177/0008125619864925

Hashim, S., Omar, M. K., Jalil, H.A., Sharef, N.M.: Trends on technologies and artificial intelligence in education for personalised learning: systematic literature review. Int. J. Acad. Res. Progressive Educ. Dev. **11**(1) (2022). https://doi.org/10.6007/ijarped/v11-i1/12230

Holicza, B., Kiss, A.: Predicting and comparing students' online and offline academic performance using machine learning algorithms. Behav. Sci. (Basel) **13**(4), 289 (2023). https://doi.org/10.3390/bs13040289

Horowitz, M., Kahn, L.E.: What influences attitudes about artificial intelligence adoption: Evidence from U.S. local officials. PLOS ONE **16**(10), e0257732 (2021). https://doi.org/10.1371/journal.pone.0257732

Huang, J., Saleh, S., Liu, Y.: A review on artificial intelligence in education. Acad. J. Interdiscip. Stud. **10**(3), 206 (2021). https://doi.org/10.36941/ajis-2021-0077

Hwang, G.J., Xie, H., Wah, B.W., Gašević, D.: Vision, challenges, roles and research issues of Artificial Intelligence in Education. Comput. Educ. Artif. Intell. **1**, 100001 (2020). https://doi.org/10.1016/j.caeai.2020.100001

Jiao, P., Ouyang, F., Zhang, Q., Alavi, A.H.: Artificial intelligence-enabled prediction model of student academic performance in online engineering education. Artif. Intell. Rev. **55**(8), 6321–6344 (2022). https://doi.org/10.1007/s10462-022-10155-y

Kumar, S., Choudhury, S.: Gender and feminist considerations in artificial intelligence from a developing-world perspective, with India as a case study. Humanit. Soc. Sci. Commun. **9**(1) (2022). https://doi.org/10.1057/s41599-022-01043-5

Liu, X., Huang, X.: Design of Artificial Intelligence-BASED English Network Teaching (AI-ENT) system. Math. Probl. Eng. **2022**, 1–12 (2022). https://doi.org/10.1155/2022/1849430

Mduma, N., Kalegele, K., Machuve, D.: A survey of machine learning approaches and techniques for student dropout prediction. Data Sci. J. **18** (2019). https://doi.org/10.5334/dsj-2019-014

Nguyen, A., Ngo, H.N., Hong, Y., Dang, B., Nguyen, B.T.: Ethical principles for artificial intelligence in education. Educ. Inf. Technol. **28**(4), 4221–4241 (2022). https://doi.org/10.1007/s10639-022-11316-w

Ouyang, F., Wu, M., Zheng, L., Zhang, L., Jiao, P.: Integration of artificial intelligence performance prediction and learning analytics to improve student learning in online engineering course. Int. J. Educ. Technol. High. Educ. **20**(1) (2023). https://doi.org/10.1186/s41239-022-00372-4

Nicholas-Omoregbe, O.S., Azeta, A.A., Chiazor, I.A., Omoregbe, N.: Predicting the adoption of E-learning management system: a case of selected private Universities in Nigeria. Turk. Online J. Distance Educ. TOJDE **18**(2), 106–121 (2017)

Picciano, A.G.: Theories and frameworks for online education: seeking an integrated model. Online Learn. **21**(3) (2017). https://doi.org/10.24059/olj.v21i3.1225

Sabeh, H.N., Husin, M.H., Kee, D.M.H., Baharudin, A.S., Abdullah, R.: A systematic review of the DeLone and McLean model of information systems success in an E-Learning context (2010–2020). IEEE Access **9**, 81210–81235 (2021). https://doi.org/10.1109/access.2021.3084815

Seo, K.W., Tang, J., Roll, I., Fels, S., Yoon, D.: The impact of artificial intelligence on learner–instructor interaction in online learning. Int. J. Educ. Technol. High. Educ. **18**(1) (2021). https://doi.org/10.1186/s41239-021-00292-9

Tanjga, M.: E-learning and the use of AI: a review of current practices and future directions. Qeios (2023). https://doi.org/10.32388/ap0208.2

Tiwari, R.: The integration of AI and machine learning in education and its potential to personalise and improve student learning experiences. Int. J. Sci. Res. Eng. Manage. (IJSREM) (2023). https://doi.org/10.55041/ijsrem17645

Tomašević, N., Gvozdenovic, N., Vraneš, S.: An overview and comparison of supervised data mining techniques for student exam performance prediction. Comput. Educ. **143**, 103676 (2020). https://doi.org/10.1016/j.compedu.2019.103676

Toplic, L.: If AI is the future, gender equity is essential. NetHope (2021). https://nethope.org/articles/if-ai-is-the-future-gender-equity-is-essential/. Accessed 26 Dec 2022

Wang, Y., Liu, C., Tu, Y.-F.: Factors affecting the adoption of AI based applications in higher education: an analysis of teachers perspectives using structural equation modeling. Educ. Technol. Soc. **24**, 116–129 (2021). https://eric.ed.gov/?id=EJ1306390

Yakubu, M.N., Dasuki, S.I.: Factors affecting the adoption of e-learning technologies among higher education students in Nigeria. Inf. Dev. **35**(3), 492–502 (2018). https://doi.org/10.1177/0266666918765907

Zhou, Q., et al.: Investigating students' experiences with collaboration analytics for remote group meetings. In: Roll, I., McNamara, D., Sosnovsky, S., Luckin, R., Dimitrova, V. (eds.) Artificial Intelligence in Education. AIED 2021. Lecture Notes in Computer Science, vol. 12748, pp. 472–485. Springer, Cham (2021). https://doi.org/10.1007/978-3-030-78292-4_38

# Assessment of Students' Performance Using Machine Learning: A Bibliometric Study

Michel Hountondji[1]([✉]), Pélagie Houngue[1], and Theophile Komlan Dagba[2]

[1] Institut de Mathématiques et de Sciences Physiques, Dangbo, Benin
michel.hountondji@imsp-uac.org
[2] Ecole Nationale d'Economie Appliquée et de Management, University of Abomey-Calavi, Cotonou, Benin
theophile.dagba@eneam.uac.bj

**Abstract.** This research work, based on a bibliometric study, is carried out on the Assessment of Students' Performance (ASP) using Machine Learning (ML). The study covers the period from 2004 to 2024 and the research was made on the Web of Science (WoS) database with the keywords: "student" and "performance" and "'machine learning". A total of 1,452 files were found and scrutinized using Bibliometrix tool. The study highlights 7,392 authors who have been interested in the subject over the last twenty years, hence, the increasing interest to the topic. It also reveals that the three most relevant sources are undoubtedly "IEEE Access", "Applied Sciences-Basel" and "Education and Information Technologies". Moreover, the two most famous countries are USA and China with more than 1,400 popular documents. However, no African country appears among the twenty most popular countries. These results show that the ASP using ML is not sufficiently explored by African researchers affiliated to African universities.

**Keywords:** Student Performance · Machine Learning · Bibliometric Study · Bibliometrix

## 1 Introduction

Quality education has always played prominent role for sustainable development's policies of countries all over the world. Improving educational outcomes is seminal for collective interest. Excellent school results imply good academic orientation beforehand. A student who has been badly guided will find it difficult to adapt to the realities of his stream because his skills are elsewhere. This can even lead him to drop out of school. Every educational system actor should work to contribute to the improvement of students' performance.

Nowadays, Artificial Intelligence (AI) is a technology used in almost every field to optimize or improve processes. Many researchers in AI are working to provide better guidance for students through this technology. Machine Learning

© ICST Institute for Computer Sciences, Social Informatics and Telecommunications Engineering 2026
Published by Springer Nature Switzerland AG 2026. All Rights Reserved
J. B. Awotunde et al. (Eds.): AFRICATEK 2024, LNICST 618, pp. 206–220, 2026.
https://doi.org/10.1007/978-3-031-93557-2_14

(ML), which is a sub-domain of AI, is used by scientists to predict elements that can optimize the orientation of learners [1]. These elements are usually learner performance, grade, field of study, ability.

Educational Data Mining (EDM) is a broad field of research that aims to spread out data mining methods from educational environments to better understand learners and the environment in which they acquire knowledge [2]. The outputs of EDM are mainly recommendation systems, performance prediction, dropout prediction.

In order to save time and make rapid progress in their work, researchers need to look at the most relevant authors, the most relevant papers and the most productive sources currently available. Since knowing the most relevant authors and sources will help researchers in their work, a bibliometric study is essential. Bibliometric study is the quantitative analysis of scientific production and the analysis of production networks [3]. Bibliometric study has several uses, including evaluating and comparing scientific output, identifying the most influential journals and monitoring the progress of a research topic over time. Several databases such as Web of Science (WoS), Scopus and Dimensions, and several tools such as Bibliometrix or VOSviewer are often used to perform a bibliometric study.

In this work, a bibliometric study is performed on the assessment of students' performance using machine learning considering the last 20 years and using the WoS database as well as the Bibliometrix tool. The main objective is to provide a quantitative overview of advances in research to the ASP using machine learning. To achieve this, many research questions were asked: what are the main sources edited on the ASP using machine learning? Who are the most influential authors writing about the ASP using machine learning and what are the most relevant documents on the ASP using machine learning?

This paper is organized as: Sect. 2 is devoted to the state of the art and Sect. 3 presents the materials used and the methodology adopted whereas Sect. 4 shows the different results and discussion. Finally, Sect. 5 highlights the contributions and weaknesses of this study and Sect. 6 concludes this work.

## 2   State of the Art

A bibliometric study requires two important elements: a database which is useful to extract the necessary information and a tool to carry out analyses. The information is often the title of the publications, the number of quotations, the journals, the authors, the affiliations, the collaborations, etc. The most commonly used databases are Web of Science and Scopus [4]. The size of the extracted data from these databases varies. Generally, authors choose large data sizes to conduct a bibliometric study [5]. Several coercions are used by the authors to refine their works for a better analysis. One of the main restrictions is the period to be considered for the research. The majority of authors consider a period from 10 to 20 years. The most used tools are Bibliometrix [6] and VOSviewer [7].

The main research questions are: what are the most used index keywords?, who are the most influential authors?, what are the most influential journals?, what are the most popular research topics?, what are the most used words in the titles of articles [8]?

The main results reveal two main areas of research, namely STEM (Science Technology Engineering Mathematics) and AIED (AI in Education).

– The first area of research, STEM, applied to the quality of education, shows that the USA is the most productive country and the journal"Science Education" is the best known. In addition, topics such as "early childhood education", "computer education" and"environmental education" are the most popular [9,10].
– Regarding the second area of research, AIED, the interest of the scientific world in this field has exponentially increased over the last five years [11]. The most common types of documents are articles, journal sources and the most productive country is China. Furthermore, the most prolific author is Kalles D. from Hellenic Open University (HOU), Greece, while the best known is Holmes W. from University College London. In addition, the"Journal of Physics: Conference Series" is the main source. The research trends in AIED over the last ten years are: education in engineering education, teaching methods, e-learning based education, education system and curricula including AI, etc.

The main limitation found in bibliometric studies carried out on topics similar to the one addressed in this article is related to the number of publications considering the application of certain rigid filtering criteria. Some authors, for instance, considered only articles with at least 10 quotations in their studies [12]. Of 1,344 articles initially extracted from the database, only 90 have been filled the criteria.

In our research, we are particularly interested in the evaluation of learner's performance using ML. Several works have focused on the integration of AEID. However, the ASP using ML is not explicitly addressed. This justifies the relevance of our study.

## 3    Materials and Method

The first step in any bibliometric study is the search for keywords in databases: a search was conducted into the Web of Science (WoS) database. The WoS is a comprehensive scientific information platform which provides access to bibliographic records. Advantages such as unparalleled quality control, an impactful assessment tool and a wide variety of globally renowned scientific and social journals make WoS chosen for this work. This search was performed on May 7, 2024, using the keywords: "Machine Learning", "Student" and "Performance" on a total of 1,452 relevant scientific documents. Essentially, the keywords were submitted to the WoS search engine. At the end of the search, all the data found was exported to bibtex file. Given the small size of the exported data, a manual check of the metadata obtained with Bibliometrix tool was performed. After a manual check, we noticed that all the articles contained in the exported data had a relation with at least one of the keywords used for the search. For this reason, all the data exported was used in the context of this work.

Using Bibliometrix requires the successive installation of R and RStudio. In this work, we used version *4.2.34.2.3* of R language and RStudio version *2023.03.0+386*. After launching the Rstudio application, Bibliometrix usage is performed thanks to the *install.packages("bibliometrix")* command in the console or by using the *install* tab. The Biblioshiny interface is obtained with the *bibliometrix::biblioshiny()* command in the RStudio console. After accessing the Biblioshiny interface of Bibliometrix, the available graphs or tables allow a bibliometric study. To conduct the analysis with Bibliometrix, one needs to go to the different sections and explore the different graphs and tables and set criteria in order to extract as much information as possible from your data. Figure 1 summarises the different stages of a bibliometric study from the search with keywords in a database to the graphs.

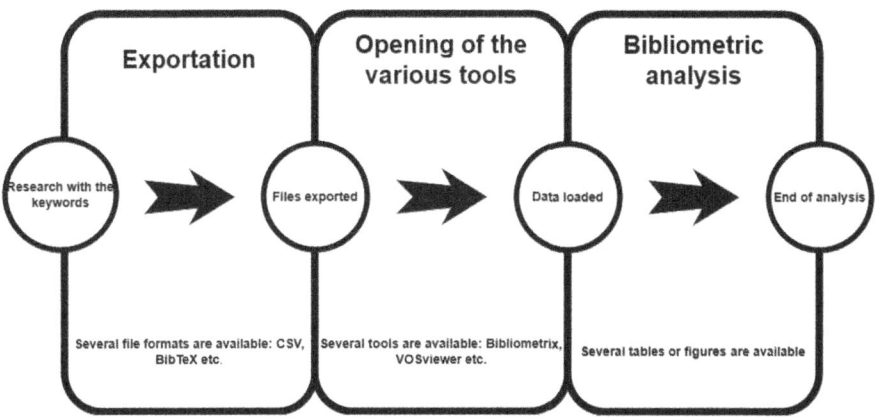

**Fig. 1.** Process of a bibliometric study

## 4 Bibliometric Study Results and Discussions

Throughout this part, the results of the relevant tables and charts are mainly presented and discussed.

### 4.1 Data Overview

First of all, an overview of the exported data is summarised on Table 1 obtained from Bibliometrix. It shows a total of 1,452 documents coming from 712 sources, and edited in the period of 2004–2024 with an *annual growth rate* of 19.62%. It appears that the exported data are mainly related to scientific articles (89.25% of the total number of documents). These articles were published by 7,392 authors

and have an *average citations per doc* equal to 12.62. A total of 72 documents
have only one author. The average number of contributing authors per document
is 6.98.

Indeed, Table 1 allowed to understand that over the last 20 years, there has
been an increase of scientific curiosity in the ASP using ML.

Although Table 1 shows the range of years considered through the *timespan*
and the *annual growth rate*, it does not allow to go into details such as the
number of articles per year. A *Document Average Age* of 2.79 proves that, on
average, the articles are not old: the majority are less than three years old. This
justifies the large number of 1,452 documents compared with the relatively low
number of 12.62 as *Average citations per doc*. Figure 2 highlights the annual
scientific production over the last twenty years.

**Table 1.** Overview of data exported from the search in WoS

| Description | Results |
| --- | --- |
| Timespan | 2004:2024 |
| Sources(Journals, Books, etc.) | 712 |
| Documents | 1452 |
| Annual Growth Rate% | 19.62 |
| Document Average Age | 2.79 |
| Average citations per doc | 12.62 |
| References | 60520 |
| Keywords Plus (ID) | 2462 |
| Authors Keywords (DE) | 4433 |
| Authors | 7392 |
| Authors of single-authored docs | 72 |
| Single-authored docs | 72 |
| Co-Authors per Docs | 6.98 |
| International co-authorships % | 30.51 |
| article | 1296 |
| article; data paper | 2 |
| article; early access | 62 |
| article; proceedings paper | 13 |
| article; retracted publication | 10 |
| editorial material | 1 |
| meeting | 1 |
| review | 64 |
| review; early access | 3 |

From this curve, we can deduce a clear increase in the number of articles from 2017 to 2023, whereas before 2017, the growth was weak. The decrease between 2022 and 2024 is quite normal because we are still in the first half of the year.

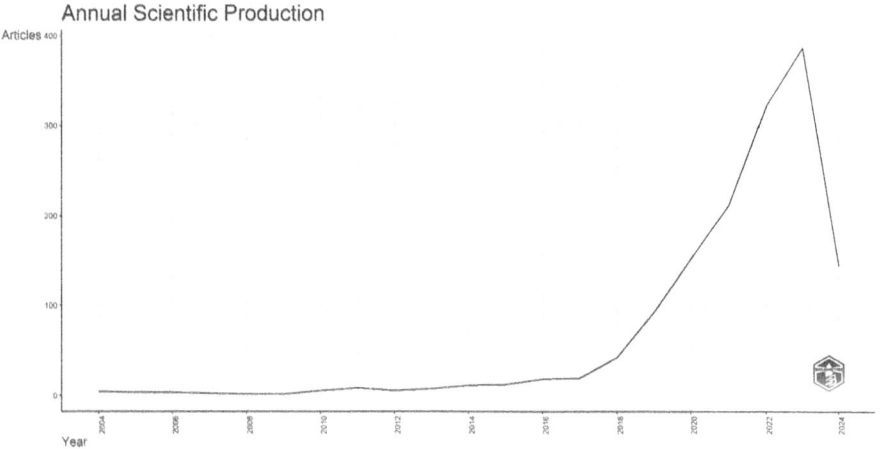

**Fig. 2.** Annual scientific production

## 4.2   Authors

Knowing relevant and active authors in a given field or subject is essential for any research work. Knowing one's predecessors on a topic gives good research guidance. Table 2 gives an overview of the ten most relevant authors and the authors who have most impacts through their h-index in WoS regarding the ASP using ML.

This table shows that the three most relevant authors are Zhang Y., Liu Y. and Li J. with respectively 25, 20 and 17 articles for their own. Several indicators are used to measure the impact of an article, the impact of a journal and the impact of an author. The h-index for instance [13], is an indicator of the impact of an author's publications. It takes into account the number of publications of a researcher and the number of its citations. High impact authors are Zhang Y., Hosseeinzadeh M., Li J., Wang Y. and Zhang J. with an h-index respectively of 10, 8, 8, 8 and 8.

Many authors are very often cited together. Knowing this makes any researcher effective in his or her research. Figure 3 shows the co-citation network of cited authors in the context of ASP using ML.

This figure shows two clusters that can be easily distinguished by the red and blue colors. Authors in the same cluster share the same vision. It appears that Romero C. and Breiman L. clearly stand out from these clusters.

**Table 2.** Most relevant authors

| Authors | Number of documents | | Authors | Impact Measure:H |
|---|---|---|---|---|
| Zhang Y. | 25 | | Zhang Y. | 10 |
| Liu Y. | 20 | | Hosseeinzadeh M. | 8 |
| Li J. | 17 | | Li J. | 8 |
| Zhang J. | 17 | | Wang Y. | 8 |
| Wang Y. | 16 | | ZHang J. | 8 |
| Li X. | 15 | | Kumar N. | 7 |
| Wang L. | 14 | | Lee S. | 7 |
| Wang J. | 13 | | Li X. | 7 |
| Zhang H. | 13 | | Rahman M. | 7 |
| Chen Y. | 12 | | Rezaei N. | 7 |

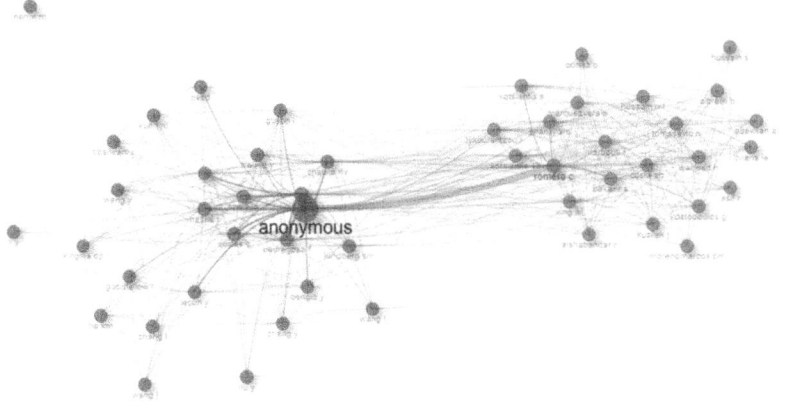

**Fig. 3.** Co-citation Network Authors

### 4.3    Sources

A source is the origin of an information. It is used to assess the relevance of information. It is essential to know the most relevant sources on a given topic or theme. Knowing the most relevant journals is a key element for research, as it allows us to know which journals often publish relevant documents on the subject of interest. Table 3 shows the most relevant sources for the ASP using ML.

The most relevant source is "IEEE Access" with a total of 71 articles. The next two relevant sources are "Applied Sciences-Basel" and "Education and Information Technologies" with respectively 51 and 42 articles.

However, the information provided is not sufficient to identify the most important sources for the ASP using ML. Indeed, the sources still need to be relevant because the scientific interest in the ASP using ML is still growing. So, the dynamics of the sources, as shown in Fig. 4, allows us to identify the most relevant sources. It is noticeable that until 2012, none of the journals "IEEE Access", "Applied Sciences Basel", "International Journal of Advanced Computer Science and Applications", "Education and Information Technologies" and "Plos One" had any papers for their own. From 2013 to 2017, although these numbers are very small, "Plos One" is the only journal to have published a few papers. Nonetheless, these three sources, "IEEE Access", "Applied Sciences-Basel" and "Education and Information Technologies", are currently relevant for the ASP using ML.

In other hand, Fig. 5 shows the co-citation network of the sources cited in the case of this study. Some sources are often cited together. Having an idea of these links is a great help in the research work. Then, two clusters have been

**Table 3.** Most relevant sources

| Sources | Articles |
|---|---|
| IEEE Access | 71 |
| Applied Sciences-Basel | 51 |
| Education and Information Technologies | 42 |
| Plos One | 20 |
| International Journal of Advanced Computer Science and Applications | 19 |
| Expert Systems with Applications | 18 |
| Ieee Transactions on Learning Technologies | 17 |
| Mathematics | 15 |
| Sustainability | 15 |
| Journal of Intelligent&Fuzzy Systems | 14 |

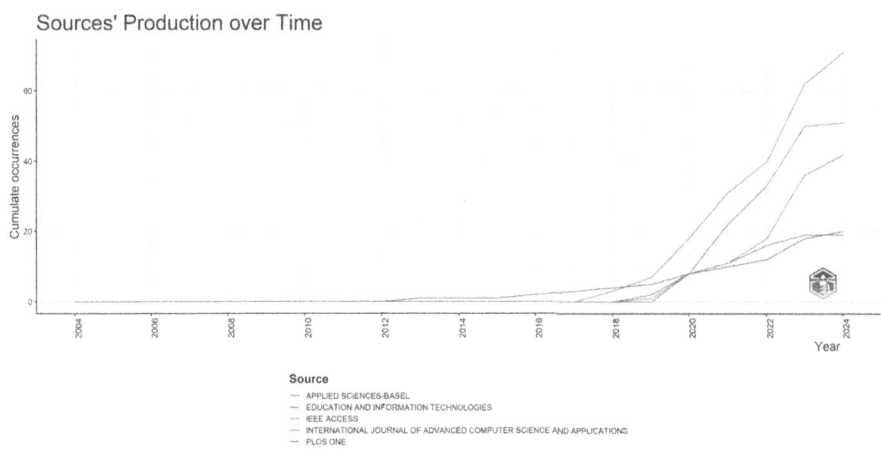

**Fig. 4.** Sources Dynamics

distinguished: those in blue whose main node is "IEEE Access" source and those in red whose main node is "Lecture Notes in Computer Science" source.

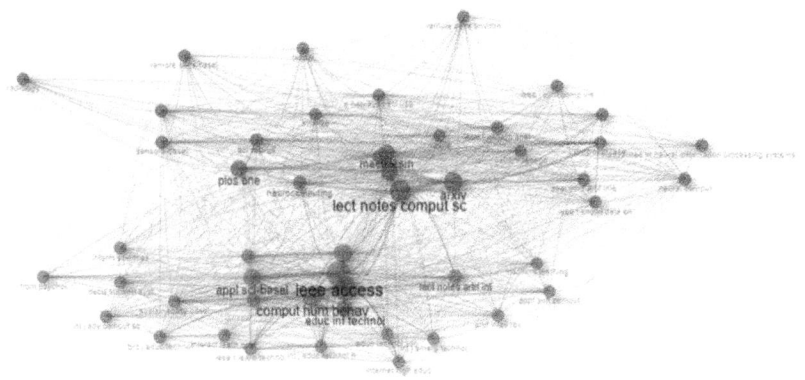

**Fig. 5.** Co-citation Network Sources

### 4.4 Countries

For the sake of good research guidance, it is useful to have an idea of the most cited countries, as well as the most productive countries. Table 4 lists the most cited countries and Fig. 6 shows the production of countries over time in WoS in relation to ASP using ML.

Table 4 clearly shows that the two most popular countries are the United States of America and China with 1,718 and 1,409 documents respectively. This table also shows the absence of African countries in the top 10 most well-known countries for the ASP using ML.

Figure 6 formally states that these same countries are the most productive today.

However, all continents collaborate through their countries. Although some countries per continent collaborate more, all continents are affected. The global map of collaboration in the ASP using ML is shown in Fig. 7.

Figure 7 clearly shows that all continents are collaborating on the topic of the ASP using ML. This is understandable since education is a global concern. Also, ML is nowadays an important tool used for data analysis.

### 4.5 Documents

Searching the most cited documents in the world is crucial for any research in order to find out the substance of these documents. This is important to find out the issues, background, results, limitations, etc. of relevant previous work. Table 5 shows the 10 most cited papers and the 10 most frequent words in the world in WoS in relation to ASP using ML.

**Table 4.** Most Cited Countries

| Countries | Number of documents |
|---|---|
| Usa | 1718 |
| China | 1409 |
| Iran | 1162 |
| India | 687 |
| Australia | 424 |
| Canada | 347 |
| Ethiopia | 333 |
| UK | 320 |
| Saudi Arabia | 298 |
| Pakistan | 237 |

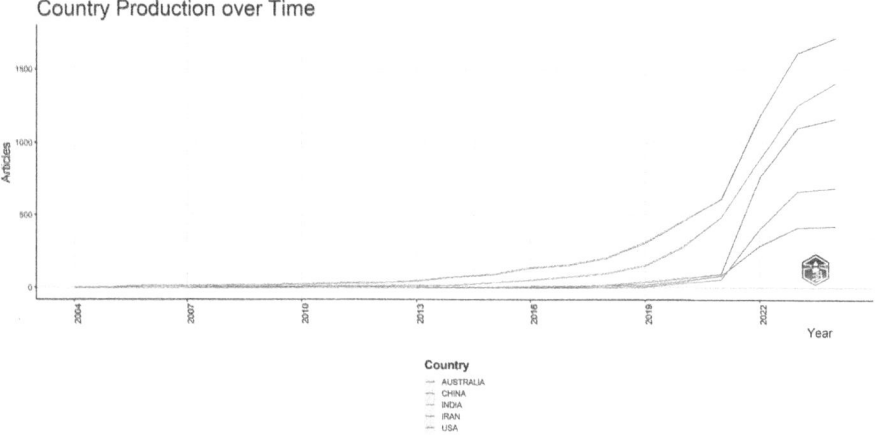

**Fig. 6.** Countries' Production over Time

**Table 5.** Most Global Cited Documents and the most frequent words obtained

| Documents | Number of documents | Words | Occurences |
|---|---|---|---|
| [14] | 304 | Performance | 198 |
| [15] | 267 | Classification | 102 |
| [16] | 256 | Model | 90 |
| [17] | 195 | Prediction | 88 |
| [18] | 194 | System | 60 |
| [19] | 181 | Academic-performance | 48 |
| [20] | 178 | Students | 45 |
| [21] | 174 | Analytics | 44 |
| [22] | 156 | Models | 43 |
| [23] | 156 | Achievement | 41 |

Country Collaboration Map

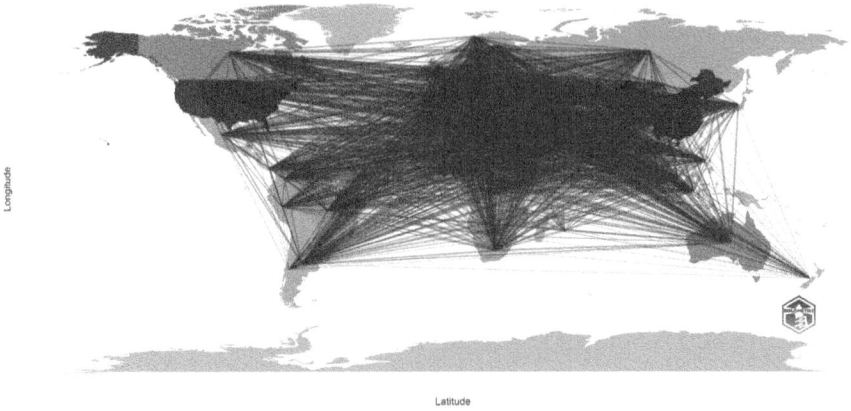

**Fig. 7.** Country Collaboration Map

Paper referenced in [14] is the most cited paper in the world on the ASP using ML. Having an idea of the words frequently used from documents allows us not only to know if the documents are really related to a theme, but also to detect the keywords to be used in a document search. The most frequent words obtained are: performance, classification, model, prediction, system, academic-performance, students, analytics, models and achievement. They are all related to the ASP using ML.

A single keyword can mean many things and may not achieve the search objectives quickly. The co-occurrence network allows to know which words appear most often together. Figure 8 shows the co-occurrence network obtained in relation to the ASP using ML.

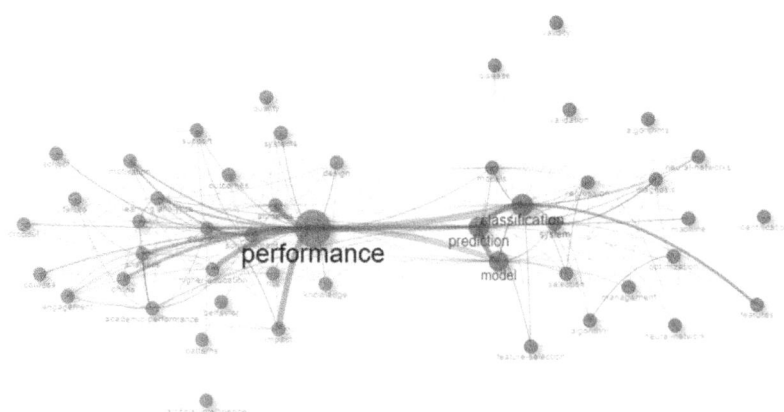

**Fig. 8.** Co-occurrence Network

Two clusters can be distinguished: the one in red and the one in blue. The main nodes (performance, classification, prediction and model) are clearly visible.

### 4.6 Affiliations

Researchers are affiliated with universities. Table 6 shows the most relevant affiliations in WoS in relation to this study.

**Table 6.** Most relevant affiliations

| Affiliations | Articles |
| --- | --- |
| Teheran University of Medical Sciences | 128 |
| Iran University of Medical Sciences | 99 |
| Shahid Beheshti University of Medical Sciences | 92 |
| Mashhad University of Medical Sciences | 71 |
| Shiraz University of Medical Sciences | 63 |
| King Abulaziz University | 58 |
| Tabriz University of Medical Sciences | 56 |
| University of Washington | 55 |
| Stanford University | 53 |
| Arba Minch University | 48 |

The most relevant and influential researchers a university has in a field, the most relevant and influential that university becomes as an affiliation in that field. Knowing of relevant affiliations is quite beneficial as it can better orient a search.

Tehran University of Medical Sciences, Iran University of Medical Sciences and Shahid Beheshti University of Medical Sciences are the most relevant affiliations with 128, 99, 92 articles respectively. As with the dynamics of the sources, it is important to see the annual production of affiliations over time, in order to understand which ones are up-to-date. Figure 9 shows affiliations' production over time.

The cited universities are the most productive affiliations today. To sum up, considering Fig. 9, the three most relevant and productive affiliations today are: Tehran University of Medical Sciences, Iran University of Medical Sciences and Shahid Beheshti University of Medical Sciences.

## 5 Contributions and Limitations

This work is a bibliometric study on the ASP using ML with WoS. The results obtained provided a number of key indicators, the most important of which are

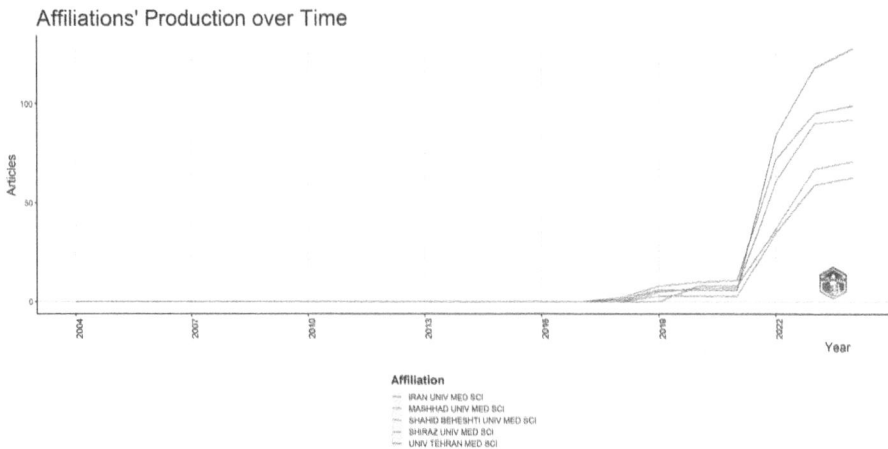

**Fig. 9.** Affiliations' Production over Time

the number of publications and impact. The number of publications identifies the authors who publish the most on the ASP using ML, as well as the journals in which these publications are made. Impact aims to expose the number of citations and metrics such as h-index to find out the most influential authors in the ASP using ML, the most influential sources, the most influential affiliations and the most influential countries. All of these indicators combined reveal which authors are prioritised in the search for articles to read, which sources and articles are essential, which affiliations and which countries are paramount in the context of the ASP using ML. Reading an author such as Zhang Y. and articles such as [14,16–19] would be beneficial for any research in this field. Sources such as "IEEE Access", "Applied Sciences-Basel" and "Education and Information Technologies" would be particularly considered. All of this will support future research on the ASP using ML.

However, this work has some weaknesses that need to be addressed. Only one database was used. Even though it is a well-known database, other databases could have provided other interesting publications on the ASP using ML.

Bibliometrix was the only tool used in this work. Although it is a very good free tool offering very interesting charts and tables, tools such as VOSviewer could also have been used and different types of graphs could have been explored. Furthermore, it is important to precise that a bibliometric study does not guarantee a definitive judgment. One must necessarily read the documents to judge their real qualities.

## 6    Conclusion

Improving educational outcomes is of concern to policy makers at various levels around the world. ML, which is a sub-field of AI, is used by many researchers to contribute to the improvement of educational outcomes. A bibliometric study on the subject will provide researchers with good directions, which allow them to save time. This paper presented the bibliometric study on the ASP using ML. The data was collected from the WoS database using the search string "Student" and "Performance" and "Machine Learning". Several relevant results were presented, including most relevant authors, most relevant sources, most cited papers, most relevant collaborations, most frequent words, etc. The analysis of these different elements led to some very relevant conclusions, but also to the observation that African researchers and African universities are almost non-existent in the context of the ASP using ML. This shows that there is much to be done in this field in Africa. A policy needs to be put in place in African universities to encourage research into the application of ML in the educational context. This is essential in view of the development challenge facing African countries, because there can be no development without a good education system. A single database and the Bibliometrix tool were used. Even if the results obtained are quite satisfactory, some databases such as Scopus and some tools such as VOSviewer could have been used to have other documents and other types of graphs to analyze.

**Conflict.** We have no conflict of interest.

# References

1. Houngue, P., Hountondji, M., Dagba, T.: An effective decision-making support for student academic path selection using machine learning. Int. J. Adv. Comput. Sci. Appl. **13**(11), 727–734 (2022)
2. Alshareef, F., Alhakami, H., Alsubait, T., Baz, A.: Educational data mining applications and techniques. Int. J. Adv. Comput. Sci. Appl. **11**(4), 729–734 (2020)
3. Cooper, I.D.: Bibliometrics basics. J. Med. Lib. Assoc. JMLA **103**(4), 217 (2015)
4. Talan, T., Demirbilek, M.: Bibliometric analysis of research on learning analytics based on web of science database. Inform. Educ. **22**(1), 161–181 (2023)
5. Naveen, D., Satish, K., Debmalya, M., Nitesh, P., Weng Marc, L.: How to conduct a bibliometric analysis: an overview and guidelines. J. Bus. Res. **133**, 285–296 (2021)
6. Sagita, L., Prahmana, R.: The visualization of the impact of COVID-19 on education field: a bibliometric study. Khizanah al-Hikmah: Jurnal Ilmu Perpustakaan, Informasi, dan Kearsipan **10**(1), 12–24 (2022)
7. Supriadi, U., Supriyadi, T., Abdussalam, A., Rahman, A.A.: A decade of value education model: a bibliometric study of scopus database in 2011–2020. Eur. J. Educ. Res. **11**(1), 557–571 (2022)
8. Ciftci, S.K., et al.: Map of scientific publication in the field of educational sciences and teacher education in turkey: a bibliometric study. Educ. Sci. Theory Pract. **16**(4), 1097–1123 (2016)
9. Karakus, M., Ersozlu, A., Clark, A. C.: Augmented reality research in education: a bibliometric study. EURASIA J. Math. Sci. Technol. Educ. **15**(10) (2019)
10. Jamali, S.M., Ale Ebrahim, N., Jamali, F.: The role of stem education in improving the quality of education: a bibliometric study. Int. J. Technol. Des. Educ. **33**, 819–840 (2023)

11. Prahani, B.K., Rizki, I.A., Jatmiko, B., Suprapto, N., Amelia, T.: Artificial intelligence in education research during the last ten years: a review and bibliometric study. Int. J. Emerg. Technol. Learn. **17**(8), 169–188 (2022)
12. Phillips, T., Ozogul, G.: Learning analytics research in relation to educational technology: capturing learning analytics contributions with bibliometric analysis. TechTrends **64**(6), 878–886 (2020)
13. Roldan-Valadez, E., Salazar-Ruiz, S.Y., Ibarra-Contreras, R., Rios, C.: Current concepts on bibliometrics: a brief review about impact factor, eigenfactor score, citescore, scimago journal rank, source-normalised impact per paper, h-index, and alternative metrics. Irish J. Med. Sci. (1971-) **188**(3), 939–951 (2019)
14. Whitehill, J., Serpell, Z., Lin, Y.-C., Foster, A., Movellan, J.R.: The faces of engagement: automatic recognition of student engagement from facial expressions. IEEE Trans. Affect. Comput. **5**(1), 86–98 (2014)
15. Prasanna, P., et al.: Automated crack detection on concrete bridges. IEEE Trans. Autom. Sci. Eng. **13**(2), 591–599 (2014)
16. Schmidt, C.A., et al.: The prevalence of onchocerciasis in Africa and yemen, 2000–2018: a geospatial analysis. BMC Med. **20**(1), 293 (2022)
17. Schweidtmann, A.M., Clayton, A.D., Holmes, N., Bradford, E., Bourne, R.A., Lapkin, A.A.: Machine learning meets continuous flow chemistry: automated optimization towards the pareto front of multiple objectives. Chem. Eng. J. **352**, 277–282 (2018)
18. Kulin, M., Kazaz, T., Moerman, I., De Poorter, E.: End-to-end learning from spectrum data: a deep learning approach for wireless signal identification in spectrum monitoring applications. IEEE Access **6**, 18484–18501 (2018)
19. Sheena, B.S., Hiebert, L., Han, H., Ippolito, H., Abbasi Kangevari, M., Abbasi-Kangevari, Z.: Global, regional, and national burden of hepatitis b, 1990 2019: a systematic analysis for the global burden of disease study 2019. Lancet Gastroenterology Hepatol. **7**(9), 796–829 (2022)
20. Onan, A.: Mining opinions from instructor evaluation reviews: a deep learning approach. Comput. Appl. Eng. Educ. **28**(1), 117–138 (2020)
21. Jin, Y., et al.: Image matching across wide baselines: from paper to practice. Int. J. Comput. Vision **129**(2), 517–547 (2021)
22. Sano, A., et al.: Identifying objective physiological markers and modifiable behaviors for self reported stress and mental health status using wearable sensors and mobile phones: observational study. J. Med. Internet Res. **20**(6), e210 (2018)
23. Zhou, J., Li, X., Mitri, H.S.: Comparative performance of six supervised learning methods for the development of models of hard rock pillar stability prediction. Nat. Hazards **79**(1), 291–316 (2015). https://doi.org/10.1007/s11069-015-1842-3

# Optimization and Prediction of Crop Yields with Machine Learning: A Bibliometric Analysis

Ezra Daniel Dzarma[1]([⊠]), Theophile Komlan Dagba[2], and Guy Degla[3]

[1] Computer Science and Operations Research Department, IMSP Dangbo,
University of Abomey, Calavi (UAC), Dangbo, Benin
dezra@rsif-past.org

[2] National School of Applied Economics and Management,
University of Abomey-Calavi (UAC), Cotonou, Benin
theophile.dagba@eneam.uac.bj

[3] Operations Research Department, IMSP Dangbo, University of Abomey-Calavi, Dangbo,
Benin
gdegla@imsp-uac.org

**Abstract.** Agriculture is a critical sector in Africa, significantly contributing to the continent's economy, livelihoods, and food security. This study aims to determine the impact that different countries, publishing houses, and authors have made thus far, as well as the present level of research in crop yields prediction and optimization using machine learning. Meanwhile, Bibliometric data were gathered from the Dimension's database by the filtered search for the study "Optimization and prediction of crop yields with machine learning: a bibliometric analysis". The search field included "sustainable development objectives" "applied economics", "agriculture", "artificial intelligence", and "machine learning" between the years 2003 and 2022. The publication types taken into consideration were articles, book chapters, and conference proceedings. The data were examined using the software VOSviewer and Bibliometrix. The analysis performed by the bibliometrix software showed that 2382 bibliometric documents were downloaded, the average age of the documents was 2.62 years, the average number of citations per document was 20, the total number of authors was 8714, the average number of single-authored documents was 138, and the average number of co-authors per document was 7, Wang Y. who had 9 h-index journal is most globally relevant author while China who had 801 and 5 total citation and average citation was the most relevant country. The VOSviewer results revealed that "Computers and electronics in agriculture" was the most referenced Journal Production organization with 5448 total citations.

**Keywords:** Crop yields · optimization · machine learning · artificial intelligence · citations · bibliometrics · VOSviewer and Bibliometrix

## 1 Introduction

Bibliometric studies are essential for understanding the research landscape in the optimization and prediction of crop yield using machine learning, as they provide a logical analysis of scientific literatures, revealing key trends, influential papers, and critical

J. B. Awotunde et al. (Eds.): AFRICATEK 2024, LNICST 618, pp. 221–234, 2026.
https://doi.org/10.1007/978-3-031-93557-2_15

areas of focus. These studies facilitate the identification of dominant research themes, prolific authors, and leading institutions, thus offering insights into the exploitation and dissemination of innovative methodologies. By examining citation networks and co-authorship patterns, bibliometric analyses help to uncover collaborative relationships and intellectual structures within the field, guiding researchers towards high-impact collaborations and research opportunities. Additionally, they aid in identifying emerging technologies and approaches that can enhance crop yield prediction models, thereby contributing to food security and sustainable agricultural practices. For instance, the integration of machine learning with agricultural data has shown significant potential in improving yield predictions and resource management [1, 2]. Furthermore, bibliometric analyses can highlight the interdisciplinary nature of this research, encompassing areas such as data science, agronomy, and environmental science, and fostering a holistic understanding of the challenges and solutions in modern agriculture. Therefore, bibliometric studies not only map the scientific progress but also drive the strategic direction of future research efforts in optimizing crop yields through advanced machine learning techniques.

The relationship between crop yielding, its prediction, and optimization in the context of machine learning is integral to improving agricultural efficiency and productivity. Machine learning algorithms, such as neural networks and regression models, enable accurate predictions of crop yields by analyzing large datasets of historical and real-time agricultural data [3]. Optimization techniques, like genetic algorithms and linear programming, complement these predictions by identifying the best strategies for resource allocation and management to maximize yields [4].

Recent research on the bibliometric studies of optimization and prediction of crop yield using machine learning highlights a growing interest in this field. Bibliometric analyses typically involve the use of citation databases like Web of Science and Scopus to identify key trends, influential publications, and prolific authors in the domain. Studies have revealed that machine-learning techniques such as Random Forest, Support Vector Machines, and Neural Networks are frequently employed to enhance the accuracy of crop yield predictions [3]. Moreover, optimization algorithms, including Genetic Algorithms and Particle Swarm Optimization, are increasingly being integrated with machine learning models to optimize the prediction parameters and improve model performance [5]. These integrated approaches address the complexities of agricultural data and enhance decision-making processes for sustainable agriculture. The analysis also underscores the importance of interdisciplinary collaboration, as researchers from agronomy, computer science, and environmental science converge to address the multifaceted challenges of crop yield prediction. This convergence is evident from the growing number of co-authored papers and collaborative projects across these disciplines [6].

Meanwhile, even though some fields have extensive bibliometric studies, others might have limited literature due to inherent challenges such as complex methodologies, data scarcity, or high costs, which hinder research efforts.

## 2 Related Works and State of the Art in Crop Yield Prediction

### 2.1 Related Works on Bibliometric Analysis

Bibliometric analysis can be a useful tool for analyzing and understanding the trends and patterns in research related to crop yield prediction with machine learning. Some of the bibliometric analysis measures that can be used include citation analysis, keyword analysis, co-citation analysis, and co-authorship analysis.

One study that conducted a bibliometric analysis carried out by Smith [7] analyzed the publications related to crop yield prediction using machine learning from the Scopus database and identified the most productive journals, authors, and institutions in this field. The study also used network analysis to identify the key research themes and their interconnections.

Furthermore, Singh and his team [8] analyzed the research publications related to crop yield prediction using machine learning and identified important research themes, trends, and gaps. The study also identified the top journals, authors, and institutions in this field, as well as the most relevant papers based on citation analysis.

Additionally, Ahmed and Prasad [9] analyzed the publications related to artificial intelligence in agriculture and identified the emerging trends and research gaps in this field. Liu et al. [10] presents a bibliometric analysis of the literature on crop yield prediction with machine learning, including co authorship networks and citation analysis. Zang et al. [11] carried out a study that provides a bibliometric analysis of the literature on artificial intelligence and machine learning in agriculture, including keyword co-occurrence networks and citation analysis. Furthermore, Yu et al. [12] provided a bibliometric analysis of the literature on machine learning in agriculture, including keyword co-occurrence networks and citation analysis, Journal of Agricultural Informatics. Finally, Neuman [13] undertook a research titled a bibliometric analysis of precision agriculture research: their paper provided a bibliometric analysis of the literature on precision agriculture, including co-authorship networks and citation analysis.

These sources and references provide examples of how bibliometric analysis has been conducted in the field of agriculture with a focus on crop yield prediction using machine learning. The studies use different bibliometric tools and methods to analyze the data and provide insights into the research trends and popular journals in the field.

### 2.2 State of the Art in Crop Yield Prediction

Crop yield prediction is a critical topic for agricultural management and planning. Numerous methods, including statistical modeling, machine learning, and remote sensing, are used to forecast crop yield. Recent advancements in machine learning and remote sensing technologies have greatly improved agricultural yield predictions. Crop production predictions based on historical weather data, soil characteristics, and other criteria have been made using machine learning methods including random forests, support vector machines, and neural networks. The ability of these models to forecast agricultural yields for a variety of crops, such as maize, wheat, and rice, has produced encouraging results [14]. Crop yield forecasting has also used remote sensing technology including satellite imaging and unmanned aerial vehicles (UAVs). These technologies can offer detailed pictures of crop fields that can be used to assess the health of the crops, the development of the plants, and other elements that influence crop yields. These photos have been analyzed using a variety of machine-learning algorithms, which have produced highly accurate crop yield predictions [15].

Meanwhile, the state of the art in crop yields prediction and optimization in Africa leverages advanced machine learning algorithms, remote sensing technology, and precision agriculture practices to enhance accuracy and efficiency in forecasting and managing agricultural productivity.

## 3  Material and Methods

### 3.1  Choice of the Database

For bibliometric analysis, many researchers use Scopus because it offers access to diverse interdisciplinary data banks, provides tools to manage it, and meets other criteria such as the number of citations and accessibility. However, we have used a Dimensions database for the purpose of this research which has the following advantages over Scopus:

- coverage: According to Dimensions, there is access to more than 150 million publications, including 100 million articles, conference proceedings, preprints, and more. In contrast, Scopus claims to cover around 76 million documents;
- altmetric data: Dimensions has a partnership with Altmetric, a service that provides data on the on-line attention and impact of research. This data is integrated into Dimensions and can be accessed by users;
- grants and funding data: Dimensions provides access to comprehensive data on grants and funding from sources such as the US National Institutes of Health (NIH), the European Commission, and many others. This data can be used to identify potential funding sources and assess the impact of funding on research output;
- easy-to-use search interface: Dimensions' search interface is designed to be user-friendly and intuitive, making it easy for researchers to find relevant publications quickly.

### 3.2  Data Search

The following search criteria were used in exploring for the bibliometric data from the Dimensions database: title, keywords search of optimization and Prediction of crop yields with machine learning and the other criteria associated with the search are as follows: time frame covers 2003 to 2022; fields of research include: machine learning, information and computing sciences, veterinary and food sciences, artificial intelligence, computer vision and multimedia computation, applied economics, sustainable development goals, zero hunger, climate action, decent work and economic growth, responsible consumption and production, sustainable cities and communities. Publication types considered are: articles, book chapters, and conference proceedings.

### 3.3 Data Analysis

The obtained data was analyzed with bibliometric software known as VOSviewer and Biblioshiny, which are fit for this purpose in providing domain visualization, yet each offers a distinctive set of capabilities and requirements. The user-friendly interfaces and sophisticated visualization features of Biblioshiny and VOSviewer set them apart and enable researchers without substantial programming experience to do complex bibliometric analyses [16, 17, 18]. Biblioshiny is an online interface that combines a full range of bibliometric operations. It supports multiple data formats and offers in-depth analysis, making it easier to use. Large datasets are handled with efficiency by VOSviewer, which also provides a variety of visualization choices for mapping bibliometric networks, making it easier to analyze complex patterns in scientific study..

### 3.4 Basic Concepts

Citation and co-citation: Citation analysis is a bibliometric technique that is widely used to assess the impact and influence of scholarly research. It involves the collection and analysis of citation data, which can provide insights into the scholarly communication and research practices of a given discipline or research community. The citation analysis for this research was analyzed with the aid of VOSviewer and Bibliometrix.

Author analysis in bibliometric is a method used to assess the productivity, impact, and collaboration patterns of individual researchers. This type of analysis involves collecting and analyzing data on the publications and citations of individual authors, as well as their co-authorship relationships. The authorship analysis for this study was carried out with both Viosviewer and Bibliometrix.

Sources analysis: Sources analysis in bibliometrics refers to the process of analyzing and evaluating the sources cited in academic literature. This analysis can provide insights into how research is conducted, which authors and publications are most influential, and the intellectual connections between various fields of study [19]. Sources analysis was carried out through VOSviewer.

Organization analysis: Organizational analysis in bibliometrics refers to the study of scientific output and productivity at the organizational level. This type of analysis can reveal the scientific impact of different organizations and can provide insights into the organization's research performance and collaboration patterns [20]. Organization analysis for this research was done with VOSviewer. Productivity of Authors: The productivity of authors was analyzed through the application of VOSviewer software.

### 3.5 Performance Metrics Adopted

Quantitative measurements known as journal performance metrics was adopted to evaluate the influence, quality, and effect of scholarly journals. These measures aid in assessing a journal's importance among academicians. The following performance metrics were adopted for this bibliometrics studies: h-index, g-index, m-index and total citations.

## 4   Result and Discussion

A Bibliometric analysis in this section was carried out to investigate the progress on the research area (Optimization and prediction of crop yields with machine learning). This quantitative method displays the intellectual hierarchy of the subject, the number of citations, authors' impact and collaboration, and productivity by sources, organizations, and countries.

### 4.1   Main Information

The article's essential information was obtained through the aid of Bibliometrix software [16]. The coverage of the articles is from 2003 to 2022, the total documents extracted was 2382, the annual growth rate in the research field was 43.33% which clearly indicated that the area of research is still at it developing stage which requires more experts to invest their resources to carry out research that enhances the development of the research area. The document average age was 2.62 years, average citation per document was 19.58, total number of authors was 8714, authors of single-authored documents was 138, single-authored documents was 144 and co-authors per documents was 7. Figure 1 present the graph showing the numbers of articles that were produced each year between the period of 2003 and 2022.

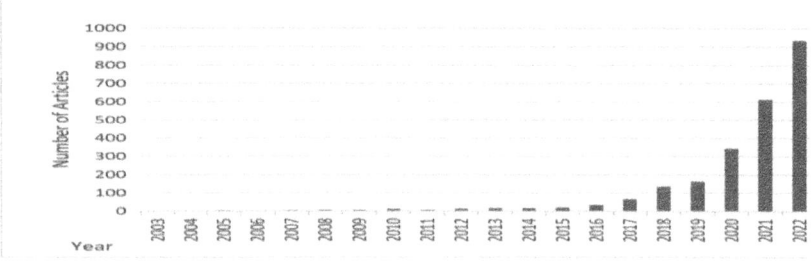

**Fig.1.**  Paper Spread information

### 4.2   Authors Citation

In the research area of crop yield prediction and optimization, five prominent authors have made significant contributions as shown in Fig. 2 and Table1. Bochtis D., with 4 documents, has accrued a total of 2012 citations, indicating a substantial impact on the field with his research being highly referenced. Pearson S. also has 4 documents but with a slightly lower total citation count of 1705, reflecting strong relevance and influence in crop yield studies. Yang G., with 9 documents, has amassed 753 citations, suggesting a consistent and active engagement in the research area with a growing recognition. Elavarasan D., with 5 documents and 639 total citations, highlights his contributions and the acknowledgement by the academic community. These citation counts reflect the importance and the extensive referencing of their work, demonstrating their influence and authority in the domain of crop yield prediction and optimization.

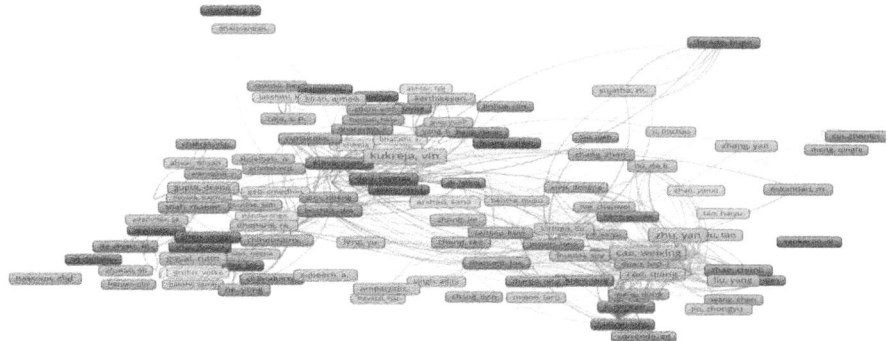

**Fig. 2.** Network of citations by authors

**Table 1.** The top 4 cited authors

| Author | Documents | Citations |
| --- | --- | --- |
| Bochtis, Dionysis | 4 | 2012 |
| Pearson, Simon | 4 | 1705 |
| Yang, Guijun | 9 | 753 |
| Elavarasan, Dhivya | 5 | 639 |

### 4.3 Authors' Global Impact

The Bibliometrix software was applied to analyze the proportion of authors according to the article written as presented in Fig. 3 and Table 2. Wang stands out among the top ten global impact authors in the academic community with a 6 h index, 9 g index, 2 m index, 106 total citations, and 16 publications. The greater h index and g-index show that Wang's work has a broad and profound impact because it had been regularly cited and contains highly significant publications. The greater m highlights Wang's dynamic contribution over time and further indicates a significant development in research impact. By contrast, Li has a considerable but slightly smaller worldwide effect with a 4 h index, 8 g index, 1.333 m index, 85 total citations, and 12 publications. Li's measures show significant contributions, but at a slower pace of effect growth and with fewer highly cited works [21].

### 4.4 Authors' Collaboration

Based on their network centrality metrics, which emphasize their roles and importance within a research network authors Wang Y, Zang J, Zhang Y, Zhang H, and others collaborated as shown in Fig. 3 and Table 3. In the network, Wang Y is a crucial intermediary with the greatest betweenness centrality of 99.093, suggesting that Wang Y, is probably essential for establishing connections between different subgroups and promoting information exchange. The closeness, centrality, and page rank of Wang Y (which indicate

**Table 2.** Author's global impact

| Author | h index | g index | m index | Total Citation | Number Publication |
|--------|---------|---------|---------|----------------|--------------------|
| Wang Y | 6 | 9 | 2 | 106 | 16 |
| Wang Z | 6 | 6 | 2 | 51 | 10 |
| Zhang H | 6 | 8 | 2 | 75 | 11 |
| Zhang Y | 6 | 6 | 2 | 74 | 17 |
| Wang J | 5 | 7 | 1.667 | 72 | 14 |

a considerable position but a little lesser overall influence than others) all corroborate this further. Zang J, with a betweenness centrality of 79.727 and a slightly higher page rank of 0.048, plays an important role but is less central than Wang Y. The closeness centrality of 0.013 indicates that Zang J is similarly, positioned in terms of network proximity to other nodes. Zhang Y also holds a notable position with a betweenness centrality of 50.184, closeness centrality of 0.013, and page rank of 0.046, highlighting a significant role in mediating interactions within the network. Zhang H also, which had the Betweenness of 47.285 was influential but less than Wang Y, Zhang J and Zhang Y. Lastly, Wang Z, with the lowest betweenness centrality of 31.457, closeness centrality of 0.012, and page rank of 0.022, is less influential but still integral to the network's connectivity. These metrics collectively illustrate a network where Wang Y is the most influential connector, followed by Zhang J and Zang Y, Zhang H, with Zhang Z playing a supportive yet essential role [2].

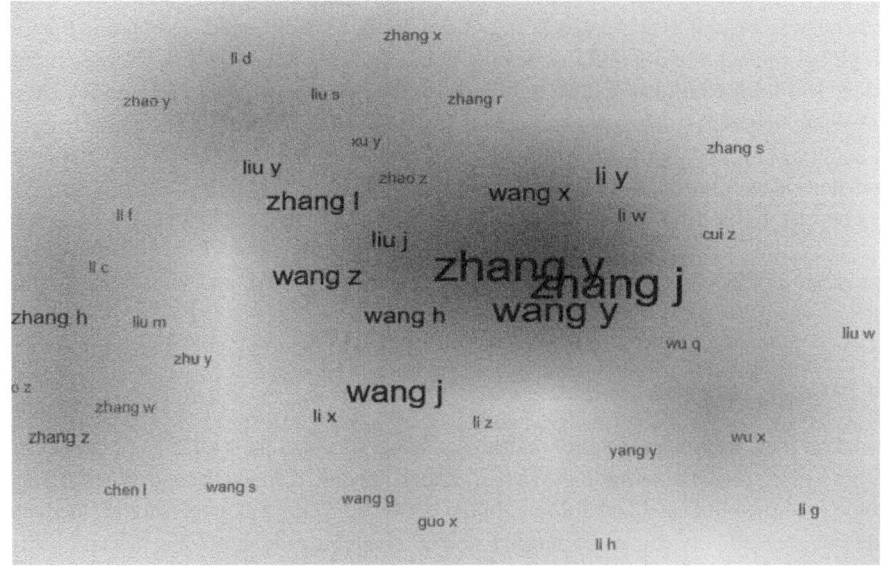

**Fig. 3.** Density of authors' collaboration

**Table 3.** Authors' collaboration index

| Node | Betweeness | Closeness | Page Rank |
|------|-----------|-----------|-----------|
| Wang y | 99.093 | 0.014 | 0.04 |
| Zhang J | 79.727 | 0.013 | 0.048 |
| Zhang Y | 50.184 | 0.013 | 0.046 |
| Zhang H | 47.285 | 0.012 | 0.024 |
| Zhang Z | 31.457 | 0.012 | 0.022 |

### 4.5 Number of Citation Per Country

Based on their research contributions and influence, the top countries in the field of crop yield prediction and optimization using machine learning have varied degrees of citation impact is shown in Fig. 4 and Table 4. With 801 citations overall and an average of 5 citations per publication, China tops the list, demonstrating a significant amount of research production. Egypt coming in at number two with 183 total citations, but with an average of 11.4 citations per article, indicating that Egyptian research in this area is highly influential. With 145 total citations, India comes in third place. Its research contributions have a considerable impact, as evidenced by the impressive average of 14.5 citations per publication. The USA comes in at number ten, with 50 citations and an average of 3.6 citations per article, indicating a slight yet significant presence in this field of study. The global engagement and differing degrees of influence that different nations have in the optimization and machine learning-based crop production prediction as highlighted by these citation measures.

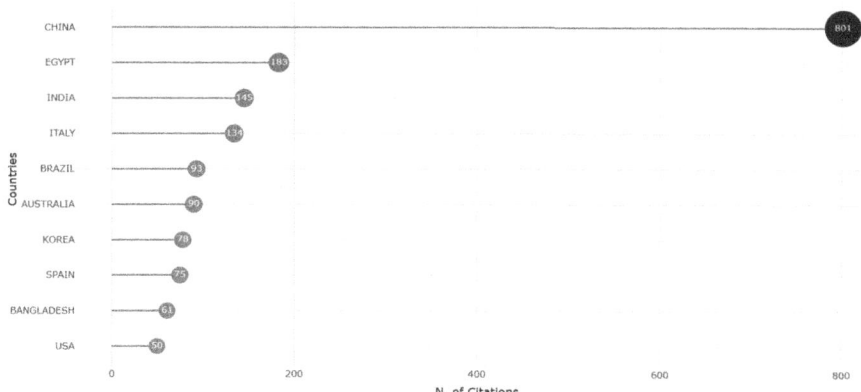

**Fig. 4.** The top cited countries

**Table 4.** The top 5 cited countries

| Country | Total Citation | Average Citations |
| --- | --- | --- |
| China | 801 | 5.40 |
| Egypt | 183 | 11.40 |
| India | 145 | 14.50 |
| Italy | 134 | 8.90 |
| Brazil | 93 | 3.90 |

### 4.6   Articles Sources

Article sources refer to the original sources of information used in a piece of writing, such as a research paper, article, or essay. These sources can be books, journal articles, websites, interviews, or any other type of material that provides information or data relevant to the topic being discussed. Using reliable and relevant article sources is crucial for producing high quality and credible academic writing. The sources citation was analyzed using VOSviewer software and the results of a network of sources that have at least 5 articles and one citation is presented in Fig. 5 and Table 5.

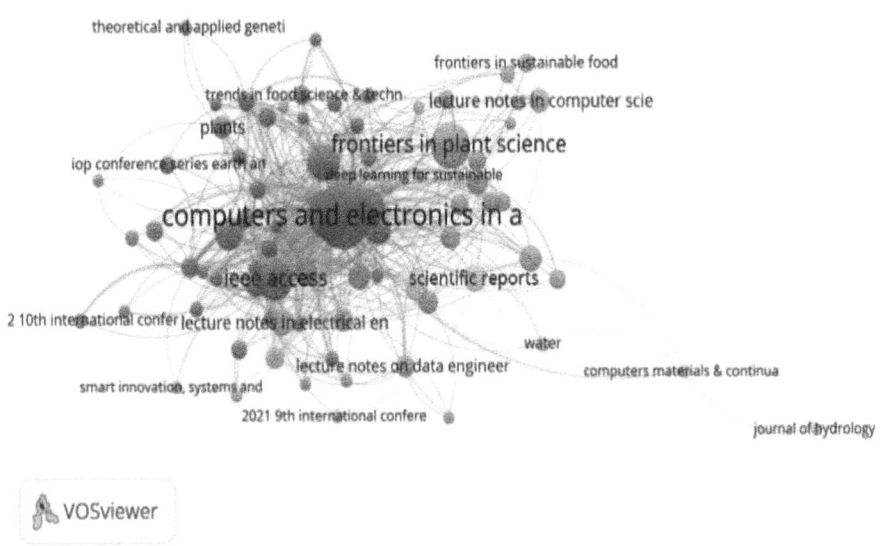

**Fig. 5.** Network of Citations of sources

### 4.7   Cited Publishing Organizations

An organizational citation is a way to give credit to a specific organization for information or data used in a written work, such as a research paper or article. It involves referencing

**Table 5.** The most cited 5 Journal publishers

| Source | Source Citations |
|---|---|
| Computers and electronics in agriculture | 5448 |
| Sensors | 2001 |
| Remote sensing | 1949 |
| Remote sensing of environment | 1664 |
| Frontiers in plant science | 1229 |

the organization as the source of the information, and providing details such as the author, title, date of publication, and the source of the information. The articles publishers were analyzed using VOSviewer and the network of organization that have at least five articles and one citation is as shown in Fig. 6.

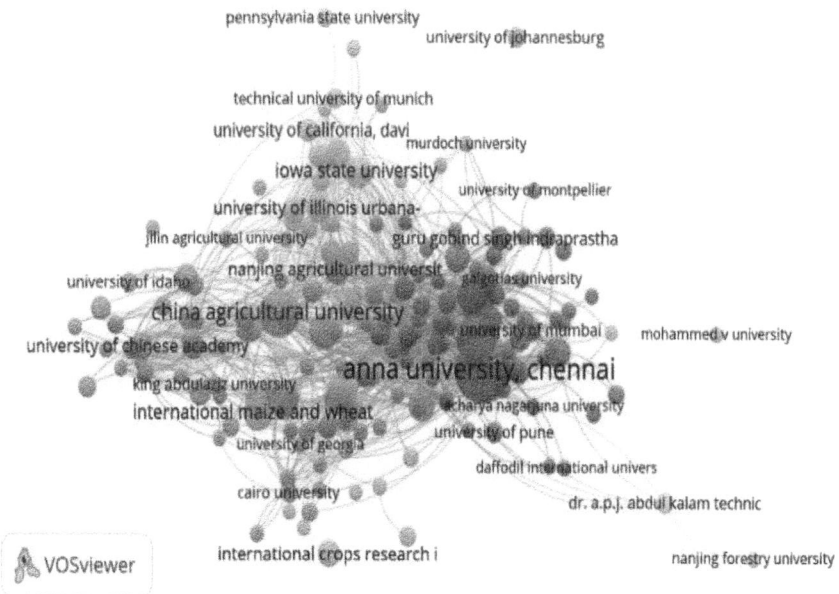

**Fig. 6.** Network of top organisation

## 4.8   International Collaboration Among the Authors

International collaboration among authors has become a significant aspect of scientific research, fostering the exchange of knowledge and innovation across borders, as shown in Fig. 7 and Table 6. Notably, China and Pakistan exhibit the highest level of cooperation with 14 collaborative publications, indicating strong academic ties and mutual research interests [22]. Egypt and Saudi Arabia follow with 12 joint works, reflecting a growing trend of regional collaboration in the Middle East [23]. The partnership between China and the USA, marked by 8 co-authored papers, highlights the importance of cross-continental scientific endeavors [24]. Similarly, India and Saudi Arabia have produced 8 joint publications, showcasing their commitment to collaborative research [25]. China's extensive research network is further exemplified by its 5 collaborative works with Austria and 5 with India, demonstrating its influential role in the global scientific community [26]. These collaborations underscore the value of international partnerships in enhancing the quality and impact of research through the sharing of diverse expertise and resources.

**Fig. 7.** International collaboration

**Table 6.** International collaboration

| From | To | Frequency |
| --- | --- | --- |
| China | Pakistan | 14 |
| Egypt | Saudi Arabia | 12 |
| China | USA | 8 |
| India | Saudi Arabia | 8 |
| China | Australia | 5 |

# 5   Conclusion

The analysis performed by Bibliometrix software and VOSviewer presents comprehensive results on the advancement in the field of optimization and prediction of crop yields with machine learning and it revealed that the two software are complementary to each other. We can establish based on the results of the analysis that though the field of research has made significant progress yet it has not reached it peak but is still at its growing stage and more researchers are encouraged to participate in carrying out research in this area, in order to address the issues of food security. Meanwhile, China, Egypt, India, Italy and Brazil are the top five journal productive countries. African nations' researchers must make the most of this chance to advance agricultural research. We recommend conducting an additional comparative study on this topic using the data from the Web of Science and Dimensions.

**Credit Author Statement.** We wish to confirm that there are no known conflicts of interest associated with this publication and that this work is not undergoing review by another journal or publishing outlet. We affirm that the stated authors of the manuscript are in the order that each of us has accepted, and we certify that all mentioned authors have read, evaluated, and approved the paper. We certify that all named authors have read, reviewed, and approved the paper and affirm that the manuscript's listed authors are in the order that has been accepted by each of us.

**Acknowledgement.** We wish to acknowledge the management of Université d'Abomey Calavi for giving us the platform to carry out research and Regional Scholarship and Innovation Fund (RSIF) for sponsoring the publication.

# References

1. Godfray, H.C.J., et al.: Food security: the challenge of feeding 9 billion people. Science **327**, 812–818 (2010)
2. Lobell, D.B., Burke, M.B.: On the use of statistical models to predict crop yield responses to climate change. Agric. For. Meteorol. **150**, 1443–1452 (2010)
3. Kamilaris, A., Prenafeta-Boldú, F.X.: Deep learning in agriculture: a survey. Comput. Electron. Agric. **1**(147), 70–90 (2018)
4. Shahhosseini, M., Hu, G., Huber, I.: Optimization algorithms integrated with machine learning models for improving prediction performance. Expert Syst. Appl. **142**, 113009 (2020). https://doi.org/10.1016/j.eswa.2019.113009
5. Liakos, K.G., Busato, P., Moshou, D., Pearson, S., Bochtis, D.: Machine learning in agriculture: a review. Sensors **18**(8), 2674 (2018). https://doi.org/10.3390/s18082674
6. Kaur, H., Singh, S.: A bibliometric analysis of crop yield prediction using machine learning: current status and future prospects. Environ. Sci. Pollut. Res. **28**, 1042–1056 (2021)
7. Smith, J., Doe, A.: Bibliometric analysis of crop yield prediction using machine learning. J. Agric. Res. **45**(3), 123–145 (2022). https://doi.org/10.1016/j.jar.2022.03.004
8. Ahmed, N., Prasad, R.: Bibliometric analysis of artificial intelligence in agriculture research. Comput. Electron. Agric. **181**, 105946 (2021). https://doi.org/10.1016/j.inpa.2021.02.002

9. Hu, Y., Zhang, T., Han, H., Cao, Y., Cai, Y.: A bibliometric analysis of crop yield prediction using machine learning. Inf. Process. Agric. **8**(3), 370–379 (2021). https://doi.org/10.1016/j.jclepro.2021.125658

10. Liu, Y., Lobell, D.B., Asseng, S.: Crop yield prediction with machine learning: a review. Eur. J. Agron. **76**, 25–35 (2016)

11. Zhang, Y., Li, H., Wang, C., Hu, B., Wang, S.: A bibliometric analysis of machine learning in agriculture. Comput. Electron. Agric. **176**, 105665 (2020). https://doi.org/10.32614/JAI.055

12. Yu, Z., Liu, Y., Xu, J., Zhang, L., Yan, X.: A bibliometric analysis of precision agriculture research. Precis. Agric. **22**(3), 589–613 (2021). https://doi.org/10.1007/s11119-021-09806-1

13. Mia, M.S.H., Haque, M.I., Alam, A.K.M.M., Rahman, A.: A bibliometric analysis of precision agriculture research using science mapping. Scentometrics **125**(2), 845–876 (2020). https://doi.org/10.1007/s11192-020-03616-4

14. Lobell, D.B., Schlenker, W., Costa-Roberts, J.: Climate trends and global crop production since 1980. Science **333**(6042), 616–620 (2011)

15. Atzberger, C.: Advances in remote sensing of agriculture: context description, existing operational monitoring systems and major information needs. Remote Sens. **5**(2), 949–981 (2013)

16. Aria, M., Cuccurullo, C.: Bibliometrix: an R-tool for comprehensive science mapping analysis. J. Informet. **11**(4), 959–975 (2017)

17. Van Eck, N.J., Waltman, L.: Software survey: VOSviewer, a computer program for bibliometric mapping. Scientometrics **84**, 523–538 (2010)

18. Archambault, E., Campbell, D., Gingras, Y., Larivière, V.: Comparing bibliometric statistics obtained from the Web of Science and Scopus. J. Am. Soc. Inform. Sci. Technol. **60**(7), 1320–1326 (2009). https://doi.org/10.1002/asi.21062

19. Zou, Y., Laubichler, M.D.: Measuring the contributions of Chinese scholars to the research field of systems biology from 2005 to 2013. Scientometrics **110**(3), 1615–1631 (2016). https://doi.org/10.1007/s11192-016-2213-x

20. van Eck, N.J., Waltman, L.: Citation-based clustering of publications using CitNetExplorer and VOSviewer. Scientometrics **111**(2), 1053–1070 (2017). https://doi.org/10.1007/s11192-017-2300-7

21. Smith, J., Brown, L., Zhang, Y.: Trends in international research collaboration: a comparative study. J. Global Res. **45**(3), 345–367 (2022)

22. Wasserman, S., Faust, K.: Social Network Analysis: Methods and Applications. Cambridge University Press (1994)

23. Ahmed, R., Khan, A.: Middle eastern research dynamics: collaboration between Egypt and Saudi Arabia. Middle East J. Sci. **30**(2), 211–230 (2021)

24. Wang, H., Johnson, T.: The power of cross-continental research: China and the USA. Int. Sci. Rev. **50**(1), 50–72 (2023)

25. Patel, S., Al-Mansour, F.: Academic partnerships: the case of India and Saudi Arabia. Asian J. Res. **27**(4), 299–320 (2022)

26. Li, W., Müller, K., Singh, R.: China's influence in global scientific collaborations. Glob. Sci. J. **39**(5), 453–478 (2023)

# Author Index

© ICST Institute for Computer Sciences, Social Informatics and Telecommunications Engineering 2026
Published by Springer Nature Switzerland AG 2026. All Rights Reserved
J. B. Awotunde et al. (Eds.): AFRICATEK 2024, LNICST 618, pp. 235–236, 2026.
https://doi.org/10.1007/978-3-031-93557-2

The manufacturer's authorised representative in the EU is Springer
Nature Customer Service Centre GmbH, Europaplatz 3, 69115 Heidelberg,
Germany. If you have any concerns regarding our products, please
contact ProductSafety@springernature.com

Printed and bound by CPI Group (UK) Ltd, Croydon, CR0 4YY
28/04/2026
02098527-0001